T0243228

EVERYDAY LIFE IN VICTORIAN LONDON

Everyday Life in Victorian London

Helen Amy

Amberley

First published 2023

Amberley Publishing
The Hill, Stroud
Gloucestershire, GL5 4EP

www.amberley-books.com

ISBN 978 1 4456 9537 2 (hardback)
ISBN 978 1 4456 9538 9 (ebook)

British Library Cataloguing in Publication Data.
A catalogue record for this book is available from the British Library.

1 2 3 4 5 6 7 8 9 10

Typesetting by SJmagic DESIGN SERVICES, India.
Printed in the UK.

CONTENTS

INTRODUCTION

Queen Victoria ascended the throne in 1837, at the age of eighteen. In her early years as Queen she was supported and guided by her Prime Minister, Lord Melbourne, with whom she had a close, even affectionate, relationship. In 1840 she married her cousin Prince Albert of Saxe-Coburg-Gotha. Albert soon became involved in Victoria's official business and she came to rely on him for advice and support.

London was the capital city of the world's richest and most advanced industrial nation, with a growing empire. It was the centre of politics, trade, finance, culture, and an important manufacturing centre, which traded with the rest of the world through its ports.

This book is about the lives of the people who lived and worked in Victorian London, but before their story is told they must be placed in their historical context.

There were four significant factors about London at the beginning of Victoria's reign: its vast and ever-increasing size, its varying and contrasting scenes, its attraction or pull factors, and its need for reform and modernisation.

London expanded rapidly throughout the Victorian period. Henry Mayhew, a journalist who worked for the *Morning Chronicle*, went up in a hot-air balloon in 1861 to survey London from above.

It appeared to him as a 'world of its own' with Belgravia and Bethnal Green as the two poles and Temple Bar as the equator, with the spreading suburbs resembling great continents. Mayhew likened London to a voracious monster consuming the surrounding countryside. The reason for this expansion was London's rapidly increasing population; in 1800 it was 1 million and by 1900 it had risen to 6.5 million.[1] This incredible rise was due to natural increase and immigration from other parts of Britain, especially from the countryside, and from abroad. London was a cosmopolitan city with inhabitants from a number of countries including Ireland, Scotland, Germany and Italy.

London was a place of great contrasts – old London, such as the remains of the medieval city and its ancient churches, contrasted with new London, to be found in the new housing developments and the railway termini. Ugly parts of the capital, such as the slums, contrasted with the splendour of such buildings as St Paul's Cathedral and Westminster Abbey. Working London, to be found in the industrial areas and the City, contrasted with London at leisure, to be found in the parks, entertainment venues and tourist spots. The noisy, colourful, bustling London during the day contrasted with the shadowy, gas-lit, night-time London.

The City, the East End and the West End were all quite different places, with their own characteristics and atmosphere. The City was changing from a centre of trade, industry, shops and residential areas to a financial centre of offices, banks and insurance companies. The East End was still a sea-faring district at the beginning of the Victorian period, where the main occupations were shipbuilding and allied trades, and silk-weaving. Many East End residents were dockworkers who lived in jerry-built houses near the river. By the middle of the century the East End was changing. Old industries were being replaced by 'noxious' industries, such as glue and soap making, previously located in the City. This area also attracted many poor people who had lost their homes in the City as it changed into a financial centre. The West End was the wealthiest district of London with its grand residential squares, expensive shopping streets and spacious parks.

People were drawn to London for a variety of reasons throughout the Victorian period. It had always been attractive as the capital city, the place where things were happening. For centuries people had come to London to seek their fortunes and this pull factor drew large numbers to the metropolis after the Industrial Revolution, including unemployed agricultural workers from the countryside searching for work. There was a huge casual labour market which attracted them; they sought employment in the industrial areas, in the docks, on building sites, in railway construction and on the streets. Sadly, for most of the new arrivals London did not live up to their expectations. Many found themselves struggling to survive among the destitute and homeless.

The metropolis also drew tourists and day visitors – there was plenty for them to see and do. Tourists came from the Continent and on steamships from more distant countries, especially America. These visitors included members of the upper class who came during the parliamentary season. While the men attended Parliament and dealt with business matters, their wives and daughters enjoyed London's many attractions and its busy social scene.

The new railways made travel simpler, cheaper and quicker than it had previously been. Handbooks, guides and street atlases were published for these tourists and visitors.

London needed to be modernised and reformed for its role as an imperial city and also to accommodate its growing population, for which the existing infrastructure was inadequate. The main problems were its overcrowded, filthy and dilapidated slums; its narrow and congested roads; its polluted rivers; its lack of clean drinking water; its inefficient public services; and its alarming crime rate.

The people of Victorian London can be divided into four social classes: the upper, middle and working classes and the underclass, often referred to as 'outcast London' or the 'submerged tenth'.

One of the greatest contrasts in Victorian London was between the lives of the rich and the poor. In his novel *Sibyl*, published in 1845, Benjamin Disraeli described the rich and poor of Victorian

England as two nations which had no conception of how the other lived. It was, said Disraeli, as if they were 'inhabitants of different planets'. The gulf between them was nowhere more apparent than in London.

The poor did not benefit from the prosperity that followed the Industrial Revolution, despite the fact that many contributed to it. Fluctuating economic conditions during the Victorian period made life uncertain and extremely hard for the poor. The 1840s, known as the 'hungry forties', was a particularly bad decade. Industry failed, unemployment rose and the cost of food increased. The repeal of the Corn Laws in 1846 and the resulting reduction in the price of bread helped the poor. The 1860s were more settled economically but there were further trade depressions at the end of the century. The poverty so evident in London was shameful and embarrassing in the capital of the world's richest nation, which was being transformed into a grand imperial city.

The lower classes expressed their discontent in the Chartist movement of the 1840s, which demanded political reform, including universal manhood suffrage. This came to nothing but it added to the fear among the better-off classes that the poor may rebel against their lot in life. This fear dated back to the French Revolution at the end of the eighteenth century and was not helped by uprisings in Continental cities in 1848.

Victorian London and its inhabitants were a source of much contemporary interest and proved popular subjects for writers, journalists, diarists, artists and photographers. Much of this contemporary evidence has survived and has been used in the writing of this book. The writings of social investigative journalists have been particularly useful in researching the lives of the poor. The most important of these was Henry Mayhew, who revealed the findings of his investigations in a series of letters to his newspaper in 1849 and 1850, some of which were subsequently published in 1851 in his book *London Labour and the London Poor*. Other journalists carried out similar investigations in the second half of Victoria's reign.

Handbooks and guidebooks written for tourists have also been consulted.

1

HOUSING

The rapidly increasing population of London throughout the nineteenth century led to a massive boom in housebuilding. To accommodate this ever-growing population London encroached more and more on the surrounding countryside. This development was helped by the existence of plenty of cheap land on which to build and the ready supply of bricks made from London clay. Charles Manby Smith, author of *Curiosities of London Life, or Phases, Physiological of the Great Metropolis* (1853), likened the growth of Victorian London to a drop of ink falling on blotting paper.

> A round, well-defined drop at first, it gradually dilates and expands in size, and assumes a ruggedness of outline as it enlarges, the little ridges flying off in every direction, radiating still farther and farther from the centre, just as the circle of London grows bigger and wider by stretching away on all sides from the original confines of the city. The comparison holds good so long as any moisture remains to be absorbed; but soon the ink dries up, and there is an end of it – which cannot be said of the bricks and mortar.[1]

Improvements in transport made it easier for workers to move to the new suburbs and many were motivated to do so by a desire to separate home and working life. There was a wide variety of housing types in London to accommodate the different social classes including mansions, detached and semi-detached villas, terraced houses and purpose-built flats.

Upper-class Homes

At the top of the social pyramid were the very wealthy titled aristocracy, who lived in vast mansions in a very small and exclusive area of London, as described in the following extract from *The World of London* by John Murray, published in *Blackwood's Magazine* in July 1841:

> Of exclusive neighbourhoods there are but few. Piccadilly, westwards from Devonshire House, decidedly takes the lead: His Royal Highness the Duke of Cambridge lends to their neighbourhood the sanction of his preference. The hero of Waterloo makes Hyde Park Corner classic ground: the Dukes of Devonshire and St Albans, the Marquis of Northampton, the Earls Cardigan and Rosebery, Lord Willoughby D'Eresby, and a host of our nobility, stamp this locality with supreme bon-ton ... there is no locality in London commanding a nobler view than that enjoyed from the windows of the mansions in Piccadilly, extending far and wide over the parks, and terminated only by the undulating outline of the distant hills of Surrey.
>
> Most of the streets that abut immediately upon the parks, overlooking the greensward, are entitled to the rank of exclusive ... Arlington Street, overlooking the Green Park, is one of those dear exclusive neighbourhoods: the fine façade of Lord Spencer's noble mansion here attracts general attention. Park Lane is another, vying with Piccadilly in the intensity of fashion. Grosvenor Square, though in a less degree, approaches exclusiveness; while Portman, Cavendish and Belgrave Squares, must be content to come within our ultra-fashionable category.

A few families who had made rather than inherited their wealth, such as the Rothschilds and the Coutts families, also lived in these exclusive and fashionable streets.

One step down the social pyramid came the untitled aristocracy. In London many of these very wealthy people lived in the Mayfair and Belgravia areas of the West End, near the Houses of Parliament and the royal court. Mayfair included Grosvenor Square, Berkeley Square, Hanover Square, Park Lane, Arlington Street and Piccadilly. The substantial eighteenth-century classical-style houses in Mayfair were the London homes of the aristocracy, who came to the capital for the parliamentary season and returned to their grand country houses for the remainder of the year.

Belgravia, with Belgrave Square at its centre, was not quite so exclusive as Mayfair. It was built in the 1820s by the famous builder Thomas Cubitt. Its residents included many wealthy merchants, bankers and top professionals. These solid, classical-style stucco-fronted houses were very grand and luxurious; many were built in squares with gardens at the centre. Hippolyte Taine, a French philosopher and historian who visited London in 1859, was impressed with these houses. This description is taken from his book *Notes on England*, written for his French readers.

> Enormous, enormous – that is the word which recurs all the time. And, moreover, rich and well-cared for, so that they must find us neglected and poor. Paris is mediocre by comparison with these 'squares', 'crescents', 'circuses', and the endless rows of monumental houses built of massive stone, with porticos and carved fronts, lining the very wide streets. There are fifty as wide as the Rue de la Paix.[2]

To keep these streets exclusive, restrictions were placed on who could lease or rent the houses. Iron gates were installed to keep people out and to keep the area quiet. There were also restrictions on the types of vehicles allowed to enter to exclude 'low vehicles', such as carts. Max Schlesinger, a German visitor to London, described these streets in his book *Saunterings in and about London* (1853).

> These fashionable quarters are as quiet as our own provincial towns. They have no shops; no omnibuses are allowed to pass

> through them, and few costermongers or sellers of fruit, onions, oysters, and fish find their way into these regions, for the cheapness of their wares has no attractions for the inhabitants of these streets. These streets, too, are macadamized expressly for the horses and carriages of the aristocracy; such roads are more comfortable for all parties concerned, that is to say, for horses, horsemen, and drivers, and the carriages are, moreover, too light to do much harm to the road. In these streets, too, there are neither counting-houses nor public-houses to disturb the neighbourhood by their daily traffic and nightly revelries. Comfort reigns supreme in the streets and in the interior of the houses. The roadway is lined with pavements of large white beautiful flag-stones, which skirt the area railings; it is covered with gravel, and carefully watered, exactly as the broad paths of our public gardens, to keep down the dust and deaden the rumbling of the carriages and the step of the horses. The horses, too, are of a superior kind, and as different from their poorer brethren, the brewer's, coal-merchant's, and omnibus horses, as the part of the town in which they eat is different from the part in which the latter work.[3]

The families who lived in these splendid houses, some of which had as many as six storeys, were looked after by a small army of servants including butlers, coachmen, footmen, housekeepers, cooks, kitchen maids, parlour maids and ladies' maids. The following description of these substantial London townhouses is taken from *The Gentleman's House* (1864) by Robert Kerr:

> The Offices accommodated on the Basement are Kitchen, Scullery, Pantry, and Larder; Butler's Pantry, Bedroom, Safe, and Cleaning-room; Housekeeper's-room, Still-room, Store-room, and Servants'-Hall; a Wine-cellar and a Closet for beer; a small Laundry, a small Housemaid's-closet, and a Sleeping-room for two men-servants; besides the usual vaults in front, and similar ones in the extreme rear, – the latter of which, it is submitted, ought to relieve the former of coals and dust. The Back-stair has a Lift from bottom to top. If these Offices are sometimes of small dimensions, it

> must be remembered that the question in London is not of what spaciousness they can be had, but whether they can be had at all. To guard against the transmission of kitchen-vapours, the door of the Kitchen is placed in a Porch; and the dinner-service would pass through a hatch within, and upwards by means of the Lift and Back-stair.
>
> On the Ground-floor we have a Dining-room at the back (as it ought to be, if possible), an Entrance-hall which is not the mere Passage of common usage, a Cloak-room and Closet, a Library, which is necessarily small, but which has only yielded to still more important considerations, a spacious Staircase-Hall, and a Service-closet for the Dining-room. The Entrance-door opens in the middle of the Front, and is not pushed away to one side in the ordinarily unstately manner.
>
> On the first-floor we have two spacious Drawing-rooms and a connecting Ante-room ... On the Second-floor there are two complete Private Bedroom-Suites, one for the heads of the family and one for guests, with a Bath-room (for gentlemen) in addition. On the next Floor we have one inferior Private Suite, three ordinary Bedrooms, a second Bath-room (for ladies), Linen-room, Soiled-linen-room, and Housemaid's-closet. The storey above accommodates a complete Nursery-suite and Bedrooms for the female-servants, one for the lady's maid being specially adapted and furnished with a Wardrobe-closet attached. Still higher, in the roof, there would be Luggage and Lumber-rooms, and any further Servants'-rooms that might be required. The lift in the Back-stair communicates with every storey throughout.
>
> The Stable-building in the rear accommodates on the Ground-floor three Stalls and a Loose-box, and two Carriage-houses; and in one of these there is provision for harness, including a fireplace. On the Upper floor there are the necessary small Loft, and a Living-room, three Bedrooms, and Closets, for the coachman.

These houses were built in rows and separated from their neighbours 'by a projection in the façade'.[4]

Middle-class Homes

The Victorian middle class was a large and diverse social group with many gradations within it, encompassing professionals such as lawyers, architects, doctors and school teachers as well as more lowly clerks and shopkeepers. Middle-class homes were located in the centre of London and increasingly, as the nineteenth century progressed, in the new suburbs. They were built in squares and streets and, particularly in the suburbs, were constructed to standard plans which gave them a uniform appearance. The new suburban homes were rented from landlords who had cashed in on the housing boom.

The homes of the wealthiest members of this class were substantial buildings, often comprising several storeys, which needed a number of servants to run them. Hippolyte Taine described some of the houses inhabited by the upper middle class in central London.

> All the surroundings of Hyde Park are covered with similar houses [to those he had previously described], but larger and handsomer and which, in the midst of London, still keep a look of the country. Each stands alone in its square of lawn and shrubbery; two floors in impeccable taste and immaculately maintained; a portico, a tradesman's bell and a visitor's bell; a basement for the kitchen and servants, with a service staircase. Very little moulding or ornament; no outside shutters; large, clear windows letting in ample light; flowers on the window-sills and the peristyle [a porch made from a row of columns]; stables in a separate building, so that the smell and sight of them be out of the way; all outside walls dressed with white stucco, shining, glossy; not a splash of mud or dust anywhere; the trees, lawns and servants all groomed like articles in an exhibition of model products … Simple, however, and feeling no need for outward show; but, on the other hand, very particular as regards neatness, cleanliness, order and comfort; and separating his [the occupier's] life from those of his inferiors.[5]

The male heads of the families who lived in these and other middle-class houses set out for work each morning while their wives stayed at home to supervise the running of the house and the care of the children, their spare time occupied with ladylike pursuits such as sewing and beadwork, paying social calls to other ladies and, possibly, some charity work.

Just below them in the social hierarchy were those members of the middle class who lived in the sort of houses described in the following paragraphs, also by Hippolyte Taine:

> Innumerable houses built for their owners' enjoyment, cottages set in lawn and trees, and in every style, Gothic, Greek, Byzantine, Medieval or Renaissance Italian, or in a mixture of every variation on these styles. As a rule they are built in rows, or in groups of five, six, twenty all identical and visibly built by the same contractor, like so many examples of the same vase or bronze. They turn out houses as we turn out Paris fancy-goods. What a multitude of easy, comfortable, of wealthy households! The whole implies large profits from quick turnover, an opulent free-spending middle-class very different from our own…
>
> The most modest houses, built of brown brick, are pretty by reason of their cleanness; the window panes are polished like mirrors, there is almost always a small garden, green and full of flowers, and the façade will be covered by a creeper or climbing plant.[6]

The typical interior of a middle-class home in London is described in detail by Max Schlesinger:

> The small space between the street-door and the stairs, hardly sufficient in length and breadth to deserve the pompous name of a 'hall,' is usually furnished with a couple of mahogany chairs, or, in wealthier houses, with flower-pots, statuettes, and now and then a sixth or seventh-rate picture. The floor is covered with oil-cloth, and this again is covered with a breadth of carpet. A single glance tells us, that after passing the threshold, we have at once entered the temple of domestic life…
>
> From the hall we make our way to the parlour – the refectory of the house. The parlour is the common sitting-room of the family,

> the centre-point of the domestic state. It is here that many eat their dinners, and some say their prayers; and in this room does the lady of the house arrange her household affairs and issue her commands. In winter the parlour fire burns from early morn till late at night, and it is into the parlour that the visitor is shewn, unless he happens to call on a reception-day, when the drawing rooms are thrown open to the friends of the family.
>
> Large folding-doors, which occupy nearly the whole breadth of the back wall, separate the front from the back-parlour, and when opened, the two form one large room. The number and the circumstances of the family devote this back parlour either to the purposes of a library for the master, the son, or the daughters of the house, or convert it into a boudoir, office or breakfast-room. Frequently, it serves no purpose in particular, and all in turn.
>
> These two rooms occupy the whole depth of the house. All the other apartments are above, so that there are from two to four rooms in each storey…
>
> In the first floor are the reception-rooms; in the second the bed-rooms, with their large four-posters and marble-topped wash-stands; in the third storey are the nurseries and servants' rooms; and in the fourth, if a fourth there be, you find a couple of low garrets, for the occasional accommodation of some bachelor friend of the family.[7]

There was also a well-equipped kitchen, a back kitchen and various storerooms. The house was lit from kitchen to attic by gaslights and there was a plentiful supply of fresh and hot water.

The middle classes were proud of their homes and family life was very important to them. By modern standards the interiors of their homes were cluttered and fussy. A typical parlour contained a sofa and chairs with frilly chintz covers, a piano, several small tables draped with a tablecloth and a carpet on the floor. On display were vases, ornaments, framed photographs, stuffed birds and waxed fruits under glass and the papered walls were covered with pictures. A cloth overmantle hid the mantlepiece above the decoratively tiled fireplace. On the fireplace wall there were portraits of Queen Victoria and Prince Albert, whose love of home and family was an inspiration to the middle classes. The contents of their home were an indication of their social status and were proudly displayed for visitors to see.

For much of the Victorian period the inhabitants of London lived in houses – either as one family or, in the case of the poor, in houses of multiple occupancy. Purpose-built flats, which were not so cost-effective to build as houses, did not appear in London until the latter years of the century.

Homes of the Lower Classes

The housing conditions of the poorest Londoners, both the working or 'deserving' poor and the unemployed or 'undeserving' poor, were truly appalling. It was not until the mid-1880s that any attempt was made to provide adequate housing for this large group of people and this only benefited a small number of the working poor. Social investigative journalists drew attention to these housing conditions throughout the Victorian period.

Unlike better-off Londoners, who could afford to move away from their workplaces, the working poor had to live near the docks, marketplaces, building sites and other places where they scratched out a living. These were the people who, together with the unemployed, lived in the numerous slum districts to be found in all areas of the capital. Some of them could not even afford to live in the slums and were forced to live on the streets.

Slums

There had been slums in London for centuries. William Hogarth vividly depicted the vile slums of Georgian times in his paintings. Those of the Victorian era, however, were even worse. The older slums had largely been confined to the City itself but, with the rapid and unprecedented increase in the capital's population, slums appeared all over London.

As the City developed into a business and commercial centre the shops moved to the West End and many people moved to the new suburbs. Those left behind were the poor who could not afford to move out and needed to be near their places of work. The houses which were not demolished for redevelopment were taken over by the poor.

Dwellings which had previously been occupied by one family became grossly overcrowded slum homes, crammed from cellar to attic with the desperately poor. Greedy landlords took advantage of the shortage of accommodation by crowding as many people as possible into their properties.

The most notorious slum districts included Seven Dials near Covent Garden, Saffron Hill near Holborn, the Old Nichol and Ratcliff Highway in the East End and Jacob's Island in Bermondsey. Many other slums were less well known but just as appalling.

A surprising fact about the slums of Victorian London is that many were situated close to affluent areas and the most exclusive shopping streets. Blanchard Jerrold commented on this in *London A Pilgrimage* (1872).

> Yet there are terrible highways and passages round about the Abbey [Westminster Abbey] still – as there are indeed about all the fairer parts of the metropolis. We appear to delight in violent contrasts. At the back of Regent Street and Oxford Street are alleys of houses where some among the most miserable of London's citizens abide. There are purlieus in Kensington, Belgravia, Westbournia, and the Regent's Park, as heart-sickening as those that skirt the highway of Shoreditch. The Palace looks out upon the common Lodging House. From the brightest of our roads, the traveller has only to make a few steps aside to light upon the haunt of the costermonger, the rough, the cadger. Worse company than that to be picked up within three minutes' walk of the Houses of Parliament, is not within the metropolitan postal district, as the detective force, whose headquarters are at hand, would willingly testify.[8]

Victorian slums were known as 'rookeries' because their inhabitants were squeezed together in colonies like rooks in their nests. Slum dwellers belonged to the underclass referred to as 'Outcast London'. Families often had to sub-let to pay their rent and more than ten people living in one room was common. There are many contemporary articles written by journalists, the clergy, mission and charity workers, and foreign visitors to draw attention to the plight of the poor and the evils of the slums. One foreign visitor who wrote about the slums of London was the German philosopher Friedrich Engels, the co-author of *The Communist Manifesto*. The following extracts come from his work *The Condition of the Working Classes in England* (1845):

> The streets themselves are usually unpaved and full of holes. They are filthy and strewn with animal and vegetable refuse. Since they have neither gutters nor drains the refuse accumulates in stagnant, stinking puddles. Ventilation in the slums is inadequate owing to the hopelessly unplanned nature of these areas. A great many people live huddled together in a very small area, and so it is easy to imagine the nature of the air in these workers' quarters. However, in fine weather the streets are used for the drying of washing and clothes lines are stretched across the streets from house to house and wet garments are hung out on them.
>
> ... St Giles is situated in the most densely populated part of London and is surrounded by splendid wide streets which are used by the fashionable world. It is close to Oxford Street, Trafalgar Square and the Strand. It is a confused conglomeration of tall houses of three or four storeys. The narrow, dirty streets are just as crowded as the main thoroughfares, but in St Giles one sees only members of the working classes. The narrowness of the roads is accentuated by the presence of street markets in which baskets of rotting and virtually uneatable vegetables and fruit are exposed for sale. The smell from these and from the butchers' stalls is appalling. The houses are packed from cellar to attic and they are as dirty inside as outside. No human being would willingly inhabit such dens. Yet even worse conditions are to be found in the houses which lie off the main road down narrow alleys leading to the courts. These dwellings are approached by covered passages between the houses. The extent to which these filthy passages are falling into decay beggars all description. There is hardly an unbroken windowpane to be seen, the walls are crumbling, the door posts and window frames are loose and rotten. The doors,

> where they exist, are made of old boards nailed together. Indeed, in this nest of thieves doors are superfluous, because there is nothing worth stealing. Piles of refuse and ashes lie all over the place and the slops thrown out into the streets collect in pools which emit a foul stench. Here live the poorest of the poor. Here the worst-paid workers rub shoulders with thieves, rogues and prostitutes. Most of them have come from Ireland or are of Irish extraction. Those who have not yet been entirely engulfed in the morass of iniquity by which they are surrounded are daily losing the power to resist the demoralising influences of poverty, dirt and low environment.[9]

The dreadful conditions described by Engels could have fitted any of the numerous slum districts of the Victorian capital. Unsurprisingly, the poor people who lived in these slums suffered badly during regular outbreaks of cholera and typhoid.

As London was modernised slums were cleared to make way for new roads and railways. This led to further crowding in the remaining slum districts, as no provision was made for the poor who were displaced. Railway building between 1857 and 1869, for example, led to the displacement of 37,000 people.[10]

The government made limited, ineffectual attempts to improve the slums in London. Attempts by the government to force landlords to improve the sanitary conditions of their properties were unsuccessful. The Torrens Act of 1868, which attempted to compel property owners to maintain rented accommodation in good repair, also failed, for various reasons. The only action on the part of landlords was to continue to take advantage of the ever-increasing demand for accommodation by putting up rents.

Incredibly in the last decades of the century slum conditions only got worse. The continued movement of people from the city, the arrival of more jobseekers from other parts of the country and further slum clearance for redevelopment led to even greater competition for housing. An influx of Jewish people fleeing persecution in Europe added to the problem. These people settled in the East End, which had become the most deprived area of London, a ghetto for the desperately poor.

Model Housing

By the middle of the century there was a growing awareness of the physical and moral evils of slum housing in London and a recognition of the need to improve housing for the lower classes. A number of associations and companies were set up to build model housing, including model lodging houses for the working poor, in central London.

One of the earliest of these bodies was the Society for Improving the Conditions of the Labouring Classes which was established in 1844. The Queen and Prince Albert were patrons of the society and Lord Shaftesbury was its chairman. In the following year the Metropolitan Association for Improving the Dwellings of the Working Classes was founded. At the Great Exhibition of 1851, held in Hyde Park, one of the most popular exhibits was a group of model houses for the poor designed by Prince Albert, which had been erected in the grounds of Hyde Park Barracks. Known as 'Prince Albert's Model Cottages', the red-brick building was divided into four flats, each with a large living room with a cooking range, a scullery, three bedrooms and a toilet. After the exhibition the building was taken down and re-erected in Kennington, where it still stands.

In 1867 the Artisans, Labourers and General Dwellings Company was established with the aim of extending model housing to the suburbs. They had the idea of building 'cottage estates' of two-storey terraced houses. The first estate was built in Shaftesbury Park, Battersea, between 1872 and 1877. This was followed by an estate in Queen's Park, West Kilburn, which was built between 1875 and 1881.

Philanthropists

Two philanthropists who helped with the problem of housing the poor of Victorian London were George Peabody and Octavia Hill. Peabody was a wealthy American businessman who left a legacy of £500,000 to provide cheap housing for the poor. The first Peabody flats, which were housed in barrack-style buildings, were opened in Spitalfields in 1864.[11] Larger estates followed in other parts of London including Islington, Poplar, Shadwell and Bermondsey. By

1882, 14,600 had been housed in 3,500 Peabody homes. Many Peabody estates still exist today.

Octavia Hill, with financial help from John Ruskin, the art critic and philanthropist, bought some dilapidated houses in St Marylebone to repair and rent out to the poor. Eventually she took on, repaired and managed a large number of properties in the poor areas of London.

Noble as these initiatives were, they only helped the working poor and very few of them. They hardly scratched the surface of the problem of housing the poorest people in London, as the capital's population continued to grow.

Council Housing

As with so many other social problems in Victorian England, the government was slow to address the desperate need for adequate housing for the poorest inhabitants of London. The efforts of charitable organisations and philanthropists had made little difference. Social investigative journalists and other writers had continued to draw attention to the problem, but it was not until the publication in 1884 of a leaflet entitled *The Bitter Cry of Outcast London* by the Reverend Andrew Mearns that the outcry became too loud and too insistent to ignore any longer. This leaflet put the government under pressure to act. Even Queen Victoria read the leaflet and added her voice to the demands for action.

A royal commission was set up in 1884 to investigate working-class housing. This led to the foundation of the East End Dwellings Company to help the abject poor living in that part of London.

Further pressure was exerted by the findings of a groundbreaking survey of poverty in London in the 1880s, which was carried out by the businessman Charles Booth. The results of this survey, which were published in 1889, revealed the horrifying extent of the deprivation in some parts of London and that the problem was far worse than had been feared.

The London County Council, which was formed in 1888, also set about solving the problem. It made use of the powers granted by the Artisans' Dwellings Act of 1875, and the Housing of the

Working Classes Act was passed in 1890 to carry out a large slum clearance programme and build the first council housing for the poor. The first London council estate was the Boundary Estate, which was built on the site of the notorious Old Nichol slum district in the East End.

The Homeless

The most desperate inhabitants of Victorian London were those who could not even afford to rent part of a room in a slum dwelling. In the words of William Booth, the founder of the Salvation Army, 'There is a depth below that of the dweller in the slums. It is that of the dweller in the street, who has not even a lair in the slums which he can call his own.'[12]

These people slept on the streets, in parks, in marketplaces, under railway bridges and the dry arches of bridges across the Thames, in doorways, or anywhere they could find some protection from the weather. Occasionally they stayed in night shelters or refuges for the homeless, the casual ward of the workhouse or, if they were able to find a few pennies, in a common lodging house.

Houses of Refuge for the Destitute Poor

Houses of Refuge for the Destitute Poor, which were often referred to as 'straw-yards', were shelters run by charities. These clean and well-run refuges provided food, washing facilities and a bed made of hay to sleep on, but they only catered for a tiny proportion of destitute people and only in the worst winter weather. Most people who sought shelter in straw-yards were turned away.

Henry Mayhew visited one of these refuges located in Playhouse Yard, Cripplegate, and described what he saw in a letter published in *The Morning Chronicle* in January 1850. This refuge was opened in 1820 by a Mr Hick, a city mace-bearer, in premises which formerly housed a hat factory. Mayhew described a crowd of ragged, shivering people waiting for the doors to open. There was room for 200 people, who were allowed to stay for three nights only. Men and women slept in separate wards and were given gruel, water and a portion of bread before going to sleep; they received the same rations the following morning before they returned to the streets. Mayhew was impressed with the way the refuge was run and the way in which the desperate people who sought shelter there were treated. He described the sleeping arrangements as follows:

> The berths, both in the men's and women's wards, are on the ground, and divided one from another only by a wooden partition about a foot high; a similar partition is at the head and feet; so that in all the wards it looks as if there were a series of coffins arranged in long catacombs. This burial-like aspect is the more striking when the inmates are all asleep, as they were, with the rarest exceptions, when I walked round at ten o'clock at night. Each sleeper has for covering a large basil (dressed sheep-skin), such as cobblers use for aprons. As they lie in long rows, in the most profound repose, with these dark brown wrappers about them, they present the uniform look and arrangement of a long line of mummies. Each bed in the coffin, or trough-like division, is made of waterproof cloth, stuffed with hay, made so as to be easily cleaned. It is soft and pleasant to the touch. Formerly the beds were plain straw, but the present plan has been in use for seven years.[13]

Another refuge for the homeless was the Field Lane Refuge in Clerkenwell. This refuge, which was for adults and children, moved in 1865 to larger premises in Saffron Hill. According to Thomas Archer, the author of *The Terrible Sights of London* (1870), its accommodation was more than adequate:

> The great wards devoted to the purpose of night-refuges, where, instead of being cramped for space, the unfortunate inmates can sit comfortably at large tables, and, on backed benches, to take their bread and cocoa, or even to read such books and magazines as are provided for them. The beds ... consist of strips of sacking stretched on iron struts from the wall, and so form a series of bedsteads about a foot apart, and covered with comfortable rugs. The great height and space of the rooms – the walls of which have been inscribed with texts and mottoes by an ornamental 'writer', who was for

some time an inmate of the institution – give plenty of ventilation, while at the same time an even temperature can be maintained.[14]

Common Lodging Houses

For 2*d* a night homeless people could sleep in one of the numerous 'common lodging houses', also known as 'low lodging houses', which were located in slum districts all over the capital. These lodging houses were dilapidated, filthy, insanitary and overcrowded. They had no privies or fresh water. The homeless shared vermin-infested beds in foul-smelling, unventilated, mixed-sex rooms. Those who could not afford to pay for a bed slept on a pile of rags on the bare floor for a penny. The only facility provided was a fire for cooking food.

People who used lodging houses included the unemployed, sailors, dock and building workers, market porters, street sellers, vagrants, beggars, pickpockets and minor criminals. The worst lodging houses were dens of iniquity and vice haunted by prostitutes and hardened criminals. Many lodging-house keepers acted as fences for stolen goods.

A man interviewed by Henry Mayhew described his experience of staying in a common lodging house:

> I myself have slept in the top room of a house not far from Drury-lane, and you could study the stars, if you were so minded, through the holes left by the slates having been blown off the roof. It was a fine summer's night, and the openings in the roof were then rather an advantage, for they admitted air, and the room wasn't so foul as it might have been without them. I never went there again, but you may judge what thoughts went through a man's mind – a man who had seen prosperous days – as he lay in a place like that, without being able to sleep, watching the sky.

The man told Mayhew that

> he had scraped together a handful of bugs from the bed-clothes, and crushed them under a candlestick, and had done that many a

> time, when he could only resort to the lowest places. He had slept in rooms so crammed with sleepers – he believed there were 30 where 12 would have been a proper number – that their breaths in the dead of night and in the unventilated chamber, rose (I use his own words) 'in one foul, choking steam of stench'.[15]

Charles Dickens visited several lodging houses in the notorious slums of St Giles parish in central London when he accompanied a police inspector on a routine night patrol. He described what he saw in an article entitled *On Duty with Inspector Field*, which was published in 1851. The following extract describes the scene in a lodging house where some Irish immigrant families were staying:

> Saint Giles's church clock, striking eleven, hums through our hand from the dilapidated door of a dark outhouse as we open it, and are stricken back by the pestilent breath that issues from within...
>
> Ten, twenty, thirty – who can count them! Men, women, children, for the most part naked, heaped upon the floor like maggots in a cheese! Ho! In that dark corner yonder! Does anybody lie there? Me, Sir, Irish me, a widder, with six children. And yonder? Me, Sir, Irish me, with me wife and eight poor babes. And to the left there? Me, Sir, Irish me, along with two more Irish boys as is me friends. And to the right there? Me, Sir, and the Murphy family, numbering five blessed souls. And what's this, coiling, now about my foot? Another Irish me, pitifully in want of shaving, whom I have awakened from sleep – and across my other foot lies his wife – and by the shoes of Inspector Field lie their three eldest – and their three youngest are at present squeezed between the open door and the wall. And why is there no-one on that little mat before the sullen fire? Because O'Donovan, with his wife and daughter, is not come in from selling Lucifers [matches]! Nor on the bit of sacking in the nearest corner? Bad luck! Because that Irish family is late tonight, a-cadging in the streets!
>
> They are all awake now, the children excepted, and most of them sit up, to stare. Wheresoever Mr Rogers [a police officer] turns the flaming eye [torch] there is a spectral figure rising, unshrouded, from a grave of rags.[16]

Lord Shaftesbury, who did much to help the poor of Victorian England, was very concerned about the condition of common lodging houses in London. In 1851, the year in which Dickens's article was published, two Acts were passed by Parliament as a result of Shaftesbury's efforts. Under the new legislation it became compulsory for lodging houses to be regulated and inspected by the police, to enforce cleanliness and to end overcrowding. As a result, the worst lodging houses were closed and there was a general improvement in the conditions of those which remained open.

Over the remaining decades of the century the number of lodging houses declined steadily. Eventually in the 1890s the remaining 500 passed into the control of the newly formed London County Council.

The Workhouse and Casual Ward

In the early to mid-Victorian period the only shelter for the destitute homeless which was not provided by charities was the workhouse. The workhouse itself provided long-term shelter, while temporary shelter could be found in the casual ward, which was usually located in the same building or nearby.

The Poor Law Amendment Act of 1834 divided the poor into the 'deserving' and 'undeserving'. The reason for this was the widely held belief that some poor people were responsible for their own plight because they were lazy, feckless and thriftless. They were not seen as victims of circumstances beyond their control. After 1834 parishes were grouped together in unions and one large workhouse was built for each union. These grim, prison-like buildings were referred to as 'bastilles'. There were forty union workhouses in London.[17] The only available relief after 1834 was inside these institutions, where conditions were deliberately made harsh as a deterrent. Any able-bodied person who sought relief had to work for it.

Many people who ended up in the workhouse were too old, sick or frail to work. These poor people had to mix there with habitual vagrants, prostitutes and criminals. The horrors of the Victorian workhouse are well known; most people preferred to endure the most severe privations rather than seek shelter in them.

Conditions in the casual wards, which also attracted undesirables as well as the destitute, were as grim and forbidding as in the workhouse itself. Conditions varied from casual ward to casual ward. As a test of destitution and industry all applicants, both adults and children, were supposed to do three hours' work in return for food and shelter. It was not always possible to enforce this regulation in London, where the pressure on workhouses was much greater than elsewhere. It had proved impossible to abolish outdoor relief completely in London, as required by the 1834 Act, due to the overwhelming level of need.

In 1866 the journalist James Greenwood spent a night in the casual ward of Lambeth Workhouse in order to write about the experience. He found it difficult to describe what he witnessed that night, as this extract from his report shows:

> No language with which I am acquainted is capable of conveying an adequate conception of the spectacle I then encountered. Imagine a space of about thirty feet by thirty enclosed on three sides by a dingy white-washed wall, and roofed with naked tiles which were furred with the damp and filth that reeked within. As for the fourth side of the shed, it was boarded in for (say) a third of its breadth; the remaining space being hung with flimsy canvas, in which was a gap two feet wide at top, widening to at least four feet at bottom. This far too airy shed was paved with stone, the flags so thickly encrusted with filth that I mistook it at first for a floor of natural earth ... At one glance my appalled vision took in thirty of them – thirty men and boys stretched upon shallow pallets which put only six inches of comfortable hay between them and the stony floor.[18]

Casual wards, like other refuges, could not accommodate all who sought shelter in them, as Charles Dickens discovered when he came across five people, including two young sisters, who had been turned away by a casual ward in Whitechapel. He was shocked and deeply disturbed by the sight of these rejected paupers, as he related in an article entitled 'A Nightly Scene in London', published in *Household Words* in January 1856:

> On the fifth of last November, I, the Conductor of this journal, accompanied by a friend well-known to the public [John Forster, biographer and critic], accidently strayed into Whitechapel. It was a miserable evening; very dark, very muddy, and raining hard.
>
> There are many woeful sights in that part of London, and it has been well-known to me in most of its aspects for many years. We had forgotten the mud and rain in slowly walking along and looking about us, when we found ourselves, at eight o'clock, before the Workhouse.
>
> Crouched against the wall of the Workhouse, in the dark street, on the muddy pavement-stones, with the rain raining upon them, were five bundles of rags. They were motionless, and had no resemblance to the human form. Five great beehives, covered with rags – five dead bodies taken out of graves, tied neck and heels, and covered with rags – would have looked like those five bundles upon which the rain rained down in the public street.
>
> 'What is this?' said my companion. 'What *is* this?'
>
> 'Some miserable people shut out of the Casual Ward, I think,' said I.
>
> We had stopped before the five ragged mounds, and were quite rooted to the spot by their horrible appearance. Five awful Sphinxes by the wayside, crying to every passer-by, 'Stop and guess! What is to be the end of a state of society that leaves us here!'
>
> As we stood looking at them, a decent working-man, having the appearance of a stone-mason, touched me on the shoulder
>
> 'This is an awful sight, Sir,' said he, 'in a Christian country!'
>
> 'God knows it is, my friend,' said I.
>
> 'I have often seen it much worse than this, as I have been going home from my work. I have counted fifteen, twenty, five-and-twenty, many a time. It's a shocking thing to see.'
>
> 'A shocking thing, indeed,' said I and my companion together. The man lingered near us a little while, wished us good-night, and went on.[19]

Dickens was so upset by what he saw that he gave each of the paupers a shilling to pay for food and lodgings for the night elsewhere.

The government was finally compelled to drop its *laissez-faire* policy and help the homeless of London during the severe winter weather of 1860 to 1861, which coincided with a trade depression. These exacerbated the already dire problem of poverty in the capital. The government set about reviewing the administration of the Poor Law. This led to the passing of the Metropolitan Houseless Poor Act in 1864 which extended the provision for 'destitute wayfarers, wanderers and foundlings', including able-bodied men, who had previously been excluded.

Further action was taken with the passing of the Metropolitan Poor Act in 1867. Under the terms of this Act sick inmates were removed from London workhouses and placed in hospitals set up for them in large boroughs.

The casual ward only offered occasional respite for those in need because of the huge demand. Seeking relief in a casual ward was made more difficult after the passing of another Act in 1882. Anyone using a casual ward had to be detained for two nights and a whole day in between, if they could not afford to pay for their accommodation. They were also forbidden from returning within thirty days. It is not surprising, therefore, that so many desperate people lived on the streets.

In the last two decades of the century many clean, respectable, well-run shelters were opened for the homeless in London by charities and church organisations. Homelessness persisted, nevertheless, and much needed to be done to solve this problem. There were nowhere near enough places in shelters for all in need.

A census by a Salvation Army officer taken one summer in the 1880s gives some idea of the extent of the problem. It revealed 368 people sleeping on the embankment between Blackfriars and Westminster; this included Covent Garden Market and bridge recesses as well as the Embankment itself.[20] These were just three of the innumerable places in the capital where the homeless slept. The problem was actually worse than these figures suggest, as they were recorded during a period of good trade in London, when more people were in work and, consequently, fewer people slept on the streets.

William Booth, the founder of the Salvation Army, described the homeless people who slept along the Embankment in his book *Darkest England and the Way Out* (1890).

> Here, between the Temple and Blackfriars, I found the poor wretches by the score; almost every seat contained its full complement of six – some men, some women – all reclining in various postures and nearly all fast asleep. Just as Big Ben strikes two, the moon, flashing across the Thames and lighting up the stone work of the Embankment, brings into relief a pitiable spectacle. Here on the stone abutments, which afford a slight protection from the biting wind, are scores of men lying side by side, huddled together for warmth, and, of course, without any other covering than their ordinary clothing, which is scanty enough at the best. Some have laid down a few pieces of waste paper, by way of taking the chill off the stones, but the majority are too tired, even for that, and the nightly toilet of most consists of first removing the hat, swathing the head in whatever old rag may be doing duty as a handkerchief, and then replacing the hat.[21]

Many of the night shelters in London were opened by the Salvation Army. Their first shelter for men opened its doors in 1888. It provided food and shelter for a small sum and men who used it were treated with kindness and respect. The following year the first Salvation Army shelter for women was opened with accommodation for up to 261. A very popular shelter was established in Blackfriars Road. A bunk bed, washing and cooking facilities were provided for 3*d* a night, or a seat on a bench in a hall and food could be obtained for a penny.[22] Salvation Army officers went out seeking homeless people to help. Soon there were shelters across London.

2

EDUCATION

The type of education a child received in Victorian England depended on their social class and gender. There was a wide range of schools in London at this time as well as institutions and facilities for further and higher education.

The Higher Social Classes

Boys' Education

Boys of the upper and middle classes usually received their early education at home, where they were taught by private tutors. They then went on to a private school or a 'public school', which, despite the name, were exclusive fee-paying establishments. The term 'public' refers to the origins of these schools – they were open to any public citizens who could pay the fees. A few scholarships were available for boys from poor but 'respectable' families. After attending these schools, boys could go on to study at Oxford or Cambridge University or one of the recently opened colleges of the University of London. They then embarked on careers in the professions or business.

There were a number of excellent, long-established public schools in London, including Westminster and Merchant Taylors' Schools, and Dulwich College.

Westminster School

Westminster School was located within the precincts of Westminster Abbey, next to the Palace of Westminster (Houses of Parliament). It was originally founded in the twelfth century by Benedictine monks and refounded in 1560 by Queen Elizabeth I. For several centuries the school was joined with the Abbey but became independent following the passing of the Public Schools Act in 1868. Admission was by open competition. Boys who passed the scholarship exams were known as Queen's Scholars. In the nineteenth century more subjects were added to the traditional classical curriculum taught in public schools.

Merchant Taylors' School

This school was founded in 1561 for boys aged nine to fourteen who were recommended by the Merchant Taylors Company, one of the ancient guilds of the City of London. It was located in Suffolk Lane in the City until 1875, when it moved to Charterhouse Square. Like Westminster School, its curriculum was extended in the nineteenth century with the addition of mathematics, science and modern languages.

Dulwich College

Dulwich College was built and endowed in 1619 by Edward Alleyn, a famous actor and proprietor of the Fortune Theatre. The following description of the college is taken from *Curiosities of London* (1867) by John Timbs:

> In 1851, the Archbishop of Canterbury, as official Visitor of the College, extended the education at the school to surveying, chemistry, engineering, and the allied sciences. In 1858 was passed an Act of Parliament, by which its educational system will be kept expanding in proportion to its wealth. There are now two Schools; an upper, which provides a more advanced education for boys of the better class, and a lower, intended for the preparation of youths for commercial life; each school about 300. The fees in the upper school amount to £8 per annum for each boy, and in the lower

to £1. In addition to these scholars there are foundation-boys in both schools, boarded and lodged at the expense of the charity. To provide for this extension, new buildings were commenced in 1866, on a site of 30 acres, between the present College and the Crystal Palace. The centre of the building is a large hall for dining and for the general gathering of the boys; there are a cloister between the two schools, and official residences for the masters. There is a Speech-day for classic and dramatic orations; and the performance of a play, preference being given to Shakespeare's.[1]

City of London School

Established in 1835, this was one of the new public schools for the sons of "respectable persons engaged in professional, commercial or trading pursuits." The school was originally located in Milk Street, Cheapside but moved to a new building on the Victoria Embankment in 1879. Its wide curriculum included English, French, German, Latin, Greek, writing, arithmetic, mathematics, book-keeping, geography and history.

Life in a Public School

Harrow School

Hippolyte Taine visited the famous Harrow School during his stay in London in the 1860s. Although it was located in Middlesex, outside the confines of Victorian London, this description of his visit gives some idea of how boys' public schools were run at that time:

> But the principal part of the machine is the company of house-masters: each of these teaches a subject – Greek, Latin, Mathematics, etc.- and, in addition, boards and lodges from ten to thirty boarders in his house. As a rule the boys are two to a room, but each of the older boys has a room to himself. House-masters with only about a dozen boarders give them their meals at their own family table. Where they are more numerous they eat at two tables presided over by ladies of the master's household. Thus the boy, when he first arrives at school, finds himself in something like his own paternal household...

> ... boys and youths together form an organised body, a sort of small, distinct State with its own chiefs and its own laws. The chiefs are the pupils in the highest class (sixth form), more especially the fifteen highest pupils in the school (monitors) and, in each house, the highest pupil. They maintain order, see that the rules are obeyed and, in general, do the same work as our ushers [Taine is making a comparison with French schools].

The pupils worked six to seven hours a day, which included sport and games. Taine concluded that in an English public school education there was 'nothing ... to attract the mind. The principal object arrived at is a good knowledge of Greek and Latin and the ability to write verse and prose in these two languages correctly.'[2]

Highgate School

Edmund Yates, a journalist and author, described his not too happy years at Highgate School in his memoir *Edmund Yates, His Recollections and Experiences* (1885).

> I look back to the six years which I passed at the Highgate School with very little pleasure. The headmaster, Dr Dyne, was a capable pedagogue enough, not more than usually narrow-minded, priggish and conventional. He was a type of the old-fashioned pedantic school, which looked upon Oxford as the 'hub of the universe', thought the study of Latin and Greek the primary object of our creation, despised modern languages and foreign countries, and believed thoroughly in the virtues of corporal punishment. A desperate 'swisher' the doctor, as I had cause to know, and not overburdened, to my thinking, with tact, judgment, or impartiality. He never liked me, and there was no particular reason why he should, for I had the theatrical taint; I was not a show-boy; I was not going to the university, where I could reflect credit on my teaching; and I was idle, mischievous, independent.
>
> I must have learned something, for I was at the head of the fifth form when I left, at fifteen years of age; but I do not suppose what I acquired did me much good. I could read, construe, and parse the principal Latin and Greek poets – I am sure I could

not do so now – but of English classics I was wholly ignorant; they formed no portion of the 'curriculum'. The study of modern language, though not absolutely tabooed, was minimised as much as possible. I do not imagine that the headmaster or any of his assistants had ever crossed the Channel, or knew a syllable even of French, for which language their contempt was as great as Mr Lillyvick's [a character in Dickens' novel *Nicholas Nickleby*].The learning of French and German was an 'extra' not supposed to be in the least necessary to an ordinary education, but to be paid for separately, and to be undergone by the boys, whose foolish parents insisted on their acquiring it, at times when the rest of the school was at play. A snuff-taking old French gentleman came once a week, and sat at the end of a table, while a dozen boys fought round it, larked, and shot paper pellets into his frizzy hair. He had no authority, poor old fellow, and there was no-one to keep order; the whole thing was a farce; and had I not had a natural inclination for French study, and an interest in my *Telemaque* and my *Henriade* sufficient to induce me to read them in my play-hours and my holidays – interest such as I never could feel in my Homer, Virgil, or Herodotus – I should have left Highgate as ignorant of modern language as did most of my compeers. But though I got little good from it, it is not to be denied that Highgate School, under Dr Dyne's management, was very successful. Its pupils took scholarships and exhibitions, and good positions later on in the class-lists; and the tone of the school, which under the doctor's predecessors had suffered terribly, was entirely restored by him; a greater feat, it will be allowed, than the quintupling the number of pupils, which Dr Dyne also accomplished during his régime.[3]

Charity Schools

There were a few schools in London which were run by charities. The personal recommendation of a governor was necessary to obtain admission and applicants were means tested, so that only children whose parents could not afford to pay for their education were admitted.

The most famous of these schools was Christ's Hospital in Newgate Street. It was founded in 1553 for poor fatherless children and foundlings. The school was commonly referred to as the 'Blue Coat School' because of its unusual uniform consisting of a blue gown, a yellow petticoat, a red girdle, yellow stockings, a clergyman-style neckband and a flat black woollen cap.

Girls' Education

It was assumed that girls of the higher social classes would marry and devote their lives to their husbands and children. For this reason it was deemed that they did not need a proper education. Their education was, therefore, limited to ornamental accomplishments such as sewing, drawing, dancing and music. They were also taught basic literacy skills and enough mathematics to enable them to manage a household budget. They were taught at home by a governess, at private schools and finishing schools. If they failed to find a husband their education was considered sufficient for them to earn a living as a governess.

Girls' Schools

In 1850 Miss Frances Buss opened the North London Collegiate School for girls. She went on to found Camden School for Girls. These schools provided their pupils with a proper education and campaigned for them to be allowed to take public examinations and attend university.

In 1872 the Girls' Day School Trust was formed which established more than thirty schools for girls in England by the end of the century.

Queen's College

In 1848 Queen's College, the first school in England established for the higher education of women, was opened in Harley Street. Its foundation resulted from the concern of supporters of the Governesses Benevolent Institution that women responsible for educating children should be well educated themselves. Miss Buss was one of its early students. The following information about the college is taken from Peter Cunningham's *Hand Book of London* (1850):

> Queen's College, London, so named by royal permission and under royal charter for general female education, and for granting to governesses certificates of qualification. The subjects of instruction are arithmetic, drawing, English grammar, French, geography, history, Latin, vocal music, natural history, reading, writing. It is at present in Harley-street.[4]

Bedford College

In 1849 a Ladies College was opened in Bedford Square to provide women with a higher education, the first college of its kind in England. Its founder, Mrs Elizabeth Reid, declared, 'We shall never have better men till men have better mothers.' According to Charles Dickens Junior's *Dictionary of London* (1888) the college gave 'a good education' to young women over the age of sixteen. Lectures were given in biology, chemistry and physics.[5] The college became a constituent college of the University of London in 1900.

The Poor

At the beginning of the Victorian era poor children were rarely educated. Basic literacy skills were taught in most Sunday schools alongside religious instruction. There were two options for parents who could afford a little money for their children's education. One was 'dame schools', run by elderly women in their own homes, which offered little more than child-minding. The other option was an elementary school run by one of two voluntary religious societies, which received some financial aid from the government. These were the National Society for Promoting the Education of the Poor in the Principles of the Established Church, established in 1811, and the British and Foreign School Society, established in 1814. Although the latter claimed to be non-secular, it was, in practice, supported by nonconformists. Pupils who attended one of these schools received a basic education in reading, writing and arithmetic (the three Rs). Parents were charged a few pennies a week, known as the 'school pence', for the education of their children.

The very poorest children, even if they had time to attend school, would not have been able to find the 'school pence'. Some children were too busy working to go to school, as their families needed the few pennies a week even small children could earn. There were also many children without families living and working on the streets of London, who received no education at all. Their days and all their energy were taken up with the struggle to survive.

Henry Mayhew came across a large number of children who had received no education and knew nothing beyond what was necessary to survive on the streets. One such child was a nine-year-old boy who worked as a mudlark on the banks of the River Thames. He was typical of the many uneducated children the journalist interviewed. Mayhew recorded the boy's responses to his questions.

> He had been one month at school before he went mud-larking. Some time ago he had gone to the ragged-school; but he no longer went there, for he forgot it. He could neither read nor write, and did not think he could learn if he tried 'ever-so-much'. He didn't know what religion his father and mother were, nor did know what religion meant. God was God, he said. He had heard he was good, but didn't know what good he was to him. He thought he was a Christian, but he didn't know what a Christian was. He had heard of Jesus Christ once, when he went to a Catholic chapel, but he never heard tell of who or what he was, and didn't 'particular care' about knowing. His father and mother were born in Aberdeen, but he didn't know where Aberdeen was. London was England, and England, he said, was in London, but he couldn't tell in what part. He could not tell where he would go to when he died, and didn't believe anyone could tell that. Prayers, he told me, were what people said to themselves at night. He never said any, and didn't know any; his mother sometimes used to speak to him about them, but he could never learn any.[6]

The government's woefully inadequate contribution to the education of the poor in London was to build five residential 'district' or 'barrack' schools. The largest of these schools was the Central London District School for Pauper Children, known as the 'monster school' with places for 1,000 pupils. It was originally in Norwood in south-east London before moving to Hanwell on the outskirts of the capital. There was, not surprisingly, a stigma attached to these 'poor law' schools. Pauper children living long-term in London workhouses received a rudimentary education in a workhouse school or were sent to local voluntary aided schools. Some were sent for industrial training to help them break out of the cycle of poverty.

Ragged Schools

Ragged schools, which had existed before the Victorian period, were set up by individuals and charities to offer free education to children too poor, ragged, dirty and rough to be accepted by other schools, such as those run by the two religious societies. The founders of ragged schools were motivated by their faith and compassion for the poor. It was through his work as a ragged school teacher in the East End that Thomas Barnardo became aware of the plight of destitute and homeless children in London and set about helping them.

Many of London's ragged schools were housed in makeshift buildings, such as old stables and filled-in railway arches in the slum areas. As well as providing a basic education with a high religious content, ragged schools provided a warm shelter and sometimes food and clothing as well. Some ragged schools were small concerns, such as one founded by Quintin Hogg, a businessman, in Off Alley near the Strand in 1864. Hogg wrote the following description of his school:

> The class prospered amazingly; our little room which was only thirty foot long by twelve foot wide got so crammed that I used to divide the school into two sections of sixty each, the first lot coming from seven to eight-thirty, and the second lot from eight-

> thirty to ten. There I used to sit between two classes, perched on the back of a form, dining on my 'pint of thick and two doorsteps', as the boys used to call coffee and bread and treacle, taking one class in reading and the other at writing or arithmetic. Each section closed with a ten minutes' service and prayer.[7]

Other schools, such as those founded by the missionaries of the London City Mission, were part of a larger organisation. The Field Lane Ragged School, opened in 1841, became one of the largest in London. A description by Charles Dickens of a visit he paid to the boys' class at this school is in marked contrast to the pleasant, orderly picture of the Off Alley School. It shows what a hard task it was to educate the rough, uncouth and unmanageable street children who attended London's ragged schools.

> The close, low, chamber at the back, in which the boys were crowded, was so foul and stifling as to be, at first, almost insupportable. But its moral aspect was so far worse than its physical, that this was soon forgotten. Huddled together on a bench about the room, and shown out by some flaring candles stuck against the walls, were a crowd of boys, varying from mere infants to young men; sellers of fruit, herbs, lucifer-matches, flints; sleepers under the dry arches of bridges; young thieves and beggars – with nothing natural to youth about them; with nothing frank, ingenuous, or pleasant in their faces; low-browed, vicious, cunning, wicked; abandoned of all help but this;- speeding downward to destruction, – and UNUTTERABLY IGNORANT.[8]

The ragged school was the only hope for these boys and Dickens was impressed by the efforts being made to help them.

A poor mother who was interviewed by Henry Mayhew praised the education her children received at a London ragged school.

> My little girl goes now to the Ragged School, and is a good scholar, and a very good girl, and never misses school ... I consider the Ragged School here has done great good. My children have had

> a good education. They can read and write well, and God knows how they would have learned that but for the school here.[9]

Thomas Archer, a contemporary author of a number of books on London, was also impressed with the education provided at ragged schools, describing them as 'a mighty power in this great city' which had 'extended their benevolent influence throughout the poorest neighbourhoods'.[10] This reflected a widely held view.

The Ragged School Union

The Ragged School Union was formed in 1844 with Lord Shaftesbury as its president, a position he held for forty years. Its purpose was to raise the profile of ragged schools, to support them and to spread their 'humanising influence'. The union also succeeded in drawing attention to the issue of educating poor children. Between 1844 and 1852 the number of ragged schools in London rose from sixteen to 110. By 1870 there were 191 of these schools in the capital, educating more than 52,000 pupils.[11] By then pupils were taught by trained teachers, monitors and volunteers.

Government Intervention

By the middle of the century there was growing pressure for the government to be involved in the organisation of education for the nation's children. In 1858 the Newcastle Commission was set up to look into the state of education in England and Wales. It reported back recommendations of the measures necessary to provide an effective and cheap education for all children. A Revised Education Code was introduced in 1862 which made the grants paid to the schools run by the two voluntary societies dependent on the attendance of pupils, and their performance in the three Rs. An additional grant was paid to schools providing religious instruction. Schools were inspected regularly by government inspectors.

In 1870 the government passed an Education Act which established state education in England and Wales. The factor which finally pushed the government into taking action was the passing of the 1867 Reform Act. This extended the right to vote to male working-class householders in towns. It was feared that if the new voters remained uneducated they would not use their vote wisely. In the words of the MP Robert Lowe, 'we must educate our future masters'.

Under the terms of the 1870 Act elementary schools were built in places where there were no church schools. These new schools, which were run by School Boards elected by ratepayers, became known as 'Board Schools'. The new purpose-built schools had assembly halls and tiered classrooms. Those in London were often large and imposing buildings of several storeys. They rose above the surrounding streets as a symbol of the growing importance of education.

The offices of the London School Board were housed in a grand, early Renaissance-style building on the Victoria Embankment. In 1896 the London School Board had nearly half-a-million children on its rolls, who were taught by nine thousand adult and pupil teachers.

The primary object of state education was to make children into good citizens and prepare them for work fitting their station in life. At a cost of a few pence a week for all but the poorest children, the curriculum covered the three Rs, religious instruction and physical education. Other subjects such as history and geography were added later. Pupils were also taught practical, vocational subjects, such as metalwork and woodwork for the boys and domestic science and needlework for the girls. The following descriptions of a board school assembly, cookery and carpentry classes are taken from *The Queen's London, A Pictorial and Descriptive Record of the Streets, Buildings, Parks and Scenery of the Great Metropolis in the Fifty-ninth Year of the Reign of Her Majesty Queen Victoria* (1896):

Morning Assembly at a Board School

Just as at the large public schools of England the boys meet together for morning prayers, so in like fashion the day begins at the Kilburn

Lane Higher Grade School ... First a hymn is sung, accompanied by the string band – numbering in all some sixty boys ... and by a youthful organist. This band is, all things considered, an excellent one, and its employment conduces greatly to the reverent interest taken by the boys in the proceedings. Prayers, read by the headmaster, follow, after which the scholars go to their respective class-rooms to enter upon the studies of the day.[12]

A Board School Cookery Class

Twenty-four girls attending the Kilburn Lane School, all with neat pinafores on, form the class. Half of them are occupied in copying recipes; while the other dozen are busily engaged in preparing various homely dishes suitable for an artisan's dinner. The expert teacher has spent the first hour of the morning in explaining how the work is to be done, and the young plain-cooks-in-the-making are now showing in practice how far they have mastered their lesson.[13]

A Board School Carpentry Class

Cookery for the girls; carpentry for the boys. Such is the programme carried out at the Kilburn Lane Higher Grade School ... Each boy in attendance receives weekly two-and-a-half-hours' instruction in practical woodwork, drawing, and the growth and structure of the different varieties of hard and soft wood. The lads are also taught how to grind and sharpen the tools they use. It is not at all astonishing that for most boys, whatever they may think of other lessons, this branch of elementary education has an irresistible attraction. The authorities are satisfied that such work fulfils its purpose, which is the training of the eyes and hands to habits of accuracy and neatness.[14]

To achieve their objective of creating useful citizens out of working-class children, schools inculcated such middle-class virtues as cleanliness, punctuality, diligence, gratitude, obedience and dutifulness. Good behaviour was rewarded and bad behaviour was punished.

From 1880 attendance became compulsory for all children aged five to ten years and School Board 'Visitors' were appointed to enforce it. Attendance figures were used to calculate government grants, so schools had an incentive to be strict about this. To encourage good attendance children received certificates and prizes. Attendance rates also improved from 1891, when the 'school pence' was abolished.

By the end of the century the school leaving age had increased to twelve years and there was a marked improvement in literacy rates. Thomas Barnardo noticed the good work done by the Board Schools which had 'brought education to the most neglected' and had contributed to the 'silent but profound revolution' which he noticed all around him in London in the last years of the nineteenth century.

The poor had been helped to help themselves, both for the present and future generations, as the journalist George Sims discovered on a visit to a Board School in 1883.

> Directly we enter we are struck with the appearance of these children. Bad faces there are among them – bruises and scars, and bandages and rags – but the bulk of these younger children have a generally better appearance than their little neighbours.
>
> There is a theory in the school, and it is borne out to a certain extent by fact, that some of the youngest and best-looking are the children of girls who just got the benefit of the Education Act before they were too old, and who in their young married life have reaped the benefit of those principles of cleanliness and thrift which the Board School inculcates. The young mothers are already a race far ahead of the older ones in this district, and the children naturally benefit by it.[15]

Further Education

In 1859 a book entitled *Self-Help* was published and soon became a best-seller. Its author was a Scottish journalist named Samuel Smiles. This book encapsulated the spirit of the age. Many readers followed Smiles' advice and took advantage of the opportunities for self-improvement which were increasingly being made available for everyone, including the working classes. This enthusiasm was helped by the improvement in literacy following the introduction of state education.

In keeping with Samuel Smiles' self-help ethic many working men's institutions, run privately or by charities, were founded in London to provide further education for the working classes.

The London Mechanics' Institution

The London Mechanics' Institution was founded by George Birkbeck, a physician and philanthropist, 'for dissemination of useful knowledge among the industrious classes of the community'. The following description is taken from *Cruchley's London in 1865: A Handbook for Strangers*:

> The London Mechanics' Institution, 29 Southampton Buildings, Chancery Lane, is the oldest, and, in fact, may be considered the originator of all the Mechanics' or Popular Institutes for education, literature, and science, in England. The late excellent philanthropist, Dr Birkbeck, founded it in 1823, deriving much assistance from the support of Lord Brougham and many other public spirited men. Its library contains 4000 volumes. There are reading-rooms, class-rooms, a capacious 'theatre' or lecture-room, in which for thirty-five years the lectures have been given weekly, and the usual appurtenances of a literary institute.[16]

Cruchley listed seven similar institutions across the capital.

Regent Street Polytechnic

According to Peter Cunningham's *Hand-Book of London* this educational and entertainment facility was founded in 1838 for 'the advancement of the Arts and Practical Sciences, especially in connexion with Agriculture, Mining, Manufactures and other branches of industry'. One of the main attractions was a cast-iron diving bell in which 'visitors may safely descend a considerable depth into the tank, which, with the canals, holds nearly ten thousand gallons of water, and can, if required be emptied in less than one minute'. Cunningham added, 'This is an interesting and instructive exhibition, worthy of a visit from every stranger in London.'[17]

In 1881 this institution was acquired by the businessman and philanthropist Quintin Hogg. Its provision was extended to include Bible classes, social and athletics clubs, lectures and technical training. These facilities were open to anyone who could afford to pay the subscription.

Northampton Institute

The Northampton Institute, which was inspired by the Regent Street Polytechnic, was established in 1891 on a site in Clerkenwell which originally belonged to the Marquess of Northampton. It provided technical education, physical training and recreation for young people of the area's poorer classes. It offered training in mechanical and electrical engineering, electro chemistry, horology (clockmaking was a local industry), crafts, domestic economy and women's trades.

The City of London College

The City of London College, located in White Street and Ropemaker Street, Moorfields, was founded in 1848 by two London clergymen. Its aim was to provide instruction in languages, arts and sciences. Its original location was in Crosby Hall, Bishopsgate, but it grew to such an extent that it was moved to Sussex Hall in Leadenhall Street, where it remained providing good service for twenty-two years. It moved to its final location in 1883. Most of its teaching was done in the evening.

The People's Palace

The People's Palace in Mile End Road was a free cultural institution for people living in the East End. It was opened by Queen Victoria in May 1887, the year in which she celebrated her Golden Jubilee. The main hall, which was used for public meetings, concerts and art exhibitions, was named the Queens' Hall because all round the building there were statues of the queens of England. The People's Palace was paid for by donations.

According to Charles Dickens Junior,

> The germ of this institution was the bequest of £12,250 by Mr Barber Beaumont, towards the founding of a Philosophical Institution for the benefit of the inhabitants of Beaumont-sq., Mile End. Since then the trust has been much extended and has erected palatial buildings for the advantage of the East End poor, out of funds subscribed by the public; the Drapers' Company having alone contributed the munificent sum of £60,000. The scheme of the trust includes the provision of a great central hall, large library, swimming baths, technical trade and science schools, gymnasia, billiard and refreshment rooms, great exhibitions, winter gardens &c; the aim, in short, being to provide a place of recreation and university for the poor of East London. Since October 1887, when active operations began, three quarters of a million people have attended the Palace, and there are now nearly 3,000 students in the evening classes. The Palace is, indeed, well worthy of a visit from all.[18]

The University of London

In the 1820s a group of politicians and scholars decided to establish a university in London which would be open to anyone who could pay the moderate fees. A site was bought in Bloomsbury and University College was opened in Gower Street in 1828. In 1831 a rival college, Kings College, was opened in the Strand.

In 1836 the University of London was established. It was incorporated by royal charter the following year, the first year of Victoria's reign. The charter gave the governing body the power to set examinations and confer degrees. A wide range of subjects was taught. In 1878 the university admitted women to all degree subjects except medicine. The following year the London Medical College for Women was founded, with the power to confer degrees.

The university, which flourished throughout the Victorian period, offered an excellent alternative to the long-established universities of Oxford and Cambridge.

Public Libraries

The introduction of free public libraries helped the poor to help themselves. The Public Libraries Act of 1850 gave local boroughs the power to establish free public libraries – prior to the Act libraries were paid for by subscription. In practice boroughs were hampered by limitations on the amount of money they were permitted to spend, but the principle of free libraries had been established.

In London the first public library was opened in Great Smith Street in Westminster in 1857. More libraries opened in the following decades, often with the financial help of philanthropists.

Putney Library was one of the libraries opened following the passing of the Public Libraries Act. It was opened in 1889 in what was described as 'a palatial and commodious structure'. It was paid for by George Newnes, a wealthy publisher. In its first ten years nearly half a million books were borrowed.

East Ham Library was partly paid for by John Passmore Edwards, editor of the journal *Building News*. According to an article in the *Municipal Journal* of 4 November 1899, there were 'few places where libraries were more appreciated. To have seen the crowds who turned out last Saturday to the opening ceremony of the new library would have convinced anyone of the keen interest the people take in the subject.' The article said of the building, 'It is architecturally beautiful, and is crowned by a handsome clock tower.'

3

WORK

There were countless ways to make a living in Victorian London. It was the centre of government, finance, commerce, an important manufacturing centre and its port was the largest in the world – all providing employment for many Londoners. As the city was being modernised, enlarged and improved there were also many opportunities for architects, engineers and builders. An army of workers was employed in different fields to cater for the needs of London's rapidly increasing population and its many tourists and visitors.

Different occupations were located in different areas of London. Clerkenwell, for example, was the centre of watch and jewellery making, Spitalfields and Bethnal Green were locations for silk and velvet weavers, the East End districts by the river were where trades connected with ships and sailing were found, and Fleet Street and the Strand were the centre of the printing industry.

Despite the many job opportunities there were not enough jobs to go round. There was great competition for casual work and many people, particularly the unskilled, were forced to scratch a living on the streets. Some were forced to beg or resort to crime to survive.

Domestic Servants

In 1851 there were around a quarter of a million domestic servants in London, most of whom were female. They were employed to do the hard physical work of running the homes of the upper and middle classes. Employing servants was a sign of respectability and even lowly members of the middle class could afford a young maid, known as a maid-of-all-work. These were the lowest and most put upon of Victorian servants.

Hannah Cullwick was a maid-of-all-work for an upholsterer in Kilburn. She worked long hours – usually from half-past six in the morning until eleven o'clock at night. Unlike most maids in her position, Hannah had another servant to help her. The following is an extract from her diary, which shows how much she was expected to do in return for a pitiful wage and board and lodging:

> Opened the shutters and lighted the kitchen fire – shook my sooty things in the dusthole and emptied the soot there, swept and dusted the rooms and the hall, laid the cloth and got breakfast up – cleaned two pairs of boots – made the beds and emptied the slops, cleared and washed the breakfast things up – cleaned the plate – cleaned the knives and got dinner up – cleared away, cleaned the kitchen up – unpacked a hamper – took two chickens to Mrs Brewer's and brought a message back – made a tart and picked and gutted two ducks and roasted them – cleaned the steps and flags on my knees, blackleaded the scraper in the front of the house – cleaned the street flags too on my knees – had tea – cleared away – washed up in the scullery – cleared the pantry on my knees and scoured the tables – scrubbed the flags round the house and cleaned the window sills – got tea at 9 for the master and Mrs Warwick in my dirt but Anne carried it up – cleaned the privy and passage and scullery floor on my knees – washed the door and cleaned the sink down – put the supper ready for Anne to take up, as I was too dirty and tired to go upstairs.[1]

Transport

Many people were employed in a variety of jobs on the trains, both above and below ground, the omnibuses, trams and steamboats which provided public transport in London. There were also countless cab drivers providing a service all over the capital.

The horse-drawn omnibuses, which were introduced in 1829, were busy from early morning until late at night in all directions across London. Henry Mayhew interviewed an omnibus conductor or 'cad' when he was investigating the lives of poor workers in the 1840s. This 'very intelligent' man, whose work was just as gruelling as Hannah Cullwick's, worked very long hours with no holiday; most of his life was taken up by his job, as this extract from the interview shows.

> 'I am thirty-five or thirty-six, and have been a conductor for six years ... The worst part of my business is its uncertainty. I may be discharged any day, and not know for what...I think I've done better as a conductor in hot weather or fine weather than in wet. Tho' I've got a good journey when it's come on to showery as people was starting for or starting from the City. I had one master, who when his buss (sic) came in full in the wet, used to say, 'This is prime, them's God Almighty's customers; he sent them.' I've heard him say so many a time. We get far more ladies and children too on a fine day; they go more a shopping then, and of an evening they go more to public places. I pay over my money every night. It runs from 40 shillings to £4.4 s., or a little more on extraordinary occasions. I have taken more money since the short-uns [short journeys] were established. One day before that I took only 18 shillings.
>
> ... I never get to a public place – whether it's a chapel or a play-house – unless, indeed, I get a holiday, and that is not once in two years. I've asked for a day's holiday and been refused ... I'm quite ignorant of what's passing in the world, my time's so taken up. We only know what's going on from hearing people talk in the bus. I never care to read the paper now, though I used to like it. If I have two minutes to spare I'd rather take a nap than anything else. We know no more politics than the backwoodsmen of America, because we haven't time to care about it. I've fallen asleep on my step as the bus was going on,

> and have almost fallen off. I have often to put up with insolence from vulgar fellows that think it fun to chaff a cad, as they call it. There's no help for it. Our masters won't listen to complaints. If we're not satisfied we can go. Conductors are a sober set of men. We must be sober. It takes every farthing of our wages to live well enough and keep a wife and family ... In winter I never see my three children, only as they're in bed, and I never hear their voices, if they don't wake up early. If they cry at night it don't disturb me, I sleep so heavily after fifteen hours work out in the air.[2]

The Newspaper Industry

During the Victorian period there was a huge increase in the publication of newspapers, helped by improving literacy rates as the century progressed. The daily newspapers included the *Times*, the *Daily Telegraph*, the *Morning Chronicle* and the *Morning Post*. Sunday newspapers were also published. There were more than a hundred newspapers in the London suburbs alone. The centre of this busy industry was in and around Fleet Street.

When the writer and journalist George Augustus Sala was researching his book *Twice Round the Clock or Hours of the Day and Night in London* (1859) he visited the offices and printing works of the *Times* in Printing House Square near St Paul's Cathedral to watch the newspaper in production. This extract describes the collection of the piles of the first edition of the paper, hot off the press.

> At five o'clock a.m., the first phase of the publication of the *Times* newspaper commences. In a large bare room – something like the receiving ward of an hospital – with a pay counter at one end, and lined throughout with parallel rows of bare deal tables, the 'leading journal' first sees the light of publicity. The tables are covered with huge piles of newspapers spread out the full size of the sheet. These are, with dazzling celerity, folded by legions of stout porters, and straightway carried to the door, where cabs, and carts, and light express phaeton-like vehicles, are in

readiness to convey them to the railway stations. The quantity of papers borne to the carriages outside by the stout porters seems, and truly is, prodigious; but your astonishment will be increased when I tell you that this only forms the stock purchased every morning by those gigantic newsagents, Messrs Smith and Son, of the Strand. As the largest consumers, the *Times* naturally allows them a priority of supply, and it is not for a considerable period after they have received their orders that the great body of newsagents and newsvendors – the 'trade', as they are generically termed – are admitted, grumbling intensely, to buy the number of quires or copies which they expect to sell or lend that day. The scene outside then becomes one of baffling noise amid confusion. There is a cobweb of wheeled vehicles of all sorts, from a cab to a hybrid construction something between a wheelbarrow and a costermonger's shallow [basket]. There is much bawling and flinging, shoving, hoisting, pulling and dragging of parcels; all the horses' heads seem to be turned the wrong way; everybody's off-wheel seems locked in somebody else's; but the proceedings on the whole are characterised by much good-humour and some fun. The mob of boys – all engaged in the news trade – is something wonderful; fat boys, lean boys, sandy-haired and red-haired boys, tall boys and short boys, boys with red comforters (though it is summer), and boys with sacks on their backs and money-bags in their hands; boys with turn-down collars; and boys whose extreme buttonedupness renders the fact of their having any shirts to put collars to, turn-down or stuck-up, grievously problematical. Hard-working boys are these juvenile Bashi-Bazouks [Ottoman soldiers] of the newspaper trade. And I am glad to observe, for the edification of social economists, with scarcely an exception, very honest boys. I don't exactly say that they are trusted with untold gold, but of the gold that is told, to say nothing of the silver and copper, they give a generally entirely satisfactory account. At about half-past seven the cohorts of newsvendors, infantry and cavalry, gradually disperse, and the *Times* is left to the agonies of its second edition.[3]

Manufacture and Trade

London was an important manufacturing centre. Its industries included tanning, brewing, ship and coach building, and the manufacture of shoes, clothes, clocks, bricks, pianos and precision instruments.

At the beginning of the Victorian era the East End of London was still a seafaring district, where the main industries were shipbuilding and associated trades, and silk weaving. By the middle of the nineteenth century the East End was changing – its old industries had declined and were replaced by 'noxious' trades, such as glue and soap making. These trades had previously been located in the City but moved to the East End when the City became a financial centre.

The Clothing Industry

The small workshops of this industry, which had a large proportion of female labour, were located in the West End, near the homes of the well-to-do. These were replaced later in the century by mass-produced, 'off-the-peg' goods.

The following detailed description of a clothes factory is taken from an article by Miss Clementine Black, Secretary of the Women's Trades Union and Provident League:

> As we go round and watch the work being done, we perceive that these girls can do things almost miraculous. Children's frocks and pinafores are being made – little delicate garments with tiny tucks and lace edgings, and minute runners of fine tape in the top hem. And these tape-runners the girls do not slip in with a bodkin; no, they like to go a quicker way, they stitch the hem, which is perhaps a quarter of an inch wide, with the tape in it. To do that and never fix it is a feat indeed. One girl I saw stitching on lace; the lace was frilled, and she frilled it with her fingers as she stitched. Nothing is tacked, and yet the exactitude and delicacy of the work are faultless ... And this work is done with very great rapidity. The whizz of the machines seems deafening to a newcomer; but the workers talk

> through it with no raising of the voice. One corner of the room is noisiest of all; it is the corner where the button-hole machines stand. The button-hole is made in a fraction of a minute; and when a garment has all its button-holes made, it is tossed to a young girl at a table to cut, for the machine does not cut. She has a little instrument with a blade precisely the right length, and laying the garment on the table, makes incision after incision. There is, of course, a certain danger of cutting the sewn edge, but with the proper instrument this danger is slight. Another young girl takes the garment, gives it a sharp shake, lays it flat on the deal table, and folds it in the twinkling of an eye.[4]

Brewing

Brewing was a major industry in Victorian London, employing many people. As well as those who made the beer, others were employed managing production, making barrels, caring for the dray horses, selling, in distribution and in the brewery offices. The main London breweries were Barclay and Perkins in Southwark, the Albion Brewery in Whitechapel, the Lion Brewery in Lambeth, Fullers in Chiswick and Whitbread's in Chiswell Street, Islington.

This description of the Lion Brewery is taken from *Curiosities of London* by John Timbs.

> The handsomest edifice of this class in the metropolis is the Lion Brewery, built for Goding in 1836, in Belvedere-road, next Waterloo-bridge, and surmounted with a colossal stone lion. The top of the building is a tank to contain 1000 barrels of water, pumped up from a well 230 feet deep, or from the Thames; this supplies the floor below, where the boiled liquor is cooled – 200 barrels in less than an hour; when cooled it is received on the floor beneath into the fermenting tuns [vats]; next it descends to the floor for fining; and lastly, to the cellars or store-vats. The steam-engine passes the beer under the Belvedere-road; loads or unloads barges; conveys malt by the Archimedes Screw or Jacob's Ladder; and pumps water and beer to every height and extreme

position, displaying the advantage of mechanic power, by its steady, quiet regularity.[5]

In *London A Pilgrimage* Blanchard Jerrold described his visit to a brewery to watch the brewing process.

A journey through the town of Malt and Hops is heavy work. The departments are many, and are all spacious. They follow in well-considered sequence. The mashing, the boiling, the cooling, the fermenting, the cleansing, the barrel-filling, the storing, the despatching, are so many departments of the government; with a sustaining aroma holding all in one atmosphere – and which keeps the mind in an unbroken train of thought even when contemplating the stables where the famous horses are kept as daintily as in the Royal Mews. Perhaps the first startling scene in the round is the mash-tun.

Mashing is the elementary process of beer making, and the object of these strange workers with wooden spades is to mix the malt thoroughly with the water. The result is an amber liquid, called wort – lakes of which we proceed to view, lying placidly in tanks. During its progression to perfect beer the sweet wort grows sour. On its way it is pumped up from the cool lakes into gigantic copper boilers, and boiled with great care – for here the experienced and learned brewer shows himself. The boiling satisfactorily done, the wort flows out into broad lakes, airily situated – where it can become rapidly cool, without getting sour; and then it gradually subsides into these prodigious gyle [quantity of beer brewed at one time] tuns, about which staircases are ranged, and in which you would have to drag carefully for the body of an elephant. In these towers, against which men look like flies, the wort ferments – and we have – porter...

... there are upwards of forty officials – who direct the coming and going, the filling and repairing, the brewing and selling of a rolling army of something like eighty thousand barrels. Their domain covers an acre of land and comprises several streets

> bridged by light iron-bridges that look slight as spider-webs from the pavement.[6]

Public Services

Public services were a major employer in Victorian London. These services included the maintenance of roads, footpaths and bridges, parks and open spaces, water supply, sewers, the fire, police and postal services, street cleaning, rubbish collection and street lighting.

In the early years of Victoria's reign responsibility for the capital's infrastructure and public services was divided between a multitude of local parishes, bodies and companies. In 1855 the Metropolitan Board of Works was formed and took over the running of most services. The City of London was responsible for its own services.

Sewage Workers

Not surprisingly, the more unpleasant, dangerous and usually badly paid jobs, such as maintaining the sewers and collecting and sifting through rubbish, were done by the poorest Londoners. Henry Mayhew interviewed a number of these poor workers, including a sewage flusher, whose story was related in a letter to the *Morning Chronicle* in November 1849.

> 'I've been at flushing four months now. I don't know how long it will last ... The best part of my work is in plunging ditches, or cleansing the open sewers. Some of them, though, are bad enough as to stenches' ... 'When we go plunging' the man continued, 'we has long poles with a piece of wood at the end of them, and we stirs up the mud at the bottom of the ditches while the tide's a-going down. We have got slides at the end of the ditches, and we pulls these up and lets out the water, mud, and all, into the Thames' ... 'We're in the water a great deal ... The sewers generally swarms with rats. I runs away from 'em, I don't like 'em ... When the slide is lifted up the rush is very great, and takes all before it. It roars away like a wild beast. We're always obliged to work according to tide, both above and below ground. When we have got no water in the sewer we shovels the dirt up into a bank on both sides, so that

> when the flush of water comes down the loosened dirt is all carried away by it. After flushing, the bottom of the sewer is as clean as this floor, but in a couple of months the soil is a foot to fifteen inches deep, and middling hard.'[7]

This man worked as one of a team of 300, for seven and a half hours every day in the foul air of the sewers.

Rubbish Collection

Another public service was provided by the dustmen, who collected the household rubbish from an estimated 300,000 houses in London and took it to the dust-yards. Many people were then employed in sifting through the rubbish, leaving only soil and dust. According to Mayhew there were ninety contractors, both large and small, involved in this business in London. He described the dustmen as wearing 'knee-breeches, with ancle (*sic*) boots or gaiters, short dirty smockfrocks or coarse gray (*sic*) jackets, and fantail hats'.[8]

They walked around the streets with a 'heavily-built high box cart, which is mostly coated with a thick crust of filth, and drawn by a clumsy-looking horse'. Two men accompanied the cart and filled baskets from the dustbins, which they emptied into the cart. They alerted residents of their arrival by crying out 'Dust. Oy-eh!' When the cart was full it was taken to one of London's many dust-yards.[9]

Mayhew visited one such dust-yard where he interviewed a rubbish sifter.

> [He] was, at the time of my visit, shovelling the sifted soil from one of the lesser heaps, and, by a great effort of strength and activity, pitching each shovel-full to the top of a lofty mound, somewhat resembling a pyramid. Opposite to him stood a little woman, stoutly made, and with her arms bare above the elbow; she was his partner in the work, and was pitching shovelfull for shovelfull with him to the summit of the heap. She wore an old soiled cotton gown, open in front, and tucked up behind in the fashion of the last century. She had clouts of old rags tied round her ancles (sic) to prevent the

> dust from getting into her shoes, a sort of coarse towel fastened in front for an apron, and a red handkerchief bound tightly round her head. In this trim she worked away, and not only kept pace with the man, but often threw two shovels for his one, although he was a tall, powerful fellow. She smiled when she saw me noticing her, and seemed to continue her work with greater assiduity. I learned that she was deaf, and spoke so indistinctly that no stranger could understand her. She had also a defect in her sight, which latter circumstance had compelled her to abandon the sifting, as she could not well distinguish the various articles found in the dust-heap. The poor creature had therefore taken to the shovel and now works with it every day, doing the labour of the strongest men.[10]

The dust that was left over after the sifting process was complete was used for making bricks.

The Lamplighter

Like many Victorian children, Alfred Rosling Bennett, author of *London and Londoners in the Eighteen-Fifties and Sixties* (1924) watched out for the lamplighter who turned on the street lamps every evening and extinguished them every morning.

> He was often an elderly man, furnished with a short ladder and a hand-lamp. The former he placed against the projecting iron arm provided for the purpose, ran up, turned the gas cock, applied his lamp, down again, and away with shouldered ladder to the next beacon. In the morning he went his round again, this time to extinguish. This system endured for many years. London was gas-illuminated from the dawn of my recollection and I do not remember anything but the ladder device until the 1870s. The gas jet was only a feeble fish-tail burner, but at all events it did not daze and dazzle as some of the modern bright lights do.[11]

The Police Force

The Metropolitan Police provided another important public service. This force was established in 1829 by the Home Secretary,

Robert Peel. It had become necessary to replace the parish constables, nightwatchmen and Bow Street Runners, who previously policed the capital, with a professional force. The new police officers were nicknamed 'Bobbies' and 'Peelers' after Robert Peel and were also known as 'Crushers'. The City of London had its own force and there were also separate forces to police the River Thames and the railways.

The new Metropolitan force was made up of twenty divisions in addition to the Commissioner's Office. Each division comprised one superintendent, inspectors, sergeants and constables. Each constable had his own beat and a 'fixed point' where he was stationed at night. In 1842 a small detective department was set up to deal with more difficult or important cases.[12]

Max Schlesinger was impressed by the policemen he met in London whom he described as follows:

> The London policeman ... knows every nook and corner, every house, man, woman and child on his beat. He knows their occupations, habits and circumstances. This knowledge he derives from his constantly being employed in the same quarter and the same street, and to – and surely a mind on duty bent may take great liberties with the conventional moralities – that platonic and friendly intercourse which he carries on with the female servants of the establishments which it is his vocation to protect. An English maidservant is a pleasant girl to chat with, when half shrouded by the mystic fog of the evening and with her smart little cap coquettishly placed on her head, she issues from the sallyport of the kitchen, and advances stealthily to the row of palisades which protect the house. And the handsome policeman, too, with his blue coat and clean white gloves, is held in high regard and esteem by the cooks and housemaids of England. His position on his beat is analogous to that of the porter of a very large house; it is a point of honour with him, that nothing shall escape his observation.
>
> ... His dress is decent and citizen-like, and yet peculiar; it differs from the dress of ordinary men; coat and trousers of blue cloth; a number and a letter embroidered on his collar; a striped band and

buckle on his arm; a hat with oilskin top, and white gloves – rather a rarity in the dirty atmosphere of London.

Schlesinger also noted that the London police were armed.

It is ... a mistake to believe ... that the London police are altogether unarmed and at the mercy of every drunkard. Not only have they, in many instances and quarters, a dirk [small knife] hidden under their great-coats, but they have also, at all times, a short club-like staff in their pockets. This staff is produced on solemn occasions, for instance, on the occasion of public processions, when every policeman holds his staff in his hand.[13]

Another foreign visitor who was impressed with the London police force was Francis Wey, author of *A Frenchman Sees the English in the Fifties* (1935). He was helped by a number of policemen when he lost his way in London.

This change of residence caused me to lose my way when trying to walk back on the first night of my stay there. Not knowing which way to turn I appealed to a policeman for help. Without a word he signed me to follow him. At the end of the street, he handed me over to another policeman with the two words 'Bond Street'. This one escorted me the length of his beat, and there another one took charge of me, and so on, till I had counted twelve. None of them spoke a single word to me, and the last one simply pointed to the door. It is a novel way of reaching one's destination! You just inform your friends that you are eight or ten peelers away, they calculate the time needed, and so can dispense with maps. I had noticed during my walk that policemen were busy testing the doors of houses, which I thought an excellent precaution. Evidently the inviolability of an Englishman's home is not respected by burglars.[14]

The Fire Brigade

Originally putting out fires was the responsibility of individual parishes. The service they provided, however, was so poor that insurance companies employed their own firemen to put out fires in buildings insured by them; if a crew arrived at a fire in a building insured by another company they would not stay to help.

This system changed after a serious fire in 1861 in warehouses in Tooley Street, Bermondsey, which took two weeks to extinguish completely. Following this fire, responsibility for fighting fires was passed to the Metropolitan Board of Works. In 1866 the Metropolitan Fire Brigade was formed. According to Charles Dickens Junior in 1888 there were 591 firemen of all ranks in the service.[15]

Thomas Burke, author of *The Streets of London* (1940), remembered the impressive horse-drawn fire engines on the streets of Victorian London.

> A street sight that disappeared with the arrival of the petrol age was the horse [drawn] fire-engine on its way to a fire ... With the glittering harness, the gleaming brass helmets, the two galloping greys going all out, the driver's arms working with them, and the crew delivering crescendo yells, it was a spectacle that brought every street to a standstill and set all eyes alight.[16]

The Legal Profession

London had been the centre of the legal profession for centuries. The four Inns of Court, the professional associations for barristers in England and Wales, were situated in central London. These were Inner Temple, Middle Temple, Lincoln's Inn and Gray's Inn; all barristers had to belong to one of them. Other legal offices were situated in and around Chancery Lane, near Lincoln's Inn and close to the Royal Courts of Justice which opened in 1882. These courts were built on a site between the Strand and Carey Street, which had once been a notorious slum.

Lesser criminal cases in London were heard at a police court, such as the one in Bow Street, which was built between 1879 and 1881. More serious cases were heard at the Central Criminal Court (Old Bailey) or at one of the London Sessions Houses. Before the Royal Courts of Justice were built the law courts were based in Westminster Hall, part of the Houses of Parliament.

George Augustus Sala watched the scene outside Westminster Hall one morning and described barristers, clerks, office-boys and others involved in the cases about to start.

> Parliament Street and Palace Yard are fair to see, this pleasant morning in Term time. The cause list for all the courts is pretty full, and there is a prospect of nice legal pickings. The pavement is dotted with barristers' and solicitors' clerks carrying blue and crimson bags plethoric with papers. Smart attorneys, too, with shoe-ribbon, light vests, swinging watch-guards, and shiny hats (they have begun to wear moustaches even, the attorneys!), bustle past, papers beneath their arms, open documents in their hands, which they sort and peruse as they walk. The parti-coloured fastenings of these documents flutter, so that you would take these men of law for so many conjurors about to swallow red and green tape. And they do conjure, and to a tune, the attorneys. Lank office-boys, in hats too large, and corduroys and tweeds too short, and jackets, stained with ink, too short for them; cadaverous office-runners and process-servers, in greasy and patched habiliments, white at the seams; bruised and battered, ruby-nosed law-writers, skulking down to Westminster in quest of a chance copying job; managing clerks, staid men given to abdominal corpulence, who wear white neckcloths, plaited shirt-frills, black satin waistcoats, and heavy watch chains and seals, worn, in the good old fashion, underneath the vest, and pendulous from the base line thereof, file along the pavement to their common destination, the great Hall of Pleas at Westminster. The great solicitors and attorneys, men who may be termed the princes of law, who are at the head of vast establishments in Bedford Row and Lincoln's Inn Fields, and whose practice is hereditary, dash along in tearing cabs; you look through the windows, and see an anxious man, with bushy grey whiskers, sitting inside; the cushions beside and before him littered, piled, cumbered, with tape-tied papers. He has given Sir Fitzroy three hundred, Sir Richard five hundred, guineas, for an hour's advocacy. Thousands depend upon the decision of the twelve

> worthy men who will be in the jury-box in the course of an hour. See! one of them is cheapening apples at a stall at this very moment, and tells his companion (who has just alighted from a chaise-cart) that in that little shop yonder Marley murdered the watchmaker's shopman. Great lawyers such as these have as many noble fortunes in their hands as great doctors have noble lives. Of the secrets of noble reputations, doctors and lawyers are alike custodians; and, trustworthy.[17]

Clerks

Clerks formed a large part of the capital's workforce. They worked in civil service departments in Whitehall and the law courts, in the city as stockbrokers', bank, counting-house, post office and general office clerks, in the offices of lawyers in and around Chancery Lane, and in the offices of factories and shops. Clerical work, which was badly paid, was a male occupation until the 1870s, when the telephone and typewriter were first used in offices.

Many clerks lived in the suburbs and commuted to work from Monday to Saturday on public transport or on foot. In *Twice Round the Clock* George Augustus Sala described clerks arriving by omnibus for work in the city.

> The vast train of omnibuses that have come from the West and from the East with another great army of clerk martyrs outside and inside, their knees drawn up to their chins, and their chins resting on their umbrella handles, set down their loads of cash-book and ledger fillers. What an incalculable mass of figures must be collected in those commercial heads! What legions of £.s.d! What a chaos of cash debtor, contra creditor, bills payable and bills receivable; waste-books, day-books, cash-books and journals; insurance policies, brokerage, dock warrants, and general commercial bedevilment! They file off to their several avocations, to spin money for others, poor fellows, while they themselves are blest with meagre stipends. They plod away to their gloomy wharves and hard-hearted counting-houses, where the chains from great cranes wind round their bodies, and they dance hornpipes in

> bill-file and cash-box fetters, and the mahogany of the desks enters into their souls. So the omnibuses meet at the Bank and disgorge the clerks by hundreds; repeating this operation scores of times between nine and ten o'clock.[18]

The Docks

London was the world's largest port and, for much of the century, a major shipbuilding centre as well. The docks, which included a vast warehouse system and underground vaults, were a major employer. Men were employed in skilled and unskilled jobs and casual workers were taken on each day, as required. Much of the work was low paid and some of it was unstable, as it was dependent on the seasons and the fluctuations in world trade.

Contemporary writers likened London to a busy beehive, which is the impression conveyed by this description of the docks, which comes from *London A Pilgrimage*:

> The perspective of the great entrepot or warehouse before us is broken and lost in the whirl and movement. Bales, baskets, sacks, hogsheads, and waggons stretch as far as the eye can reach; and there is a deep murmur rising from the busy fellows within. The solid carters and porters; the dapper clerks, carrying pen and book; the Customs' men moving slowly; the slouching sailors in gaudy holiday clothes; the skipper in shiny black that fits him uneasily, convoying parties of wondering ladies; negroes, Lascars, Portuguese, Frenchman; grimy firemen – and (shadows in the throng), hungry-looking day-labourers landing the rich and sweet stores of the South, or the breadstuffs of the generous West – all this makes a striking scene that holds fast the imagination of the observer; who has just skirted the dull outer wall of a great dock…
>
> … We thread our way round the busy basins, through bales and bundles and grass-bags, over skins and rags, and antlers, ores and dye-woods; now through pungent air, and now through a tallowy atmosphere – to the quay – and the great river where fleets are for ever moored.[19]

The French writer Hippolyte Taine, who was greatly impressed by the London docks, described them as follows –

The manifold, the innumerable riggings, stretch a vast circle of spider-web all round the rim of the sky. This, surely, is one of the mighty spectacles of our planet; to see a comparable agglomeration of buildings, works, men, ships and trade, one would have to go to China.[20]

Street Sellers

A huge number of poor people scraped a living in London by selling a variety of goods in the marketplaces, on the streets and door-to-door in the residential areas. According to Henry Mayhew's estimation, the costermongers (sellers of fruit, vegetables and fish) alone numbered 30,000 in 1851.[21] Despite the plentiful supply of customers who included day-trippers, tourists and office workers, this was a very hard way to make a living due to the fierce competition from other sellers. It was also arduous because it entailed working long hours, in all weathers. Street sellers also had to watch out for the police who continually harassed people working on the streets and moved them on.

Black Jack

A door-to-door salesman known as 'Black Jack' was interviewed by John Thomson, one of the authors of *Victorian London Street Life* (1877). This extract also provides information about how Black Jack's mainly poor customers earned a living:

During winter I deal in coke, which I get at the gas works at five shillings a load of six sacks. Wholesale, a sack fetches me one and six; but it pays best to sell it to poor folks, my chief customers, in small lots at a penny and twopence a lot. I carry no weights, a basket is my measure, it goes much further that way. Coke measures better than it weighs. But if one be fairly honest – some ain't by half so honest as they should be – it makes not such mighty odds in the end which way the coke is sold. I don't know as its fair, but the poorer folks be, the more 'ave they to fork out

> for everything. Costers, most 'on 'em, could not live if they did everything on the square. Many buy dear, and sell dearer. My customers are poor, wonderful poor, living round Battersea and thereabouts. I don't believe some of 'em women and children 'ave clothes to cover 'em, so they use coal or coke in winter to get up some heat. Many of my best customers I never see, though they deal 'reglar.' I see no more of 'em than a dirty 'and, or lean arm, stuck out with the coppers through half-closed doors. Summer's the time for such like folks, when the sun's out and warm. They take 'art then and come out with some cheap rags on. Most of the men are labourers when they can get work, and loafers when they can't. The women, many of 'em, work in the dust-yards, picking rubbish. That is in fine weather. They make about two shillings a day, and they tell me they gets the bones and rags that turns up. The best men can make four shillings or four and six a day labouring at the gas works. When I set up, as I said, part of my traps was borrowed. Everything in our line can be 'ad on hire, from a basket or weights to a donkey, and stock can be got by going shares in the profits. But it don't pay to borrow or hire. You 'ave to pay as much for the hire of a basket or a pot in a fortnight as would buy the article.[22]

In summer Jack sold sand which he bought from a dealer in Old Kent Road. The red sand was used in livery stables and the white for taproom floors and for polishing pewter pots, horse harnesses and other items.

Seasonal Hawkers

Alfred Rosling Bennett recalled poor people hawking their wares and services in Islington, where he grew up in the 1850s and '60s. He remembered that sellers sold different items depending on the season.

> Summer had hawkers peculiarly its own – he or she who vociferated, 'Ornaments for your fire-stoves!' and carried, hung from poles, apron-like confections in curly paper of many colours,

designed to fill and hide domestic grates from which King Sol had temporarily banished the hissing yule-log; and the vendor of fly-traps whose cry was 'Catch 'em-alive, oh!' and whose merchandise consisted of crude devices for inveigling the domestic pests which then throve and multiplied even more than in the present year of grace.

Autumn likewise produced a seasonal hawker – he of the sawdust bags used for excluding draughts, articles which resembled long sausages and were uniformly coloured red. People used to lay them on window sills and frames and along the bottom of doors, and then blame the weather if they caught cold and their coal-merchant if the fires wouldn't burn. The Fresh-air Fiend hadn't been born then. Folks were only lately emancipated from night-caps (the woolly with tassel sort) and many were still partial to bed-curtains.

Certain wretchedly-clad men hawked groundsel, and had regular customers amongst canary fanciers. There seemed something debasing about this weed, for I never saw a decent vendor of it; but there were a few hawkers of periwinkles who ran them close in sordidness.

In winter roasted-chestnut and baked-potato merchants were more in evidence than they are to-day; chestnuts were not yet the Italian monopoly they appear to have become of recent years...

Bawling costermongers selling fruit and vegetables from barrows often traversed the streets. One article of their commerce – strawberries in pottles – is known no more. A pottle in London – it had other attributes in country places, I believe – was a fragile basket of conical shape, like a huge candle extinguisher (if that is not likewise too obsolete to be useful as an illustration for this present generation) holding a pint or so of berries – usually fine ones on top and tiny or damaged ones below.[23]

Markets

London's wholesale markets, where shopkeepers, market traders and street sellers bought food, produce, fish, meat and flowers to sell, provided employment for many people. As well as the people who produced the goods, there were the porters and wagon drivers. This description of a busy morning at Covent Garden Market is taken from *London A Pilgrimage*:

> Covent Garden Market ... is the most famous place of barter in England:- it has been said, by people who forget the historical *Halle* of Paris – in the world. A stroll through it, and around it, when the market is opening on a summer morning, between four and five, affords the visitor a score of points of interest, and some matter for reflection. As at Billingsgate and in the Borough, the surrounding streets are choked with waggons and barrows. The street vendors are of all kinds – and of the poorest of each kind – if the coffee stall keepers be excepted. The porters amble in all directions under loads of prodigious bulk. Lifted upon stalwart shoulders, towers of baskets travel about. From the tails of carts producers or 'higglers' are selling off mountainous loads of cabbages. The air is fragrant with fruit to the north, and redolent of stale vegetables to the south. The piazzas, of pleasant memory ... are alive with stalls, scattered sieves, market-gardeners, greengrocers, poor women and children in troops (these are everywhere on our way), and hawkers old and young eagerly on the look out for an advantageous transaction with a higgler, or direct from the producer. Within the market enclosure the stacks of vegetables, and the piles of fruit baskets and boxes, are of startling extent. The scene is not so brilliant as that we used to see about the old fountain at the Paris *Halle*, where the water seemed to spring from a monster horn of plenty; but these Irish women, these fresh-coloured Saxon girls, these brawny Scotch lasses, in their untidy clothes and tilted bonnets, who shell the peas, and carry the purchaser's loads, and are ready for any of the hundred-and-one jobs of a great market; fall into groups wonderfully tempting to the artist's pencil.[24]

Street Scavengers

Another way of surviving in London at this time was by finding or scavenging things to sell. This group included pure finders who collected dogs' faeces to sell to the tanneries of Bermondsey, where it was used in the leather-making process, and cigarette or 'hard-up' finders, who picked up cigarette ends to dry and sell to the poor. Others gathered rags and bones or worked as sewer scavengers known as 'toshers'. Scavenging in the sewers became popular when work began on the construction of Joseph Bazalgette's new sewage system.

Mudlarks

A large group of scavengers were the mudlarks, who raked the muddy foreshore of the River Thames when the tide was out in search of anything worth selling. The following description of a group of mudlarks comes from *Life in the London Streets or Struggles for Daily Bread* (1881) by Richard Rowe:

> Some baker's dozen of mudlarks could be seen from the stairs: an old man dressed in what seemed to have been once a woman's caped cloak, the black stripes and the green ground of the pattern equally almost obliterated by grease; an old woman with a nut-cracker nose and chin, which almost dipped into the filthy slush into which she peered, and dirty flesh as well as a scrap or two of dirty linen showing through the slashes of her burst gown, over which, for 'warmth's sake', she wore a tippet of ragged sack-cloth; and a flock of frowsy, touzled-headed youngsters – a good many with no covering to the touzled heads – of every variety of grimy tatteredness: some with their petticoats kilted or their trousers tucked up mid-thigh high, but most with petticoats and trousers which saved their owners trouble in that way, through being normally abbreviated to the regulation wading-measure. With their bags and their baskets ... with their old hats, and kettles, and pots and pans – the mudlarks, young and old, groped backwards and forwards along the hard, which plum-pudding-stoned their bare feet with little pebbles, paddled in the chilly slush, or splashed like shrimpers in the margin of the water.[25]

The scavenged items included pieces of coal, coins, bottles, jars, rope, pieces of timber, old iron or lead, which were sold for a few pence in the marine stores in the streets near the river.

Richard Rowe also recorded this description of his work by a rag and bone scavenger.

> Rags and bones and metal, – that's what I go out for. Now and again I find a halfpenny, or a penny, that's been dropped; or maybe, but that isn't nigh so often, – and neither very often, – a little bit of silver; a threepenny bit, or a Joey [slang name for 3d]. Yes, I've found sixpences, but I never found a shilling. Once I found a half-crown. I'd been out beyond Upper Clapton, and, as I was working round by the Seven Sisters' Road, I hooked out of the ditch what I thought at first was a bit of sacking, but it turned out to be the rotten half of a tweed waistcoat, and there was a hole in the lining of the pocket, so the half-crown had slipped through and slid down to the corner. That's the greatest bit of luck I ever had in the way of money finding.
>
> Metal's what pays best, if it's any weight; but a few rusty old nails in laths is about the best I ever come across ... There's the sorting as well as the finding. When I was respectable I used to look down on rags and bones, and them that dealt in 'em; but rags and bones are my living now...
>
> I've been grubbing for many a year now. I hain't got strength for anything else.[26]

Selling Services

Some poor people survived in London by selling their services on the streets or door-to-door. These street service providers, or 'street labourers' as Henry Mayhew described them, included clock, umbrella and kettle menders, knife and hat cleaners, knife and razor grinders, and grease removers. Alfred Rosling Bennett remembered the chair menders of the 1850s and '60s.

> 'Chairs to mend!' was a very familiar cry! Cane and rush-bottomed seats were much more common than at present. Bentwood furniture was not yet, and there was little intermediate between the light and convenient cane-thatched chair and the heavy and massive mahogany and horse-hair, or the solid wood. Poor people, men and women, often of gipsy aspect, brought round bundles of canes and

> rushes, and, settling on your doorstep or in your front garden, deftly and cheaply repaired the ravages of time or wear and tear.[27]

'Caney'

One of the men who survived by mending chairs was Caney, whose story was related in *Victorian London Street Life.*

> A pedlar took compassion on him and initiated Caney into the art and mystery of mending umbrellas, and with a few hints and a little practical assistance from others as poor as himself, he was able to eke out a wretched existence at desultory and humble labour, now mending umbrellas, now making wire work, now dabbling in tinker's work of all descriptions, and thus avoiding while health lasted, both starvation and the workhouse. But of all the work he undertook, that of mending chairs seems to have brought him the most constant employment. In all cases his friends are of this opinion, for they have unanimously dubbed him 'Caney' and it is under this sobriquet that he is best known in the purlieus of Drury Lane.[28]

Street Performers

Like other street occupations, street performing was a very difficult way to earn a living. Performers worked long hours in all weathers and often walked miles each day carrying heavy equipment. Rewards were poor, especially in the winter months. Street performers included musicians, dancers, puppeteers, jugglers, clowns, acrobats, tightrope and stilt-walkers, reciters and performing animals. There were street performers from many different countries including Ireland, Scotland, Italy and Germany, reflecting the cosmopolitan nature of London's population.

Henry Mayhew interviewed many street performers in the 1840s. One was a 'well-looking young man, dressed in full Highland costume, with modest manners', who gave him the following account of himself:

> I am a native of Inverness, and a Grant. My father was a soldier and a piper in the 42nd. In my youth I was a shepherd in the hills

until my father was unable to support me any longer. He had 9d. a day pension for 17 years' service, and had been thrice wounded. He taught me and my brither the pipes; he was too poor to have us taught any trade, so we started on our own accounts. We travelled up to London, having only our pipes to depend upon. We came in full Highland dress. The tartan is cheap there, and we mak it up oursels. My dress as I sit here, without my pipes, would cost about £4 in London. Our mithers spin the tartan in Inverness-shire, and the dress comes to maybe 30s., and is better than the London. My pipes cost me 3 guineas new. It is between five and six years since I first come to London and I was twenty-four last November. When I started I thought of making a fortune in London, there was such great talk of it in Inverness-shire, as a fine place with plenty of money; but when I came I found the difference. I was rather a novelty at first, and did pretty well. I could make a £1 a week then; but now I can't make 2s. a day, not even in summer. There are so many Irishmen going about London and dressed as Scotch Highlanders, that I really think I could do better as a piper even in Scotland. A Scotch family will sometimes give me a shilling or two when they find out I am a Scotchman. Chelsea is my best place, where there are many Scotchmen. There are now only five real Scotch Highlanders playing the bagpipes in the streets of London, and seven or eight Irishmen that I know of. The Irishmen do better than I do because they have more face. We have our own rooms. I pay 4s. a week for an empty room, and have my ain furniture. We are all married men, and have no connection with any other street musicians. 'Tullochgorum,' are among the performances best liked in London. I'm very seldom insulted in the streets; and then mostly by being called an Irishman, which I don't like; but I pass it off just as weel as I can.[29]

Alfred Rosling Bennett also remembered the street performers. Among his favourites were 'two tribes' of organ grinders,

one with a tall-backed instrument which tinkled like Queen Elizabeth's virginals and must, I think, have been the forerunner of the present street piano. This was played by a crooked handle at one end. The other was a wind-and-reed affair in a rectangular box, much fuller in tone, resembling its rival only in being invariably and desperately out of tune. Both were carried on the back – always by foreigners of sorts – and supported on sticks when performed on. The square box of the latter excruciator often served as stage for a wretched monkey, gaudily attired, which was forced to dance or to pretend to go through a few tricks. We boys had a favourite grinder (with monkey, of course) who was sometimes admitted to the front garden, where, screened from vulgar observation by the brick wall, we played his organ and teased his (and our) Simian [resembling monkeys] relative. Once poor Jacko escaped and climbed the laburnum tree, which was covered with its poisonous pods. He was fortunately too wise or too frightened to taste them, and was ultimately persuaded to come down by the aid of a pair of steps and a clothes-prop.[30]

Prostitution

Another way to survive in Victorian London was by prostitution. This was not, in itself, a criminal offence, although keeping a disorderly house and pimping were. There were both male and female prostitutes in London, but the men who worked in the sex trade were much fewer in number.

Some women and girls chose to be prostitutes because, compared with other means of survival, it was a relatively easy way to make money. Others turned to prostitution temporarily, when they were desperate for money, or when they needed to supplement their earnings from respectable, but poorly paid, work. Henry Mayhew discovered that seamstresses often took up prostitution when work was scarce.

Although prostitutes were to be seen all over the metropolis, certain areas were notorious for them. The Haymarket and the Strand were well known for higher-class prostitutes, particularly in and around the theatres and other amusement places. Waterloo Road was another haunt for prostitutes and people who lived off their earnings. The most violent, disreputable and diseased prostitutes were to be found in the slums and riverside areas of the East End. There were many brothels in this area to serve sailors home on leave.

Throughout this period female prostitution was widely regarded as a great, but necessary social evil. As so many men from the better-off classes used prostitutes, the problem was largely ignored. Nevertheless, prostitution was a blight on London, and an embarrassment to the capital of the world's richest nation.

Flora Tristan, a French socialist, who visited London in the late 1830s and recorded her impressions in a journal which was later published, was shocked at the sight of prostitutes everywhere she went in London. She described what she and two friends saw in the streets around Waterloo Road.

> ... then we sat upon the bridge to watch the women of the neighbourhood flock past, as they do every evening between the hours of eight and nine, on their way to the West End, where they ply their trade all through the night and return home between eight and nine in the morning. They infest the promenades and any other place where people gather, such as the approaches to the Stock Exchange, the various public buildings and the theatres, which they invade as soon as entry is reduced to half-price, turning all the corridors and foyers into their receiving-rooms. After the play they move on to the 'finishes'; these are squalid taverns or vast resplendent gin-palaces where people go to spend what remains of the night.[31]

4

TRANSPORT

Roads and Traffic

In the early Victorian period the streets of London were narrow and chronically congested. They were also in a bad state of repair and covered in mud, dust, soot and dung. Traffic was uncontrolled and impeded by many obstructions, including animals being driven to market, repairs being carried out to public utilities and the many tollbars and turnpikes erected in the previous century which still existed. There were tolls on all bridges except London Bridge. Temple Bar at the bottom of Fleet Street, which marked the old border between Westminster and the City, was a major cause of hold-ups along this busy stretch of road. With all these obstructions traffic jams were a daily feature of life in London and accidents were a regular occurrence. Horses slipped on the muddy roads and tripped on uneven surfaces. Accidents led to chaos, as shown by the following description by Max Schlesinger:

> One of the wheelers of a four-horse omnibus slipped on the pavement and fell down at the foot of the Holborn-side obelisk, between Fleet-street and Ludgate-hill. There's a stoppage. The horse makes vain endeavours to get up; there is no help for

> it, they must undo reins, buckles and straps to free him. But a stoppage of five minutes in Fleet-street creates a stoppage in every direction to the distance of perhaps half a mile or a mile. Leaning as we do against the railings of the obelisk, we look forwards towards St. Paul's, and back to Chancery-lane, up to Holborn on our left, and down on our right to Blackfriars-bridge; and this vast space presents the curious spectacle of scores of omnibuses, cabs, gigs, horses, carts, brewers' drays, coal wagons, all standing still, and jammed into an inextricable fix. Some madcap of a boy attempts the perilous passage from one side of the street to the other; he jumps over carts, creeps under the bellies of horses, and, in spite of the manifold dangers which beset him, he gains the opposite pavement. But those who can spare the time or who set some store by their lives, had better wait. Besides it is pleasant to look at all this turmoil and confusion.[1]

An additional hazard in winter was the notorious London smog, a combination of fog, smoke and the foul fumes from the polluted River Thames, which impeded vision and made breathing difficult. This was worst in the areas nearest the river. Nathaniel Hawthorne, an American writer, described walking home one foggy evening in 1847.

> I went home by way of Holborn, and the fog was denser than ever, – very black, indeed, more like a distillation of mud than anything else; the ghost of mud, – the spiritualised medium of departed mud, through which the dead citizens of London probably tread, in the Hades whither they are translated. So heavy was the gloom, that gas was lighted in all the shop-windows; and the little charcoal-furnaces of the women and – boys, roasting chestnuts, threw a ruddy, misty glow around them.[2]

Inadequate street lighting added to the difficulties and dangers of travelling in the capital. In some areas streets were lit only by smoking oil lamps.

On Foot

London's pavements were in the same poor state as the roads. Until 1855 their upkeep was the responsibility of a number of local bodies, who often failed to maintain them. Like the roads they were coated with mud or dust, depending on the weather, and smoke from countless chimneys. Some parts of London, including the slums, were not paved at all. The pavements were just as congested as the roads and guidebooks for tourists advised against stopping on the pavement because of the risk of being pushed or kicked. Among those jostling for pavement space with pedestrians were numerous street sellers and performers, crossing sweepers, people carrying advertising boards and dogs. Max Schlesinger wrote the following paragraph on the subject of walking in London:

> The necessity of expeditious and cheap locomotion in the streets of London has called forth a variety of methods of travelling. The cheapest, simplest, oldest, and most natural of them is walking. In the narrow and crowded streets of the City, where conveyances make but little progress, this method is certainly the safest, and, withal, the most expeditious. Strangers in London are not fond of walking, they are bewildered by the crowd, and frightened at the crossings; they complain of the brutal conduct of the English, who elbow their way along the pavement without considering that people who hurry on, on some important business or other, cannot possibly stop to discuss each kick or push they give or receive. A Londoner jostles you in the street, without ever dreaming of asking your pardon; he will run against you, and make you revolve on your own axis, without so much as looking round to see how you feel after the shock; he will put his foot upon a lady's foot or dress, exactly as if such foot or dress were integral parts of the pavement, which ought to be trodden upon; but if he runs you down, if he breaks your ribs, or knocks out your front teeth, he will show some slight compunction, and as he hurries off, the Londoner has actually been known to turn back and beg your pardon...

> ... you had better walk with your eyes wide open. Don't stop on the pavement, move on as fast as you can, and do as the others do, that is to say, struggle on as best you may, and push forward without any false modesty. The passengers in London streets are hardened; they give and receive kicks and pushes with equal equanimity.[3]

Horse-drawn Vehicles

A variety of horse-drawn vehicles were to be seen on the roads of Victorian London, including private carriages, hackney carriages, cabs, tradesmen's and delivery vehicles, carts, goods wagons, omnibuses and, from the 1860s, trams. Traffic began to build up early in the morning, while Londoners still slept, and kept going well into the night, as the following extract from an article published in *The Leisure Hour* magazine in 1877 shows:

> People who live in the heart of London are so accustomed to the rattling and rumbling of wheels as to be in a manner insensible to the prodigious noise they make; the racket and the din begin in the morning before they are awake, and go on without an instant's intermission for an hour or two after they are asleep; and they sometimes tell that, although the continuous uproar never disturbs their rest, the cessation of it often does, and that they are actually raised out of sleep by the unwonted silence which prevails for a time during the small hours that precede the dawn. It may not be uninteresting to glance for a few minutes at locomotive London and see how far we can analyse and catalogue the endless swarm of vehicles which every day and all day long are traversing the thoroughfares of the metropolis.

Omnibuses

The main form of public transport, until the 1860s, was the omnibus, which replaced stagecoaches and provided an alternative to cabs. The omnibus, which was a French invention, was introduced in London in 1829 by George Shillibeer, a coachbuilder. The first route ran from Paddington to the Bank of England.

These single-deck vehicles, which were usually pulled by three horses, were cramped and uncomfortable. Initially, there were no proper stops for picking up and putting down passengers. Drivers stopped wherever they were hailed and alighting passengers had to attract the driver's attention to get off.

The omnibus soon became popular and before long a number of companies were running them across the capital from early morning until midnight. The various colours of the different companies' vehicles added to the colour of the London streets. There was fierce competition for passengers and, as shown by the following letter to *The Times* dated 5 May 1845, they also fought for possession of the roads:

> Sir, – If the police can spare any time from the persecution of such poor persons as try to keep themselves out of the Workhouse, by selling fruit and other commodities in the street, it would be well for them to bestow it on the alarming nuisance of racing between rival omnibuses. At this very time the most desperate contest is being waged between two sets of omnibus proprietors for the sole possession of the road from Sloane-square to Holloway. In my way home this afternoon I have met no fewer than seven omnibuses between the White Horse Cellar and Wilton-place, all going from Chelsea to Islington and Holloway, and all being driven at such a rate, that at first sight it might be imagined that all the inhabitants of Chelsea were going to drive with all the inhabitants of Islington, and were afraid of being too late. A second glance, however, shows that nothing of the kind is going on, for all the passengers contained in the whole seven omnibuses might have been accommodated in one, and have left room to spare. But no matter! The drivers, as if they did it for mere brutal gratification, were flogging their horses and galloping through Piccadilly with no more regard to men or cattle than the Khan of Bokhara [Islamic kingdom] has for the lives of a few Christians. If there be no remedy for this, we passengers must do the best we can to take

care of our worthless lives, but if, as I believe, such wanton and furious driving is an offence in the eye of the law, let those who are paid to put laws in force look to it, before "cruelty to animals" is succeeded by destruction of human life.

I remain, Sir, your most obedient servant,
A. Walker

By the 1850s most of the operating companies were taken over by the London General Omnibus Company. Over time the design of these vehicles improved and seats were added on the roof, back to back, with ladders to reach the top deck. These became known as knifeboard omnibuses.

According to George Augustus Sala it was safer to ride on the top of an omnibus than inside where you were exposed to a number of risks.

Never ride inside an omnibus ... A friend of mine had once his tibia fractured by the diagonal brass rod that crosses the door; the door itself being violently slammed to, as is the usual custom, by the conductor. Another of my acquaintance was pitched head foremost from the interior, on the mockingly fallacious cry of 'all right' being given – was thrown on his head and killed. Inside an omnibus you are subjected to innumerable vexations and annoyances. Sticks or parasols are poked in your chest and in the back of your neck, as a polite reminder that somebody wants to get out, and that you must seize the conductor by the skirt of his coat, or pinch him in the calf of the leg, as an equally polite request for him to stop; you are half suffocated by the steam of damp umbrellas; your toes are crushed to atoms as the passengers alight or ascend; you are very probably the next neighbour to persons suffering under vexatious ailments, such as asthma, simple cold in the head, or St Vitus's dance; it is ten to one but that you suffer under the plague of babies; and, five days out of the seven, you will have a pickpocket, male or female, for a fellow-passenger. The rumbling, the jumbling, the jolting, and the concussions – the lurking ague in the straw when it is

> wet, and the peculiar omnibus fleas that lurk in it when it is dry, make the interior of one of these vehicles a place of terror and discomfort; whereas outside all is peace. You have room for your legs, you have the fresh air; you have the lively if not improving conversation of the driver and the conductor ... Finally, you have the inestimable advantage of surveying the world in its workings as you pass along.[4]

The omnibus was mainly a middle-class form of transport, as members of the working class could not afford the fare, although these eventually became cheaper. The upper class did not use omnibuses because they could afford their own carriages or to hire cabs. The omnibus played an important part in the development of the suburbs, as it enabled workers to live outside the centre of London and travel back in to work.

Cabs

Another popular from of transport was the cab, of which there were two types: the two-wheeler, two-seater Hansom cabs; and the four-wheeler, four-seater Clarence. Charles Dickens was a regular user of cabs and had a favourite cab driver, who appears from the following description to have been quite a colourful and eccentric character:

> Of all the cabriolet-drivers who we ever had the honour and gratification of knowing by sight – and our acquaintance in this way has been most extensive – there is one who made an impression on our mind which can never be effaced, and who awakened in our bosom a feeling of admiration and respect, which we entertain a fatal presentiment will never be called forth again by any human being. He was a man of most simple and prepossessing appearance. He was a brown-whiskered, white-hatted, no-coated cabman; his nose was generally red, and his bright blue eye not unfrequently stood out in bold relief against a black border of artificial workmanship; his boots were of the Wellington form, pulled up to meet his corduroy knee-smalls

> [breeches that reached only to the knees], or at least to approach as near them as their dimensions would admit of; and his neck was usually garnished with a bright yellow handkerchief. In summer he carried in his mouth a flower; in winter, a straw – slight, but to a contemplative mind, certain indications of a love of nature, and a taste for botany.
>
> His cabriolet was gorgeously painted – a bright red; and wherever we went, City or West End, Paddington or Holloway, North, East, West or South, there was the red cab, bumping up against the posts at the street corners, and turning in and out, among hackney-coaches and drays, and carts, and waggons, and omnibuses, and contriving by some strange means or other, to get out of places which no other vehicle but the red cab could ever by any possibility have contrived to get into at all. Our fondness for that red cab was unfounded.[5]

Cab drivers had a reputation for over-charging, probably because they did not have a regular wage. They were also known for being surly and not very civil.

Trams

Horse-drawn trams first appeared on two routes in London in the 1860s but the raised rails were not good for horse-drawn vehicles and caused traffic jams at crossroads. The tramlines were pulled up and trams were not introduced again until the Tramways Act was passed in 1870. Over the next two decades the tram network spread across London but they were not allowed in the busy streets of the West End and the City. Trams were cheaper than omnibuses, they could carry more passengers and they ran for longer hours.

Commuter Steamboats

The River Thames was another important part of the transport infrastructure of Victorian London. It was just as busy as the streets. Many people used the passenger steamboats run by various companies to get to work; they were the quickest means of getting across the capital from east to west until the arrival of underground trains and they were cheaper than the omnibuses.

Alfred Rosling Bennett remembered that the boats run by the Citizen Steamboat Company, which were of the 'paddle-wheel type', were the most numerous.

> They were built of iron, had flush decks with below-deck cabins fore and aft; were painted black; carried black funnels with one red band and an open-work bell-mouthed top. The paddle-boxes bore the City arms with a large capital letter in the centre, from which the boats were known as Citizen A, Citizen B, etc. up to, I think, Citizen N.[6]

In *Twice Round the Clock* George Augustus Sala described the commuter traffic on the Thames.

> So the omnibuses meet at the Bank and disgorge the clerks by hundreds; repeating this operation scores of times between nine and ten o'clock. But you are not to delude yourself, that either by wheeled vehicle or by the humbler conveyances known as 'Shanks's mare,' and the 'Marrowbone stage,' – in more refined language, walking – have all those who have business in the city reached their destination. No; the Silent Highway has been their traveling route. On the broad -would that I could add the silvery and sparkling – bosom of Father Thames, they have been borne in swift, grimy little steamboats, crowded with living freights from Chelsea, and Pimlico, and Vauxhall piers, from Hungerford, Waterloo, Temple, Blackfriars and Southwark, straight by the hay-boats, with their lateen sails discoloured in a manner that would delight a painter, straight by Thames police hulks, by four and six-oared cutters, by coal-barges, and great lighters laden with bricks and ashes and toiling toward Putney and Richmond; by oozy wharves and grim-chimneyed factories; by little, wheezy, tumbledown waterside public-houses; by breweries, and many-windowed warehouses; by the stately gardens of the Temple and the sharp-pointed spires of city churches, and the

> great dome of [St] Paul's looming blue in the morning, to the Old Shades Pier, hard by London Bridge. There is landing and scuffling and pushing; the quivering old barges, moored in the mud, are swaying and groaning beneath trampling feet. Then, for an instant, Thames Street, Upper and Lower, is invaded by an ant-hill swarm of spruce clerks, who mingle strangely with the fish-women and the dock-porters. But the insatiable counting-houses soon swallow them up: as though London's commercial maw were an hungered too, for breakfast, at nine o'clock in the morning.[7]

With the arrival of the underground railway the use of the River Thames for public transport began to decline. In 1876 the five main steamboat companies combined to form the London Steamboat Company and eight years later the company went bankrupt.

The Railways

The railway arrived in London in 1836 when a line was opened between London Bridge and Greenwich. London Bridge was the first mainline station in the capital. Trains, which were a quicker, easier and cheaper form of transport than the stagecoach, soon became very popular.

In 1837 a station was built in Euston Square, which became the terminus for the London to Birmingham line. Over the next three decades more stations were built around the edge of central London by different railway companies. By 1865 there were twelve stations connecting the capital to every corner of the country.

These stations, which included booking offices, waiting and refreshment rooms, were built in a variety of architectural styles. There was an element of rivalry among the architects and engineers involved in their construction. Paddington station, which was designed by Isambard Kingdom Brunel and Digby Wyatt, was made of glass and iron. Its design was influenced by the Crystal Palace built for the Great Exhibition of 1851. Kings Cross, with its classical vaulting, was the work of the great Victorian builder Lewis Cubitt. The most splendid of all was St Pancras station, the Gothic creation of George Gilbert Scott. Grand hotels were built near these stations to accommodate the ever-increasing number of passengers using the railway. From 1848 WH Smith opened bookstalls on station platforms selling books, newspapers and magazines.

The following descriptions, taken from *The Queen's London,* of St Pancras station give some idea of its splendour:

> Without question, the London terminus of the Midland Railway Company can challenge favourable comparison with any other station in the world. The station itself is not so extensive as the Great Eastern terminus, in Liverpool Street, but it is said to have the largest roof, unsupported by a single pillar, in existence. This roof of glass and iron, upheld by girders of an uncommon kind, which are in keeping with the style of the hotel, is no less than 243 feet broad and 690 feet long, covering in its huge span four platforms, eleven lines of rails, and a broad road for cabs ... [On] the west side, are the booking offices, and from this side the trains depart, the eastern platforms being reserved for arrivals. This triumph of construction was designed by Mr Barlow.
>
> If the interior of St Pancras railway station be remarkable, what shall be said of the exterior? This splendid Gothic pile, designed by Sir Gilbert Scott, is ornate to a degree seldom seen in such structures, and is of a rich red well calculated to defy the begriming effects of London atmosphere. The front, facing the Euston Road, constitutes the Hotel – a necessary supplement nowadays to every great railway station ... The lofty clock tower is the finest feature of the façade.[8]

Carriages

There were three classes of railway carriage. The first-class carriages, which accommodated eighteen passengers, had upholstered seats, gaslights and dining cars. Second-class carriages, which also accommodated eighteen passengers, were not so luxurious. Third-class passengers had to sit on uncomfortable wooden benches. George Augustus Sala took the seven o'clock train from Euston to the north of England one morning in 1859 and described the wide range of people travelling third-class.

> But hark! The train bell rings; there is a rush, and a trampling of feet, and in a few seconds the vast [booking] hall is almost deserted ... Let us follow the crowd of third-class passengers on to the vast platform. There the train awaits them, puffing, and snorting, and champing its adamanthine [unable to be broken] bit...
>
> But what a contrast to the quietude of the scarcely-patronised first and second-class wagons are the great hearse-like caravans in which travel the teeming hundreds who can afford to pay but a penny a mile! ... What a hurly burly; what a seething mass; what a scrambling for places; what a shrill turmoil of women's voices and children's wailings, relieved ... by the deep bass voices of gruff men! What a motley assemblage of men, women and children, belonging to callings multifariously varied, yet all marked with the homogenous penny-a-mile stamp of poverty!

Among the 'motley assemblage' were soldiers, sailors, railway navvies, servant-maids, labourers, charwomen and a prisoner in handcuffs seated between 'two stern guardians'.[9]

Local Railways

Local and suburban railway lines were also built, which, like the omnibuses, enabled better-off workers to live outside the centre of London and commute in to work. Stations were built in small villages, which soon became busy suburbs. In the 1860s railway companies were compelled by the government to run some cheap trains for workmen, as compensation for the displacement of large numbers of workers by the building of the railways. In 1883 the Cheap Trains Act was passed. All railway companies had to offer cheap fares for working men in the early morning and late evening.

The following description of the new local and suburban lines was written by Max Schlesinger in 1853:

> There are, moreover, railways especially intended for London and the suburbs; among these, are the lines to Greenwich and Blackwall, which communicate with that extraordinary railroad which, forming an enormous semi-circle, facilitates the communication between the eastern and the whole of the northern parts of London.
>
> This peripatetic line is essentially a London railway; it does not, on any one point, travel beyond the boundaries of that monster town. It is laid out between garden-walls and back-yards, between roofs, and chimneys; it is bridged over canals and crowded streets, or laid on viaducts for many miles through the poorer quarters, almost touching the houses, and passing hard by the windows of the upper storeys. In other places, according to the peculiarities of the ground, the line is carried on through tunnels under the houses, cellars, sewers, and aqueducts. It is a miraculous railway, and one which has been constructed at an enormous outlay of ingenuity and money: but it enables the Londoners to go to the northern suburbs for sixpence, in a first-class carriage too, and in less than twenty minutes. There is no cessation in the traffic of this line; the trains are moving from early morning till late at night; every quarter of an hour a train is despatched from either terminus, and these trains stop at all the intermediate stations.
>
> The journeys being so short, and time, speed and cheapness the chief objects in view, the railway company have paid little attention to the comfort of the passengers. And here I ought to add, that with the exception of greater speed, which, after all, is the main object, all the English railways are inferior to those of the Continent. In London, and in short journeys, the want of comfortable carriages, and convenient waiting-rooms is not a very painful infliction...[10]

Disadvantages of the Railways

Unfortunately, not everyone shared in the undoubted benefits which the railways brought to London and Londoners in the

Victorian period. Apart from those, largely poor, people who were displaced to make way for stations, train sheds, goods yards, tracks, bridges and viaducts, the railways also led to increased noise and pollution. Another disadvantage was that the railways added to the severe congestion of the capital's streets and pavements, due to the increasing number of people attracted to the capital and the increase in the number of goods vehicles.

The Underground Railway

The severe road and pavement congestion in London were eased by the introduction of the underground railway in 1863. The idea for this novel form of public transport was one of a number put before a Select Committee on Metropolitan Communications, which was set up in 1855 to solve the problem of connecting the main railway stations. The suggestion of an underground railway was made by the Surveyor of the City of London. Despite a number of objections, fears about tunnelling underground and setbacks, such as flooding by the River Fleet which flowed beneath the capital, the first line was opened between Paddington and the City on 10 January 1863. Six hundred and fifty people were invited to the opening, including Prime Minister William Gladstone and his wife. They travelled on the new line to Farringdon Street, where a grand banquet was held. The *Illustrated London News* described this occasion in that day's edition.

> The Metropolitan Railway was fairly opened to the public on the 10th inst. and it was calculated that more than 30,000 persons were carried over the line in the course of the day. Indeed, the desire to travel by this line on the opening day was more than the directors had provided for, and from nine o'clock in the morning till past mid-day it was impossible to obtain a place on the up or Cityward line at any of the mid stations. In the evening the tide turned, and the crush at Farringdon Street station was as great as at the door of a theatre on the first night of some popular performer. Notwithstanding the throng, it is gratifying to add that no accident occurred and the report of

> the passengers was unanimous in favour of the smoothness and comfort of the line.

As with the overground railway, there were three classes of carriage for underground passengers. Those travelling third class had to sit on wooden benches in open carriages. All the passengers had to breathe an unpleasant mixture of smoke, gas, sulphur and coal dust. The carriages were lit by gas.

Despite these discomforts the underground railway became a popular way to travel in the capital. The network spread across London and out to the suburbs in the last decades of the century. The open carriages were replaced with closed ones and the trains, which were originally powered by steam engines, were electrified from 1890.

Bridges

Ten new bridges were built across the Thames to take pressure off heavily congested London and Westminster Bridges. These included Chelsea Bridge, completed in 1858, and Hammersmith, Putney and Battersea Bridges which were all built in the 1880s. Westminster Bridge was rebuilt between 1854 and 1862. Holborn Viaduct was completed in 1869, after six years of construction. This connected Holborn with Newgate Street, spanning the steep sides of the valley of the Fleet. Bridges such as Hungerford and Wandsworth were also built to carry the railway across the Thames into central London.

The following descriptions of Blackfriars Bridge, taken from Charles Dickens Junior's *Dictionary of London*, and Battersea Bridge taken from *Cruchley's London in 1865* show that the bridges built in the Victorian era were just as splendid and ornate as the new mainline railway termini:

> Blackfriars Bridge – One of the handsomest in London ... It was built in 1864-9, at a cost of £265,000, from the designs of Mr J.Cubitt ... It crosses the river in five spans, the centre span being 185 feet. The piers are of granite, surmounted by recesses

resting on short pillars of polished red Aberdeen granite, and with ornamental stone parapets. The parapet of the bridge itself is very low, which, with the extreme shortness of the ornamental pillars at the pier ends, gives the whole structure rather a dwarfed and stunted look; but the general outline is bold and the ensemble rich, if perhaps a trifle gaudy, especially when the gilding, of which there is an unusual proportion, has been freshly renewed.[11]

The new and graceful iron bridge which crosses the Thames near Chelsea Hospital, and affords the inhabitants of Pimlico a ready access to Battersea Park, is sometimes called *New Battersea Bridge*, and sometimes *Chelsea* or *Pimlico Bridge*. It was erected in 1857-8, from the designs of Mr T.Page, at a cost of £85,319, and has received much commendation on account of its graceful proportions and elegant decorations. Length, outside the abutments, 951 ft.; within the abutments, 915 ft. Span between the two towers, 347 ft., and height of the headway in the centre, 21 ft. above Trinity high water mark. Toll,1/2d.[12]

Road Improvements

The widening and strengthening of existing roads and the construction of new ones began in the 1840s, to alleviate the severe traffic congestion. One of the earliest of the new roads was New Oxford Street, which connected Oxford Street to Holborn. More roads were built after the establishment of the Metropolitan Board of Works in 1855, which was empowered to levy rates to pay for improvements. As with the railways, many poor people were displaced to make way for these new roads.

Roads constructed in the 1870s and '80s included Northumberland Avenue, Queen Victoria Street, Shaftesbury Avenue and Charing Cross Road. Pedestrians benefited from the new roads as well as road users because more direct routes were established across London. Northumberland Avenue, for example, linked the Victoria Embankment to Trafalgar Square. Northumberland House, the London home of the Duke of

Northumberland, was demolished to make way for the road. As well as the new roads built in the centre of the capital, roads were also constructed to connect the centre to the suburbs.

Another improvement was the embankment of the River Thames, the main purpose of which was to put an end to flooding. The ancient stairways down to the river and the muddy foreshore disappeared. The Victoria, Albert and Chelsea Embankments were constructed between 1864 and 1870.

Once the Thames was contained it changed from a slow, wide river to a narrower, faster one. This helped to speed up traffic and ease congestion on the river. The Victoria and Albert Embankments also eased road congestion by offering an alternative route to Fleet Street and the Strand. Another purpose of the embankments was to carry water, sewage and gas pipes underground as well as a tunnel for the underground railway.

Many acres of land were released by the embankments, including 37 acres from the Victoria Embankment alone. This provided more land for new buildings including St Thomas' Hospital. The Embankment Gardens were also built on this reclaimed land.

The following entry from Charles Dickens Junior's *Dictionary of London* describes the significant impact made by the Victoria Embankment:

> Victoria Embankment extends along the left bank of the Thames, from Westminster to Blackfriars, about a mile and a quarter, and was constructed by Sir Joseph Bazalgette, the engineer to the Metropolitan Board of Works. The whole of the space now occupied by the Embankment was covered by water or mud, according to the state of the tide, and few London improvements have been more conducive to health and comfort. The substitution of the beautiful curve of Embankment, majestic in its simplicity, with its massive granite walls, flourishing trees, and trim gardens, is an unspeakable improvement on the squalid foreshore, and tumble-down wharves, and backs of dingy houses, which formerly abutted on the river.[13]

In the East End roads were constructed to the new docks built between 1855 and 1880.

Other measures were taken to ease London's traffic congestion. In 1855 Smithfield Market was closed and a new one opened in Copenhagen Fields, Islington. This ended the presence of livestock on the capital's streets. The removal of road and bridge tolls, and Temple Bar between the Strand and Fleet Street all helped to speed up the flow of traffic. Improvements in road and pavement surfaces did not come until asphalt was first used in the 1870s.

5

RIVER THAMES

Friedrich Engels opened his book *The Condition of the Working Class in England* with the following paragraph:

> I know nothing more imposing than the view which the Thames offers during the ascent from the sea to London Bridge. The masses of buildings, the wharves on both shores, especially from Woolwich upwards, the countless ships along both shores, crowding ever closer and closer together, until, at last, only a narrow passage remains in the middle of the river, a passage through which hundreds of steamers shoot by one another; all this is so vast, so impressive, that a man cannot collect himself, but is lost in the marvel of England's greatness before he sets foot upon English soil.[1]

The River Thames was one of the reasons why London was chosen by the Romans as a settlement place. The river was tidal and navigable, making access from the sea and the rest of the Roman Empire easy. The Romans named their new settlement Londinium.

At the beginning of the Victorian era the Thames was a wide and slow-flowing river. It regularly flooded onto surrounding low-lying areas such as Battersea, Bermondsey, Lambeth, Wandsworth and Wapping. Occasionally the river dried to a narrow stream.

'The Silent Highway', as the Victorians named it, served a number of purposes. It was a major trade route leading to the largest port in the world, into which raw materials were imported and out of which manufactured goods were exported. Sailing ships, and later steamships, steamboats, and goods barges, were constantly arriving and departing from the docks. The river was also a source of drinking water for much of London as well as a dump for raw sewage and industrial waste, such as lime and cyanide. The Thames provided occupations for many thousands of people and was the source of a huge turnover of money annually. The following description of the scene from a small steamer was written by Max Schlesinger:

> What an astounding spectacle the Thames presents at this very point below London Bridge! In autumn, when the great merchantmen, heavily laden, coming in from all parts of the world, cast their bales and casks on the shore, from whence a thousand channels of trade convey them to and distribute them over the whole of the earth – in autumn, I say, this part of the river presents a spectacle of a mighty, astounding activity, with which no other river can vie. The vessels are crowded together by fifties and hundreds on either side. Colossal steamers, running between the coast-towns of France, Germany, and Scotland, have here dropped their anchors, waiting until the days of their return for passengers and merchandise. Their little boats dance on the waves, their funnels are cold and smokeless, their furnaces extinct. Sailors walk to and fro on the decks, looking wistfully at the varying panorama of London life. In a semi-circle round those steamers are the black ships of the North. They are black all over; the decks, the bows, the sides, the rigging, and the crew, have all the same dusky hue. These vessels carry the dark diamond of England – they are colliers from Newcastle.[2]

As well as ships, the river traffic included barges, tugs, police vessels, yachts, and fishing, commuter, pleasure and rowing boats.

The river was managed by the City of London from the twelfth century until 1867, when an Act of Parliament passed control to a Board of Conservancy, which later became the Thames Conservancy. According to Charles Dickens Junior,

> The principal matters to which the rules and bye-laws of the Conservancy apply, are the navigation of the river; the lights to be carried by vessels; the regulation of the carriage of explosive substances, and of petroleum; the fisheries; the regulating of boat races.[3]

Pleasure Boats

As well as the steam-powered commuter boats described in the previous chapter, there were many steam pleasure boats run by a number of companies. Larger than the commuter boats, they took day-trippers to Margate, Ramsgate, Gravesend, Southend, Herne Bay and Sheerness. The pleasure gardens at Rosherville near Gravesend were a popular destination for day-trippers.

Small steamboats could be hired for the day. According to Charles Dickens Junior, these boats were a nuisance on the busy river. He expressed his feelings about them in his *Dictionary of the Thames* (1887).

> Steam Launches are too often the curse of the river. Driving along at an excessive rate of speed, with an utter disregard to the comfort or necessities of anglers, oarsmen and boating-parties, the average steam-launch engineer is an unmitigated nuisance. There are some owners who show consideration for other people, but their number, unfortunately, is very limited, and for the most part the launches are navigated with a recklessness which is simply shameful. Perhaps the worst offenders are the people who pay their £5.5 s. a day for the hire of a launch, and whose idea of a holiday is the truly British notion of getting over as much ground as possible in a given time. Parties of this kind, especially after the copious lunch which is one of the features of the day's outing, stimulate the engineer to fresh exertions, and appear to enjoy themselves considerably as they contemplate the anxiety and discomfort of the occupants of the punts and rowing-boats which are left floundering helplessly in

> their wash. Should there be ladies on board a boat in difficulties, their terror proportionately enhances the amusement of these steam-launch 'Arries. Unfortunately, these excursionists are not alone in their offences against courtesy and good behaviour. Too many people who ought to know very much better keep them in countenance by their selfish example.[4]

In 1883 Parliament passed an Act making special provision with respect to steam launches navigating the Thames above Kew Bridge. Steam launches and owners had to be registered and had to produce a certificate to any officers or Conservators when required, or pay a 40 shilling penalty. Other requirements and restrictions were put on steamboats to improve safety and the conduct of those navigating them. Further bye-laws were introduced in 1886.

Accidents and Disasters

Steamboats sometimes departed too quickly before all the passengers had got off on or off. This happened in 1843, when thirteen children were thrown in the river and drowned.

On 27 August 1847 the steamboat *Cricket* was about to leave the Adelphi pier, with around 100 passengers on board, when it exploded. An over-pressurised boiler had burst. The passengers on the aft deck were blown to pieces. A group of coal heavers and watermen rescued passengers from the river. Fifty people were injured and up to thirty people were thought to have died.[5]

On the evening of 3 September 1878 Britain's worst inland waterway disaster occurred on the Thames. The *Princess Alice* pleasure boat was returning to London with between 750 and 800 passengers, who had spent the day at Rosherville Gardens, Gravesend. At Triplock Point near Woolwich the boat collided with the collier *Bywell Castle*, a vessel four times her size. The *Princess Alice* broke in two and sunk in four minutes. According to a survivor,

> It was eventide, and the loud laughter was succeeded by the wildest and most pitiful shrieks that could rend the still air. All of

> us seemed to drop down like skittles. Then there was a frightful struggle on the deck. Men, women and children rolled over and clutched and tore at each other; and all through were the ceaseless screaming and appeals for help. How, in such a sudden and unexpected catastrophe, could help be given?[6]

More than 600 people died in the disaster.

The Thames Police

The Thames Division of the Metropolitan Police patrolled the river in boats. Its headquarters were at Wapping which, in the words of Charles Dickens Junior, had 'a pleasant look-out over the river, just at the junction between the Upper and Lower Pool'. In 1887 the Superintendent of the Thames Division was George Stead, whose teams comprised forty-four inspectors, four sergeants and 124 constables. According to Dickens,

> Both night and day several boats patrol the river in different parts; a fresh boat starting from the station-hard every two hours to relieve the one whose watch is up. Each boat contains an inspector and two men, the latter of whom do the rowing, and a careful system of supervision is maintained by which the passing of each boat is checked at varying points. Two steam launches are also employed.[7]

One of the duties of the river police was to search for and deal with the bodies of suicides, murder victims and people who had accidentally drowned.

Old Warships

Also moored on the Thames were several old warships, enjoying a second lease of life. The *Chichester* and the *Aresthusa* were moored off Greenhithe. They had been lent by the government to the committee of the National Refuge for Homeless and Destitute Children. From 1868 to 1874 between them they provided accommodation for 400 boys aged between fourteen and seventeen, and trained them for a life at sea in the Royal Navy and the merchant services. The *Worcester*, moored in the lower reaches of the Thames, was used as a training ship by the Officers Training Ship Society, which trained boys for a naval career.[8]

Due to serious overcrowding in London's prisons, thousands of prisoners were housed aboard prison hulks such as the *Defiance* and the *Warrior*. These old warships were moored in the Thames Estuary, off the north Kent coast.[9]

Bad Weather

The busy Thames quickly came to a standstill in adverse weather conditions. When fog was really thick there was a danger of ships colliding, as happened twice in 1840. Hurricanes also caused havoc as ships could not move and laden barges were smashed to pieces, scattering debris everywhere.

The Thames froze over several times during the nineteenth century, but never as severely as in the previous two centuries, known as the Little Ice Age, when frost fairs were held on the frozen river. Alfred Rosling Bennett remembered when the river froze in February 1855.

> a long stretch of the river was completely iced over near Hampton Court. Some of the ships in the Pool below bridge became immovable, and their crews walked ashore opposite Billingsgate and Custom House Quay ... Some forty years elapsed before I knew a frost in London approaching this one in severity.[10]

The risk of the river freezing over was reduced following the rebuilding of London Bridge in 1831 with fewer arches, allowing the water to flow more easily, and the building of the embankments which resulted in a narrower and faster river.

The Great Stink

Until a proper sewage system was built in the 1860s the River Thames was a repository for human and industrial waste, making it smelly and unpleasant. During the summer of 1858 a spell of very hot weather caused the waste matter in the river to ferment, resulting in the most foul and unbearable stench. In his memoir Alfred Rosling Bennett wrote about the 'Great Stink', as this was called, and the consequent danger of a cholera outbreak. He recalled the numerous newspaper articles on the subject and 'the newly discovered disinfectant, chloride of lime' being used.

> I remember great tubs of it being mixed and allowed to empty slowly into a black sewer–like stream that meandered, openly and unashamed, between the Old Kent Road and the Bricklayers' Arms Branch of the South-Eastern Railway; and I heard that Father Thames and his various tributaries were being treated in the same manner. In those days and for long afterwards mud-banks in the river exposed at low water swarmed with bright red worms, which lent quite a charming tint to the landscape, especially when the sun shone on them. The boys called them blood-worms, and it was no misnomer.[11]

After a new sewage system was built the health of Londoners improved, and travelling and working on the Thames became a more pleasurable experience.

Royalty on the River

Every year the royal family enjoyed a holiday at Balmoral Castle in Scotland. They set off from the quay at London Bridge in the Admiralty barge, which took them to the royal yacht *Victoria and Albert*. Crowds always gathered at the quayside to see them off.

On 30 October 1849 Prince Albert, the Prince of Wales and the Princess Royal travelled by river to open the Coal Exchange in Thames Street in the City. The queen was too unwell to attend. The royal party embarked on *Prince Frederick's Barge*, one of the royal barges used for state processions, at Whitehall Stairs. This luxurious barge was built for Frederick, Prince of Wales, the son of George II. It was over 65 feet (20 metres) long and was decorated with ornate carvings, gilded with 24 carat gold relief. After the ceremony the party returned the same way. Crowds of people, as usual, had gathered on boats, barges and along the river to see them.[12]

On 2 February 1858 Prince and Princess Frederick William of Prussia set sail from Gravesend for Germany in a snowstorm. The Princess was the eldest daughter of Queen Victoria and Prince Albert. The couple had married at Windsor on 25 January and were starting out on their married life.

Prince Albert, the Prince of Wales, Prince Alfred and the Duke of Cambridge were there to see them off. The Queen watched from a royal yacht. A cheering crowd lined the decorated pier, across which was a banner with the word 'Adieu' made out in flowers. Many small boats full of well-wishers waved them off. The guns of Tilbury Fort opposite Gravesend fired a royal salute. Afterwards there was a firework display and a bonfire on Windmill Hill, Gravesend.[13]

Princess Alexandra of Denmark arrived at Gravesend on the royal yacht *Victoria and Albert* on 7 March 1863 for her forthcoming marriage to the Prince of Wales, the Queen's eldest son. The Prince led his bride along the decorated Terrace Pier. Her parents, the future King and Queen of Denmark, and other family members accompanied Alexandra to England. On 14 March 1863 the *Illustrated London News* reported that a 'bevy of pretty maids, who, ranged on each side of the pier, awaited, with dainty little baskets filled with spring flowers, the arrival of the Princess, to scatter these, Nature's jewels, at the feet of the Royal lady'.

On 7 March 1874 the Duke and Duchess of Edinburgh arrived at Gravesend. Prince Alfred, Duke of Edinburgh, who was the Queen's second son, had recently married her Imperial Highness Grand Duchess Marie Alexandrovna of Russia at the Winter Palace in St Petersburg. They had travelled to England in the royal yacht *Victoria and Albert*. The young couple were greeted with cheers and salutes as they stepped onto the decorated Terrace Pier, with the word 'Welcome' in gold letters along the front of the roofing. On this occasion, only ticket holders were allowed onto the pier to watch. The young couple then travelled by train to London to be met by Queen Victoria and other members of the royal family.[14]

The Lord Mayor's Coronation

Each year, following the inauguration of the new Lord Mayor of London, there was a coronation procession which started on the streets and then continued along the River Thames. This dazzling spectacle was witnessed and described by Max Schlesinger.

> This [the inauguration] done, he is Lord and King of the City, and sets out upon his coronation procession, surrounded by his lieges and accompanied by the ex-Mayor, the Aldermen, Sheriffs, the dignitaries of his guild, the City heralds, trumpeters, men in brass armour, and other thrones, principalities, and powers. The road which the Lord Mayor is to take is not prescribed by law; but according to an old custom, the procession must pass through that particular ward in which the King of the City acted as Alderman. The ward participates in the triumph of the day; and the cheers in that particular locality are, if possible, louder than anywhere else.
>
> The procession turns next to the banks of the Thames. The Lord Mayor, according to time-honoured custom, must take a trip in a gondola from one of the City bridges to Westminster. Fair weather or foul, take the water he must; and the broad river presents a spectacle on such occasions as is never seen in any town of Europe, since the Venerable Doges and their nuptials with the Adriatic have become matter for history.
>
> Splendid gondolas richly gilt, glass-covered and bedecked with a variety of flags and streamers, bear the Lord Mayor and his suite. Previous to starting, a supply of water is taken on board – thus hath custom willed it. The Lord Mayor's gondola is either rowed by his own bargemen, or it is taken in tow by a steam-tug. And round the gondolas there are boats innumerable with brass bands; and the bridges and the river banks are covered with spectators, and the river is more full of life, gladness, and colour, than on any other day of the year.
>
> The Lord Mayor and his suite land at Westminster Bridge. In Westminster he repairs to the Court of Exchequer, where he is introduced to the Judges.[15]

After the conclusion of the ceremonies at Westminster the Lord Mayor and his retinue returned by river to Blackfriars Bridge.

Chinese Junks

In March 1848 the Royal Chinese Junk *Keying*, manned by a Chinese crew, arrived in London. It moored at Blackwall, before moving near to Waterloo Bridge, and soon became a popular tourist attraction.[16] According to an article published in the *Illustrated London News* on 29 July 1848, the junk's Grand Saloon was 'gorgeously furnished in the most approved style of the Celestial Empire'. The newspaper told its readers,

> The *Keying* is now open for Exhibition, from ten to six, in the East India Docks, adjoining the Railway and Steam-boat Pier, Blackwall. – Admission, one shilling. During the limited period which the Royal Chinese Junk will remain in London, the charge for admission will be reduced to One Shilling. This most interesting Exhibition, which has been justly called "the greatest novelty in Europe," has been visited by Her Majesty the Queen, all the Royal Family, and an immense number of persons, including nearly all the nobility and foreigners of distinction in London. Junk Tickets, including fare and admission, are issued by the Blackwall and Eastern Counties Railways. Omnibuses direct, and conveyance also by Steam-boat from all the Piers between Westminster and Woolwich; fare 4d. Catalogues obtainable only on board, price 6d.

The exhibition contained a collection of Chinese curiosities. Souvenirs and commemorative medals were sold to visitors.

Another Chinese junk arrived in London in 1851. It was captained by a Chinese man who appeared unexpectedly at the opening of the Great Exhibition in Hyde Park. He joined the procession which preceded the opening by the Queen. It was assumed that he was one of the VIPs invited to attend, but no one was quite sure who he was. For the price of a shilling curious visitors could look over his ship, which was moored near London Bridge.

The Boat Race

The annual boat race between Oxford and Cambridge Universities was an important event for Londoners. From the following account of the race by Blanchard Jerrold, it seems that everyone in London turned out to watch. Jerrold watched the race from the terrace of a house in Mortlake.

All London at Boat Race

Listen! The Gun! There is a heaving of the entire mass: a low, full murmur rolls along the river banks. A spasm of intense excitement passes through the two or three hundred thousand people who have packed themselves along the shores to see the prowess of a few University lads. Desperate fellows along the towing paths, take walls by assault, force their way into boats, hoist themselves upon the shoulders of their neighbours.

They are coming!

Far away in the distance we catch the cheering, to which the low hum and vibration of excitement under our Terrace is the bass accompaniment. From the haze, where the shores wind, beyond the bridge, roll waving echoes of the wild agitation that stirs the steep hedges of humanity. The boats are thrust and bullied from the central way.

They come!

Amid frantic shouting, amid a snow-storm of pocket handkerchiefs and delirious ravings of purple-faced betting men, two lithe, trim, swift boats, dipping one dip and feathering one flame of light – skim along the shining way.

Men and women dance: men who were stern of aspect a moment since, make trumpets of their hands, and bawl their joy, like bulls. The excitement is too much for many – who absolutely turn away, and mechanically echo the general cry. Cambridge – no Oxford! Oxford – no Cambridge! Bravo Oxford! Give it 'em Cambridge!

Direct and sharp as swordfish after prey – They pass!

And then a white ocean of faces bursts upon us. Helter skelter at fullest speed, hidden under their human burden and gay with

> bunting, the steamers, serried like guardsmen – a moving wall bearing a convulsed multitude – close behind the fighting crews. The roar dies out slowly, and with expiring bursts, like a nearly spent storm; and then rises and rumbles away from us to the winning post.[17]

Shipbuilding

London was an important shipbuilding centre until the 1860s. When ships' hulls began to be built from iron instead of timber, shipbuilding moved to the Clyde and Tyneside yards, which had more space to build and launch ships.

The famous *Great Eastern* designed by Isambard Kingdom Brunel, which was built to carry passengers from England to Australia, was constructed at the Napier Yard at Millwall. As a young boy Alfred Rosling Bennett saw the *Great Eastern* in Millwall Dock. It was the highlight of a pleasure boat trip he took to Gravesend in the diamond funnel steamer *Nymph*.

> This was late in 1857, and the trip was memorable because we passed, at Millwall, Scott Russell's giant steamship *Great Eastern,* afterwards renamed *Leviathan* and then, when her continued run of ill-luck induced fears that Providence was angry at the use of a biblical term in a more or less boastful sense, *Great Eastern* again. She stood on the stocks unlaunched and, it was feared at one time, unlaunchable. Her five funnels and six masts were not yet in position, but her whole hull was out of the water, and seemed tremendous. The 60-feet paddle-wheels were fixed and painted red; huge as they were they yet appeared insignificant against the vast dark sides.[18]

The *Great Eastern* was finally launched on 31 January 1858, after several unsuccessful attempts. She had to be launched sideways due to her vast size. Huge crowds of spectators gathered to watch.

The Docks

Large ships, steamboats and barges constantly unloaded their cargo at London Docks. Goods from all over the world were unloaded by casual workers – whippers, lumpers and lightermen – and stored in massive dockside warehouses. There were also extensive underground vaults for wine. The docks were one of the tourist sights of London and members of the public were allowed to tour the warehouses. The attraction of the docks is evident in Hippolyte Taine's vivid description of the scene as he approached London by ship in 1858.

> More and more ships and warehouses; one is aware of getting nearer to a great city. Small embarkation jetties, thrusting fifty paces out into the river above gleaming mud left high and dry by the ebb-tide. Every quarter of an hour, the mark and presence of man, the power with which he has transformed nature, become more obvious. Docks, warehouses, ship-building and repairing yards, workshops, dwelling-houses, part-processed materials, accumulations of goods; to the right, we pass the iron carcase of a church, being made here for assembly in India. Astonishment at last gives way to indifference; it is too much. Above Greenwich the river becomes no more than a street, a mile and more wide, with an endless traffic of ships going up and down stream between two rows of buildings, interminable brick and tile files, a murky red, fenced behind huge piles driven into the mud for the mooring of ships which tie-up there to load or unload. More and more warehouses – for copper, stone, coal, ship's gear, and the rest; more and more great piles of bales, sacks being hoisted, barrels rolled, cranes turning and creaking, capstans squeaking. The sea reaches up to London by way of the river; it is a great port in the midst of the land. It is here that New York, Melbourne, Canton and Calcutta touch first. But what carries the impression it makes, to its zenith is the number of canals by which the docks open into the body of the river; they are streets set at right angles, but they are streets of ships; you suddenly come upon them – in an endless vista: from Greenwich; which I visited last year, going to the hill-top, the horizon is completely composed of masts and rope.[19]

The Customs House

The Customs House of the Port of London was a vast and impressive building, made of Portland stone, on the northern bank of the Thames. It was built between 1814 and 1817 to replace the previous Customs House, which was destroyed by fire. In 1896, 2,000 officials worked there including eighty clerks who worked in the grand Long Room, which was 190 feet long by 66 feet wide. It was built on a quay which, according to *Mogg's Strangers' Guide to London* (1837), was

> enlarged by a substantial embankment, forms in fine weather a beautiful promenade; – and the view of the Thames from thence is considerably enlivened in the summer by the passage of steam-boats and other vessels that are perpetually navigating this noble river.[20]

The entrance to the Customs House, which was open daily to the public, was via Lower Thames Street. As well as the fine building and the excellent view of the river, there was an interesting museum about smuggling.

Tower Bridge

A bridge which allowed tall ships to reach the Pool of London had been necessary for some time. Work on Tower Bridge began in 1886. The following description is taken from *The Queen's London*:

> Further communication across the Thames at this point had been urgently needed for many years. The necessary Act was passed in 1885, the foundation-stone laid by the Prince of Wales on June 21, 1886, and the work completed, at a cost of about a million sterling, in 1894. The bridge, designed by Mr Wolfe Barry, C.B., is of somewhat peculiar construction, the low-level passage being on the 'bascule' principle: i.e. the centre span of 200 feet is divided into two, each half being pivoted and furnished with a counterpoise, and hauled upward and back against the towers when the

waterway is opened ... A high-level footway is also carried across nearly at the top of the towers, access to this being afforded by lifts in the latter. The side spans are on the suspension principle.[21]

New Docks

In the 1850s it became evident that London's docks could no longer cope with the increase in volume and size of shipping. The Pool of London became very congested and vessels had to wait a long time – sometimes months – to be unloaded. This provided a good opportunity for pilfering. New deeper, larger and enclosed docks were needed. The Victoria Dock was opened in 1855, Millwall Dock in 1868 and the Royal Albert Dock in 1880. These new docks, which were enclosed by high walls, were able to accommodate the largest ocean-going ships.

6

SHOPS AND SHOPPING

Small Shops

In the early Victorian period there were no large shops in London; shops were small, independent businesses owned and run by the shopkeeper. They were open for long hours and offered credit and home delivery. Shops selling the same goods were often located together in the same street. Tailors shops, for example, could be found in Saville Row and drapers and furniture shops in Tottenham Court Road.

Upper- and middle-class Londoners had fresh meat, fish, poultry, fruit, vegetables and milk delivered daily to their door. Other groceries came from small shops such as Harrods, which was originally a grocery shop. There were relatively few bakers shops as bread was still largely baked at home. The poor, who were not welcome in respectable shops and had little money to spend, bought their food from street markets or street sellers.

As the suburbs were developed and expanded shops were often built onto living accommodation. Goods were displayed outside and around doorways. London came to life each morning with the removal of shop shutters, as described by George Augustus Sala in *Twice Round the Clock or The Hours of the Day and Night in London.*

> There is another ceremony performed with much clattering solemnity of wooden panels, and iron bars, and stanchions, which occurs at eight o'clock in the morning. 'Tis then the shop-shutters are taken down.
>
> Now, all over London, the shops start into new life. Butchers and bakers, and candlestick-makers, grocers and cheesemongers, and pastrycooks, tailors, linendrapers, and milliners, crop up with mushroom-like rapidity.[1]

These shutters were not put back again until ten or eleven o'clock at night.

The West End

Prior to the Victorian period London's main shopping streets were in or near the City, which was still a residential area. These streets included the Strand, Holborn, Ludgate Hill, Cheapside and St Paul's Churchyard. As people moved from the City to the new housing developments in the West End the location and character of the capital's shops changed. As new areas of the West End developed shops opened to provide for all their needs. The new residents were largely wealthy people who were in London during the spring and early summer and returned to their country houses for the rest of the year.

The most exclusive shopping streets in the West End were Regent Street and Bond Street. The former, which was built between 1813 and 1820 to the designs of John Nash, was described by Peter Cunningham in his *Handbook of London* (1850) as the 'most handsome street in the metropolis'.[2] In 1848 Nash's Quadrant, a covered arcade in Regent Street, was removed which opened up the street. In his book *European Life and Manners* (1845), the writer Henry Colman wrote that 'one of the most beautiful sights' in London was seen

> on a ride down Regent Street on the box-seat of an omnibus, in the evening, when the streets are crowded with people elegantly dressed, and the shops in long ranges, with their illuminated

windows of immense length, and their interior, exhibiting an almost indefinite perspective, are in all their glory.

An article published in the *Illustrated London News* on 21 April 1866 shows that Regent Street was just as interesting a spectacle during the day.

For Regent Street to be seen to the best advantage, it should be visited on a summer's day in the afternoon, when the splendid carriages, and elegantly attired pedestrians, evince the opulence and taste of our magnificent metropolis.

The brilliant ever-shifting scene presented daily in Regent Street is dizzying in its confusion. The fire-flies of fashion glance rapidly hither and thither, and the West End streets are thronged with a promiscuous jungle of carriages, horsemen and horsewomen, cabs, omnibuses and wagons; the pavements being crowded with fashionable loungers. With what dignified ease and gorgeously bedizened footmen attend their mistresses or lounge about in attitudes of studied grace.

The 'Carriage Trade'

The West End shops catered for what was called the 'carriage trade'. The smart carriages of the well-to-do waited in the streets while they shopped or shop assistants brought sample goods to the carriage door, as described in this extract from *101, Jubilee Road* (1948), a memoir of life in Victorian London by Frederick Willis:

The shops and people radiated quality. The reputation of this area was owed to the fact that the best tradesmen plied their trades there and the "quality" went there to patronise them…

… The gleaming carriage and high-spirited horses pulled up at the entrance, the coachman sat rigidly at attention, the tiger [a groom or footman in a striped waistcoat] jumped nimbly down and opened the carriage door with a flourish. First he removed the opulent rugs that were essential to protect the precious burden from the rude breath of Boreas [the north wind], then he

> stood aside, holding the door open with one hand and bearing the rugs over his unoccupied arm, an incredible figure ... with his spotless fawn coat, top boots, white doeskin breeches and top hat decorated with a cockade. My lord and lady then alighted and sailed across the pavement to the obsequious doorman who swung open the door for them to enter. If the weather was wet the doorman advanced with a huge umbrella to escort them across the pavement, and he also carried a curved wicker protector to place over the carriage wheel in case my lady's voluminous dress should be fouled by contact with it while alighting. All this was done as naturally as you or I might pop into a teashop for a cup of tea.[4]

Oxford Street was not as grand or exclusive as its neighbours Regent Street and Bond Street, and it did not attract the same aristocratic customers. The shops there included many drapers shops as well as shoemakers, butchers and cheesemongers.

Department Stores

The first department stores appeared in the West End during the second half of the nineteenth century. They were originally small drapers shops which extended over time into neighbouring premises and enlarged the range of goods they sold. Among the earliest of these stores were 'Swan and Edgar' and 'Dickens and Jones' in Regent Street, and 'John Lewis' and 'Peter Robinson' in Oxford Street. Their goods were all reasonably priced, prices were fixed and they only dealt in cash as credit was not allowed. After the introduction of plate glass, department stores could display more goods in their windows and window shopping became a pleasurable pastime. Department stores also became more inviting to customers after the introduction of electric lighting. Amenities such as cafés, restaurants and lavatories encouraged shoppers to spend whole days shopping.

Around the same time some of the small furniture shops in Tottenham Court Road grew into much larger stores, these included Heals and Maples.

Department stores appeared in prosperous suburban high streets, such as Kensington and Knightsbridge. Whiteley's in Westbourne Grove, Kensington, was probably the most famous of the new department stores. It claimed to be 'the universal provider'. Its wide range of goods and services included food, ironmongery and a hairdressing salon. The first large food store in London was opened by J. Sainsbury in Drury Lane in 1869 and the first purpose-built department store, Bon Marché, was opened in Brixton in 1877.

As the following letter published in *Punch* in May 1868 shows, some shoppers, who were used to doing their shopping in lots of small shops specialising in different goods, found the new department stores rather mystifying:

The Pleasures of Shopping

Dear Punch,

I am one of the old school, and like the old ways. Judge then, my old friend, of the shock to my equanimity the other day. I required six pennyworth of coat buttons, and went into the first shop which looked like one for the sale of that article. On entering, I walked up to the counter and said to the man, 'I want some buttons.'

'Oh, Sir!' said he, 'please go to the other side, to the "Button Department", this is "Baby Linen"'

I went to the other side, and 'I want some buttons,' said I.

'What do you want them for?'

'For my coat.'

'Oh then, Sir, if you please, to the next shop, this is the "Ladies' Button Department".'

I was accordingly ushered by a perfumed Ladies' Button Department gentleman, through several gilded corridors, then up one pair of stairs, and down another, and finally found myself roaming at large in the 'Gentlemen's Department General'. I went up to the first counter, and repeated my request.

'Oh, Sir, if you please,' said the attendant, 'the other side; this is the "Gentlemen's Flannel Department".'

> It is needless to describe the thing any further. Suffice it to say that, after applying at the 'Gentlemen's Hosiery Department', running a tilt at the 'Gentlemen's Pantaloon Department', and being nearly stranded on the 'Gentlemen's Fancy Shirt Department', I got what I wanted, sixpennyworth of buttons
>
> Ever yours, dear Punch,
> John Strong

Later in the century, particularly after the introduction of department stores, the West End shops began to attract different customers and no longer catered solely for the upper classes during the season. They now traded throughout the year for the middle classes and shoppers from outside London. Workers in the offices, which were now appearing in this area of London, also patronised the shops there. Improvements in transport and an increased demand for consumer goods, driven by the housing boom in the capital, both helped to attract shoppers to the West End. From the 1860s, when Kensington and Knightsbridge were developed, shops were opened there creating a 'new West End'.

Bazaars and Arcades

Bazaars were permanent covered markets patronised by the better-off shopper. Their exclusivity was preserved by beadles who kept out undesirables. One of the earliest bazaars in London was the Soho Bazaar, which was opened in 1816 in an old warehouse. It sold ornaments, trinkets, lace, hats, gloves, jewellery and potted plants. Its stalls and mahogany counters were hired out to vendors by the day.

The largest and most famous of the London bazaars was the Pantheon Bazaar in Oxford Street which opened in 1834.The following description is taken from *Knight's London* (1842) by the writer and historian Charles Knight:

> The Pantheon Bazaar ... was originally a theatre, one of the most fashionable in London; but having met with the discomfitures

> which have befallen so many of our theatres, it remained untenanted for many years, and was at length entirely remodelled and converted into a bazaar. When we have passed through the entrance porch in Oxford Street, we find ourselves in a vestibule, containing a few sculptures, and from thence a flight of steps lead up to a range of rooms occupied by a picture gallery. These pictures, which are in most cases of rather moderate merit, are placed here for sale, the proprietors of the bazaar receiving a commission or percentage on any picture which may find a purchaser. From these rooms an entrance is obtained to the gallery, or upper-floor of the toy-bazaar, one of the most tasteful places of the kind in London. We look down upon the ground storey, from this open gallery, and find it arranged with counters in a very systematical order, loaded with uncountable trinkets. On one counter are articles of millinery; on another lace; on a third gloves and hosiery; on others cutlery, jewellery, toys, children's dresses, children's books, sheets of music, albums and pocket-books, porcelain ornaments, cut-glass ornaments, alabaster figures, artificial flowers, feathers, and a host of other things, principally of a light and ornamental character. Each counter is attended by a young female, as at the Soho bazaar. On one side of the toy-bazaar is an aviary, supplied with birds for sale in cages; and adjacent to it is a conservatory where plants are displayed in neat array.[5]

There were also bazaars selling large items. The Pantechnicon Bazaar, which was located in two huge buildings near Belgrave Square, sold carriages, furniture, pianos and carpets. It also had a wine department. The Baker Street Bazaar, which was originally a place to buy horses, sold harnesses and other equine equipment, carriages, furniture, stoves and ironmongery.

Arcades were covered avenues of shops. Like bazaars, arcades had beadles to keep out the poor and other unwanted people. The most famous and most exclusive of the London arcades was the Burlington Arcade in Piccadilly, which was opened in 1819. It is described in *The Queen's London*.

> Burlington Arcade, a covered walk between a double row of shops, connecting Piccadilly with the street known as Burlington Gardens, was built in 1819 for Lord George Cavendish, afterwards Earl of Burlington, and part of the gardens of old Burlington House was taken for the site ... From the first, many of the shops have been occupied by foreigners (who are more familiar in their own countries with Arcades than are Englishmen): and the goods displayed are chiefly articles of wearing apparel. Burlington Arcade, once a more fashionable haunt than it is now, is closed in the evenings and ill-behaved persons are occasionally astonished to find themselves summarily ejected therefrom into the public roads.[6]

The Lowther Arcade, built in 1830, located opposite Buckingham Street in the Strand, was a very popular place to shop. It consisted of twenty-five small shops which sold mainly cheap toys and jewellery. It was described in *Cruchley's London in 1865* as the 'plebeian sister' of Burlington Arcade. He added that 'to the uninitiated stranger, it will probably appear a perfect labyrinth of toys through which it would be a Herculean feat to pass uninjured or uninjuring'.[7]

Other arcades included the Exeter Arcade in Well Street which opened in 1850, the Royal Arcade, near Bond Street, and Princes Arcade, near Jermyn Street, both of which were opened in the 1880s.

The Lady Shopper

Shopping became a popular activity for Victorian ladies with money and time on their hands. In 1844 the satirical magazine *Punch* published this article containing tongue-in-cheek advice for lady shoppers and likening their enthusiasm for shopping to the male passion for sport.

> Shopping is the amusement of spending money at shops. It is to a lady what sporting is to a gentleman; somewhat productive, and very chargeable. Sport, however, involves the payment of one's own

shot; shopping may be managed by getting it paid for. Ride all the way till you come to the shopping-ground in a coach, if you can; in an omnibus, if you must; lest you should be tired when you get there. If you are a lady of fashion, do not get out of your carriage; and when you stop before your milliners, particularly if it is a cold, wet day, make one of the young women come out to you, and without a bonnet, in her thin shoes, stand on the kerb-stone in the damp and mud.

The best places for shopping are fashionable streets, bazaars, and the like. Street-shopping principally relates to hosiery, drapery and jewellery of the richer sort. Bazaar and Arcade-shopping, to fancy articles, nick-nacks, and perfumery. In street-shopping walk leisurely along, keeping a sharp look-out on the windows. In bazaar-shopping, beat each stall separately. Many patterns, colours, novelties, conveniences, and other articles will thus strike your eye, which you would otherwise have never wanted or dreamt of. When you have marked down some dress, or riband, for instance, that you would like, go and inquire the price of it; haggle, demur, examine and, lastly, buy. You will then be asked "whether there is any other article to-day?" Whether there is or not, let the shopman show you what wares he pleases; you will very likely desire one or more of them. Whatever you think very cheap, that buy, without reference to your need of it; it is a bargain. You will find, too, as you go on, that one thing suggests another; as bonnets – ribands for trimming, or flowers; and handkerchiefs – perfumery. In considering what more you want, try and recollect what your acquaintances have got that you have not; or what you have seen worn by strangers in going along. See if there is anything before you superior in any respect to a similar thing which you have already; if so, get it instantly, not reflecting whether your own will do well enough. You had better finish your streets before you take your bazaars and arcades; for there the shopping, which one might otherwise call cover-shopping, though excellent sport, refers mostly to articles of no manner of use; and it may be as well to reserve toys and superfluities to the last. Married ladies, when they have laid in all they want for themselves, are recommended to show their thoughtfulness by purchasing some little trifle for their husbands, who, of course, will have to pay for it in the end.

Advertising

The increased demand for goods and services led to a blitz of advertising on the streets of London. Shops and service providers used a variety of advertising methods including hand-bills, posters, sandwich-boardmen, advertising vans and huge lettering on buildings. Max Schlesinger described the different types of advertisement he saw all over London during his visit to the capital in 1850.

> The Advertisement is omnipresent. It is in the skies and on the ground; it swells as the flag in the breeze, and it sets its seal on the pavement; it is on the water, on the steam-boat wharf, and under the water in the Thames Tunnel; it roosts on the highest chimneys; it sparkles in coloured letters on street lamps; it forms the prologue of all the newspapers, and the epilogue of all the books; it breaks in upon us with the sound of trumpets, and it awes us in the silent sorrow of the Hindoo. There is no escaping from the advertisement, for it travels with you in the omnibuses, in the railway carriages, and on the paddle-boxes of the steamers.
>
> At this hour there is not an arch in a London bridge but has its advertisement painted on it.[8]

Schlesinger was shocked at the amount of gas used by one shop in Holborn to advertise its products.

> Holborn is inundated with gas-light; but the brightest glare bursts forth exactly opposite to us. Who, in the name of all that is prudent, can the people be who make such a shocking waste of gas? They are 'Moses and Son,' the great tailors and outfitters, who have lighted up the side-fronts of their branch establishment. All round the outer walls of the house, which is filled with coats, vests

and trousers, to the roof, and which exhibits three separate side-fronts towards three separate streets, there are many thousands of gas-flames, forming branches, foliage, and arabesques, and sending forth so dazzling a blaze, that this fiery column of Moses is visible to Jews and Gentiles at the distance of half a mile, lighting up the haze which not even the clearest evening can wholly banish from the London sky.

Among the fiery flowers burns the inevitable royal crown, surmounting the equally unavoidable letters V.R. To the right of these letters we have Moses and Son blessing the Queen in flaming characters of hydro-carbon'; to the left they bless the people.[9]

Second-hand Shops

Pawnbrokers

Pawnbrokers shops could be found in the poor districts of London, where their customers lived. Unredeemed items were sold off cheaply. This description of a pawnbrokers shop window near Drury Lane, taken from *The Little World of London* by Charles Manby Smith, shows the wide variety of goods on sale in these shops.

A pawnbroker's shop-window has brought us up with a sudden pull on our morning perambulations, and fascinates us with its manifold contents. Where to begin our observations, that is the question. The *embarrass de richesses* which has sprung from the embarrassments of poverty is so puzzling and perplexing, that it is next to impossible to make a choice. The window has a thousand voices waiting to speak – a thousand memorials which seem watching but to catch our eye to pour out the narrative of their sorrowful experience. These memorials are the hypothecated hostages left to guarantee the fulfilment of treaties which have all been violated, and abandoned to the uncompassionated destiny which avenges a forfeited pledge. Among them are the garments of both sexes and all ages, the personal trinkets and adornments of hopeful youth and fading age – books, the solace of the student and the companions of the solitary – musical instruments, the incentives to harmless mirth or delicious melancholy; watches, clocks, gold chains, necklaces, bracelets, brooches, snuff-boxes, work-boxes, writing-desks, surgical implements, mathematical and scientific instruments, microscopes, telescopes and stereoscopes; knives, forks, and spoons, and all the adjuncts of the dinner-table; and a thousand things besides, comprising everything 'between a flatiron and a diamond ring,' both inclusive; not omitting an unassorted collection of workmen's tools condemned to rust for a while in base inaction through the misfortunes or follies of the quondam owners.[10]

Marine Shops

Marine shops, which were located in the poor districts near the river, from where most of their customers came, originally supplied items required for ships' voyages. Some of the items sold in these shops were stolen goods. As Charles Dickens shows, in the following extract from his article *Brokers and Marine-Store Shops* (1836), they were little more than junk shops.

Look at a marine-store dealer's, in that reservoir of dirt, drunkenness and drabs: thieves, oysters, baked potatoes, and pickled salmon – Ratcliff-highway. Here, the wearing apparel is all nautical. Rough blue jackets, with mother-of-pearl buttons, oil-skin hats, coarse checked shirts, and large canvas trousers that look as if they were made for a pair of bodies instead of a pair of legs, are the staple commodities. Then, there are large bunches of cotton pocket-handkerchiefs, in colour and pattern unlike any one ever saw before, with the exception of those on the backs of the three young ladies without bonnets who passed just now. The furniture is much the same as elsewhere, with the addition of one or two models of ships, and some old prints of naval engagements in still older frames. In the window, are a few compasses, a small tray containing silver watches in clumsy thick cases: and tobacco-boxes, the lid of each ornamented with a ship, or an anchor, or some such trophy. A sailor generally pawns or sells all he has before he has

> been long ashore, and if he does not, some favoured companion kindly saves him the trouble. In either case, it is an even chance that he afterwards unconsciously repurchases the same things at a higher price than he gave for them at first.[11]

Clothes

The wealthier classes in London had their clothes made to measure by dressmakers and tailors. In the later Victorian period they had the option of buying clothes off the peg in department stores. The poorest Londoners bought their clothes from market stalls or second-hand shops which were located in the poor areas where they lived.

Monmouth Street (now Shaftesbury Avenue) in the Seven Dials slum district contained mainly second-hand clothes shops and market stalls selling old clothes. Charles Dickens, who enjoyed looking around the shops in Monmouth Street and observing the people shopping there, made the following observations in his article *Meditations in Monmouth Street* (1839):

> We have hinted at the antiquity of our favourite spot. 'A Monmouth-street laced coat' was a by-word a century ago; and still we find Monmouth-street the same. Pilot great-coats with wooden buttons, have usurped the place of the ponderous laced coats with full skirts; embroidered waistcoats with large flaps, have yielded to double-breasted checks with roll-collars; and three-cornered hats of quaint appearance, have given place to the low crowns and broad brims of the coachman school; but it is the times that have changed, not Monmouth-street. Through every alteration and every change, Monmouth-street has still remained the burial-place of the fashions; and such, to judge from all present appearances, it will remain until there are no more fashions to bury.

Dickens liked to 'walk among these extensive groves of the illustrious dead' and, while looking at the old clothes, tried 'from the shape and fashion of the garment itself to bring its former owner to the mind's eye'.[12]

Street Markets – Wholesale and Retail

There were a large number of markets, both wholesale and retail, in Victorian London. The main wholesale markets were Billingsgate Market near London Bridge, which sold fish; Leadenhall Market in Gracechurch Street, which sold meat, poultry, fish, vegetables, leather and hides; Covent Garden Market near Drury Lane, which sold fruit, vegetables and flowers; and Smithfield Market near the ancient city walls, which sold livestock. Smithfield Market was relocated to Copenhagen Fields in Islington in 1855. The old Smithfield site was rebuilt and reopened in 1868 as a meat market. The main customers of the wholesale markets were small shopkeepers, market traders and street sellers.

Blanchard Jerrold, the author of *London A Pilgrimage*, described the lively and interesting scene he encountered at Billingsgate Market early one morning.

> The opening of Billingsgate market is one of those picturesque tumults which delight the artist's eye. The grey chilly morning; the river background with masts packed close as arrows in a quiver; the lapping of the tide; the thuds of the paddles of hardly perceptible steamers; the tiers of fishing boats rich in outline and in accidental shades and tints; and then the varieties of shouting, whistling, singing and swearing men, who are landing insatiable London's first course (first and last to many thousands); the deafening vociferation, where the fish auctions are going on in the steamy open shops of the salesmen; the superb confusion and glistening of the mounds which the porters are casting into the market from the boats! It is well worth the chilly journey through the silent streets, to see.[13]

The small retail markets, where the poor bought their food, were located in streets all over the capital. Goods were sold on stalls by market traders and by peripatetic street sellers. On the periphery of these street markets there were cheap shops which were also largely patronised by the poor.

The many street markets included Borough Market located in New Cut off Waterloo Road in Lambeth, Clare Market near the Strand, the Brill Market in Somers Town and Sclater Street, Brick Lane, Petticoat Lane, Whitechapel and Spitalfield Markets, all in the East End. Some of the central London markets were displaced by new streets and railways. One of these was Hungerford Market, which was demolished to make way for Charing Cross station.

London's street markets sold a wide variety of goods. It was claimed that at Whitechapel Market, for example, everything could be bought 'to furnish a house, feed a family and plant a garden'. The same could be claimed for New Cut Market in Lambeth, which was described by Henry Mayhew in *London Labour and the London Poor*.

> At the New-cut there were, between the hours of eight and ten last Saturday evening, ranged along the kerb-stone on the north side of the road, beginning at Broadwall to the Marsh, a distance of nearly half a mile, a dense line of itinerant tradesmen – 77 of whom had vegetables for sale, 40 fruit, 25 fish, 22 boots and shoes, 14 eatables, consisting of cakes and pies, hot eels, baked potatoes and boiled whelks; 10 dealt in nightcaps, lace, ladies' collars, artificial flowers, silk and straw bonnets; 10 in tin ware, such as saucepans, teakettles, and Dutch-ovens; 9 in crockery and glass; 7 in brooms and brushes; 5 in poultry and rabbits; 6 in paper, books, songs, and almanacs; 3 in baskets; 3 in toys; 3 in chickweed and watercresses; 3 in plants and flowers; 2 in boxes; and about 50 more in sundries, such as pigs' chaps, black lead, jewellery, marine stores, side combs, sheep's trotters, peep-shows, and the like.[14]

Mayhew stated that there were fifteen such street markets held throughout London every Saturday night and Sunday morning and that they were

> perfectly free, any party being at liberty to stand there with his goods, and 'the pitch' or stand being secured simply by setting

> the wares down upon the most desirable spot that may be vacant. In order to select this the hucksters usually arrive at the market at four o'clock in the afternoon, and having chosen their 'pitch', they leave the articles they have for sale in the custody of a boy until six o'clock, when the market begins ... The class of customers at these places are mostly the wives of mechanics and labourers.[15]

Saturday night markets were always busy and crowded as poor workers, who had just received their week's wages, went to them to buy food for the following week. They were noisy places with vendors trying to cry their wares above the hubbub of the crowd. With their bright lights and colourful stalls they were more like fairs than markets, as this description of London's street markets on a Saturday night, also by Henry Mayhew, illustrates:

> There are hundreds of stalls, and every stall has its one or two lights; either it is illuminated by the intense white light of the new self-generating gas-lamp, or else it is brightened up by the red smoky flame of the old-fashioned grease lamp. One man shows off his yellow haddock with a candle stuck in a bundle of firewood; his neighbour makes a candlestick of a huge turnip, and the tallow gutters over its sides; whilst the boy shouting 'Eight a penny, stunning pears!' has rolled his dip in a thick coat of brown paper, that flares away with the candle. Some stalls are crimson with the fire shining through the holes beneath the baked chestnut stove; others have handsome octohedral lamps, while a few have a candle shining through a sieve: these, with the sparkling ground-glass globes of the tea-dealers' shops, and the butchers' gaslights streaming and fluttering in the wind, like flags of flame, pour forth such a flood of light, that at a distance the atmosphere immediately above the spot is as lurid as if the street were on fire.[16]

Street Sellers

There were thousands of street sellers in Victorian London; they included small children, the elderly and many disabled people unable to make a living by any other means. There was a steady stream of customers for the street sellers, who went wherever there was a profit to be made. Their customers included office, shop and manual workers, day-trippers and tourists. Many of their customers were people as poor as themselves, who were not welcome in respectable shops.

Some street sellers stayed in one place on their own established pitch; others wandered around the streets and often walked many miles a day. They could be seen in all the main thoroughfares of London, in the City itself, in the West End, in poor slum districts, at railway stations, in tourist spots, in public places and gardens, and outside theatres and public houses. As they had no premises or fixed stalls these street sellers carried their goods on their backs, in baskets on their heads or on trays slung around their necks. Street sellers were frequently harassed by the police and moved on.

A huge variety of goods were sold on the streets of the capital. Most sellers sold small items with low start-up costs such as matches, flypapers, shoe and boot laces, cutlery, toys, spectacles, flowers, nuts, oranges and watercress. They cried out their wares like market traders.

Street sellers worked long hours, and worked weekends as well as weekdays. Although there was no shortage of customers it was difficult to make a living this way because of the fierce competition from other sellers and market traders. This competition increased in 1851 with the huge influx of visitors to London to see the Great Exhibition in Hyde Park. Many unemployed people seized the opportunity to make money by joining the ranks of street sellers.

A rich source of information about the street sellers and their customers are the articles and books written by social investigative journalists. Some interviewed the street sellers and recorded their responses verbatim. The following extract, recording a young female flower seller describing her work, is taken from *Life In the London Streets: Or Struggles for Daily Bread* by Richard Rowe:

Above: Dudley Street in the Seven Dials slum district. (*London: A Pilgrimage*)

Right: Outside a night shelter. (*London: A Pilgrimage*)

Left: Town houses in Tavistock Square. (*The Nineteenth Century in London* by E. Beresford Chancellor)

Below: Merchant Taylors' School. (*Rambles in London* by W. J. Loftie)

Bottom: Assembly at a board school. (*The Queen's London*)

University College. (*The Queen's London*)

Above left: Dustmen at work. (*London Labour and the London Poor* by Henry Mayhew)

Above right: Brewery workers. (*London: A Pilgrimage*)

Temple Bar. (Yale Center for British Art, Paul Mellon Collection)

Above left: A 'bone grubber'. (*London Labour and the London Poor*)

Above right: A congested London street. (*London: A Pilgrimage*)

Shillibeer's omnibus. (*Travel in England* by Thomas Burke)

The Port of London. (Yale Center for British Art, Paul Mellon Collection)

Inside the docks. (*London: A Pilgrimage*)

Westminster Bridge and Westminster Abbey. (Yale Center for British Art, Paul Mellon Collection)

Orange Market, Duke's Place. (*London Labour and the London Poor*)

Regent Street. (*The Queen's London*)

Burlington Arcade. (*The Queen's London*)

Hyde Park. (Yale Center for British Art, Paul Mellon Collection)

Above left: The Parrot Walk, Zoological Gardens. (*London: A Pilgrimage*)

Above right: The end of the University Boat Race. (*London: A Pilgrimage*)

The Crystal Palace. (Yale Center for British Art, Paul Mellon Collection)

Exhibits on display at The Great Exhibition. (Yale Center for British Art, Paul Mellon Collection)

Guy's Hospital. (*The Queen's London*)

At the entrance to St Bartholomew's Hospital. (*Unsentimental Journeys Through the Modern Babylon* by James Greenwood)

Highgate Cemetery. (*The Queen's London*)

Above: Westminster Abbey. (*The Queen's London*)

Right: St Magnus the Martyr Church. (Yale Center for British Art, Paul Mellon Collection)

Above: Wesley's Chapel. (*The Queen's London*)

Left: The exercise yard at Newgate Prison. (*London: A Pilgrimage*)

Above: Holloway Prison. (*The Queen's London*)

Right: 'The Bull's Eye'. (*London: A Pilgrimage*)

Above left: 'The Wallflower Girl'. (*London Labour and the London Poor*)

Above right: 'The Mudlark'. (*London Labour and the London Poor*)

Left: 'Found in the Street'. (*London: A Pilgrimage*)

The Foreign and Commonwealth Office. (*The Queen's London*)

The Natural History Museum. (*The Queen's London*)

Above: The Royal Albert Hall. (*The Queen's London*)

Left: Queen Victoria. (Yale Center for British Art, Paul Mellon Collection)

Common Garding [Covent Garden] I goes to. O' course I buys what's in, an' then splits up the bunches. Oh yes, I know the names o' flowers well enough, sich as I sells. There's roses, an' lilies o 'the walley, an wi'lets, an' wall-flowers, an' primroses, an' snowdrops, an' mignonette, an' cloves, an' camillers, when I can run to 'em, an' sich like; an' then there's green lavender, an' dry lavender, too. I s'pose that's some kind of a flower, though 't is dry. I wish t'others would sell as well when they was withered...

Oh! I don't stick to one place in 'tickler. Sometimes I stands by the Bank, an' sometimes I go about the City...

Yes, sometimes I works the Strand, but I goes anywhere I can sell best. If folks 'ont buy in one place I tries another. Where 'busses stops is orfen a good pitch, like as they do at the corner o' Tot'nam Court Road, 'cept that the chaps with papers sometimes shoves ye away. Yes, omblibus men sometimes buys. Some on 'em is wery smart, and likes to have a rose or a bunch of wi'lets in their button'oles. Oh, all sorts o' folk buy o'me, when they does buy, 'cept 'tis poor folks' children. If they've got a penny o' course they'll spend it on grub or sweeties, instid o' flowers, – they'd be flats if they didn't. Little swell gals is fonder 'o flowers than the boys. One day, when I was standin' by St Martin's Church, a gen'leman as was goin' by wi' his little gals come back an' bought hevery bunch I'd got, 'cos the littlest had axed him for one.

I go a goodish way sometimes, – yes, where there's flowers in the front gardings. There's pleny o' houses that ain't got none, 's far as I've seen, an there ain't so many flowers where there is any that the folks they belongs to is in a 'urry to pick'em; – 'sides, there's the people in the streets to sell to.

Sometimes of a Sunday I do tidyish. 'Tween the corner o' the 'ampstead Road an' Park Square I orfen work. There's a good lot o' men goes along there, when it's fine, an' they buys pretty free, – them as is dressed smart; how can I tell what they are? P'r'haps they're shopmen wantin' to be took for swells, but them as is dressed smart is the ones as buys. Them as has worky day clo'es on doesn't.[17]

Food and Drink Stalls

There were also many stalls on the streets selling food and drink for immediate consumption, such as hot eels, picked whelks, pea soup, baked potatoes, sheep trotters, pies, pastries, buns, muffins, gingerbread, tea, coffee, cocoa, ginger beer, lemonade and hot cordials. These stallholders' customers included workers, tourists, shoppers and other street sellers, who did not have time for proper meal breaks. Henry Mayhew described coffee-stall keepers in *London Labour and the London Poor*.

> The coffee-stall keepers generally stand at the corner of a street. In the fruit and meat markets there are usually two or three coffee-stalls, and one or two in the streets leading to them ... the stalls abound in all the great thoroughfares, and the most in those not accounted 'fashionable' and great 'business' routes, but such as are frequented by working people, on their way to their day's labour...
>
> The coffee-stall usually consists of a spring-barrow, with two, and occasionally four, wheels. Some are made up of tables, and some have a tressel (sic) and board. On the top of this are placed two or three, and sometimes four, large tin cans, holding upon an average five gallons each. Beneath each of these cans is a small iron fire-pot, perforated like a rushlight shade, and here charcoal is continually burning, so as to keep the coffee or tea hot, with which the cans are filled, hot throughout the early part of the morning. The board of the stall has mostly a compartment for bread and butter, cake, and ham sandwiches, and another for the coffee mugs. There is generally a small tub under each of the stalls, in which the mugs and saucers are washed. The 'grandest' stall in this line is the one before-mentioned, as standing at the corner of Duke-street, Oxford-street ... It is a large truck on four wheels, and painted a bright green. The cans are four in number, and of bright polished tin, mounted with brass-plates. There are compartments for bread and butter, sandwiches, and cake. It is lighted by three large oil lamps, with bright brass mountings, and covered in with an oil-cloth roof. The coffee-stalls, generally, are

lighted by candle-lamps. Some coffee-stalls are covered over with tarpaulin, like a tent, and others screened from the sharp night or morning air by a clothes-horse covered with blankets, and drawn half round the stall.

Some of the stall-keepers make their appearance at twelve at night, and some not till three of four in the morning. Those that come out at midnight, are for the accommodation of the 'night-walkers' – 'fast gentlemen' and loose girls; and those that come out in the morning, are for the accommodation of the working men.[18]

7

ENTERTAINMENT AND LEISURE

Growing prosperity and more free time for some Londoners led to an increase in the number and variety of entertainment and leisure facilities on offer in the Victorian capital. There was something for people of all classes to enjoy; even the poorest, who had little or no money for entertainment, could enjoy the numerous street performances.

These facilities were also used by tourists and day-trippers, who could now reach the capital easily by train. Many guidebooks and street maps were published for the use of the ever-increasing number of visitors. The guidebooks listed old attractions such as the Tower of London, the Monument to the Great Fire of London, St Paul's Cathedral, Westminster Abbey, and the Royal Naval College at Greenwich as well as newer attractions like Buckingham Palace and the recently rebuilt Houses of Parliament. They included bus and train timetables, descriptions of sights to see and places to visit, and even instructions on how to find a policeman.

Parks

The many parks and open spaces in the capital were known as the 'lungs of London'. In the centre of London were the royal parks which were owned by the monarchy; these were Hyde Park,

St James' Park, Regent's Park and Kensington Gardens. They had amenities such as bandstands and boating lakes, and were open to the public. They were used by people of all social classes, although there was a notice on the gates of St James' Park which stated, 'The park keepers have orders to refuse admittance to the park to all beggars, any person in rags, or whose clothes are very dirty, or who are not of decent appearance and bearing.'[1]

Hyde Park

Hyde Park, which had its own police station, was a popular haunt of the upper classes, who paraded along Rotten Row in their fashionable carriages. It was also a popular place for the nannies of the wealthy to bring their young charges and to meet other nannies and children. The Serpentine in Hyde Park was used for skating when it was frozen over in winter.

Max Schlesinger, in *Saunterings In and Around London*, described a visit to Hyde Park in 1851, when he saw the Queen, Prince Albert and the Duke of Wellington.

> Hundreds of equestrians, ladies and gentlemen, gallop to and fro. How fresh and rosy these English girls are! How firmly they sit! What splendid forms and expressive features! Free, fresh, bold, and natural. The blue veil flutters, and so does the riding-habit; a word to the horse and movement of the bridle, and they gallop on, nodding to friends to the right and left, the happiness of youth expressed in face and form, and no idea, no thought, for the thousand sorrows of this earth ... Then comes an old man, with his horse walking at a slow pace, his low hat pushed back that the white hair on his temples may have the benefit of the breeze. His head bent forward, the bridle dangling in a hand weak with age, the splendour of the eyes half-dimmed, his cheeks sunken, wrinkles round his mouth and on his forehead, his aquiline nose bony and protruding; who does not know him? His horse walks gently on the sand; everyone takes off his hat; the young horse-women get out of his way, and the Duke smiles to the right and to the left. Few persons can boast of so happy a youth as this old man's age.

He turns round the corner; the long broad row becomes still more crowded; large groups of ten or twenty move up and down; fast riding is quite out of the question, when all of a sudden a couple come forward at a quick pace. There is room for them and their horses in the midst of Rotten-row, however full it may be, for everyone is eager to make way for them: it is the Queen and her husband, without martial pomp and splendour, without a single naked sword within sight. The crowd closes in behind her; the young women appear excited; the old men smile with great glee at seeing their Queen in such good health. Dandies in marvellous trowsers (sic), incredible waistcoats, and stunning ties, put up their glasses; the anglers on the lake crowd to one side in order to see the Queen; the nursery-maids, the babies, and the boys with their hoops come up to the railings; the grass plots, where just now large groups of people sat chatting, are left vacant, and the shades of the evening are over the park. The sun is going down behind the trees; its parting rays rest on the Crystal Palace with a purple and golden glare, whose reflection falls on Rotten-row and its horse-men.[2]

St James' Park

St James' Park, situated close to Buckingham Palace, is the oldest of the royal parks in London and was much frequented by Londoners, tourists and visitors. Among its attractions were a small lake and a collection of waterfowl. The following evocative description of the park is taken from Hippolyte Taine's *Notes on England*:

What pleases me most here are the trees. Every day, when I leave the Athenaeum, I go and sit for an hour in Saint James's Park. The lake gleams softly beneath its covering of mist, and dense foliage hangs above its still waters. The rounded trees, great domes of green, compose a sort of architecture far more delicate than that of masonry. The eye is rested by shapes not clearly defined, colours washed pale...

Yesterday at eight in the evening, from Suspension Bridge: the weather was fine yet all things looked vaporous; the last glow of light melted into a whitish, smoky haze; to the right, a vestige of redness, the surface of the Thames and the rest of the sky a pale slaty (sic) colour. Such tints are to be seen in Rembrandt's landscapes and Vermeer's twilights. The drowning light, the air peopled by mists and vapours, the imperceptible and continuous changes in that vast exhalation which softens and erodes all outlines, shading them with blue, all leaves the impression of a vast, vague life, diffuse and melancholy, the life of the humid land itself.[3]

Suburban Parks

A number of parks were built for public use in the suburbs of the capital during Victoria's reign, including Battersea Park and Victoria Park. Battersea Park was built on a site on the south bank of the Thames and was opened in 1858. A lake was added in 1860 and a sub-tropical garden in 1864.

Victoria Park in the East End was built on marshland filled in with earth excavated from the rebuilding of the London docks. Its amenities included a football pitch, a boating lake and an ornamental lake with an island on which stood a Chinese temple. Victoria Park was mainly used by the poor people who lived in the surrounding area. The entry for Victoria Park in *Dickens's Dictionary of London* reads as follows:

> One of the largest and finest in London, lies in what is at present the extreme North East corner of the town. It is very prettily laid out with ornamental water, & c., and differs from the West End parks in being supplied with various appliances for amusement, usually on summer evenings very liberally patronised. Victoria-pk. is one of the things which no student of London life should miss seeing, and its most characteristic times are Saturday or Sunday evenings – or both, for each has its distinct features – and Bank Holidays.[4]

Sport

There was an increase in spectator sport during the Victorian period and there was a variety of sports for the public to enjoy in London. Cricket became a national sport and two cricket grounds, Lord's in north London and The Oval in south London, were opened in 1814 and 1845 respectively.

Football was also popular, especially with the working classes, many of whom finished work at lunchtime on Saturdays and headed straight for the football grounds. Many football clubs were formed in London during this period as well as the Football League. The first FA Cup Final took place in the 1871-2 season. Alfred Rosling Bennett recalled that cup finals were 'very modest' when he was a boy.

> They were often played in public parks, without charge for admission. I have in mind one decided in West Ham Park in the early 1880s. It was between Upton Park and Preston North End, the second or third round in the English Association Cup. There was neither gate nor gate money; no stands, no seats, while the spectators numbered 300 at most.[5]

Many sporting associations were founded at this time including the Lawn Tennis Association in 1888. The first men's singles championships were held at Wimbledon in 1877, organised by the All England Croquet Club.

The safety bicycle was invented in the 1880s and cycling became a craze in London. Battersea Park was used by cyclists and races were held there. The Crystal Palace at Sydenham was used for archery contests.

Epsom Races

A sporting event which Londoners looked forward to was Epsom Races, which were held on Epsom Downs, 17 miles from London, in May. Londoners of all social classes used a variety of vehicles to get to the racecourse, to enjoy this annual spectacle or to make money from the racegoers. With the booths, tents, fortune-tellers, serenaders, and refreshment sellers there was a carnival atmosphere on race day. Blanchard Jerrold spent a day at the races in 1869 and wrote this description:

> Clear the course! We suddenly find the crowd tighten about us. A flutter goes through the sea of heads on the Grand Stand: the men climb to the roofs of the carriages: the general murmur deepens:

the betting men are in a fever of excitement: a fight or two may be descried from the vantage-ground of a rumble [back of a carriage].

They're off! The emotion is quiet at first. The Grand Stand suddenly becomes white with a thousand faces turned in one direction – an observer remarks, 'like the heads of geese upon a common.' Then a low, hoarse sound travels about the Downs, deepening in waves of thrilling vibration at every instant. Then a roar breaks upon the frantic people, answered by a second roar. The multitude is divided into two prodigious camps. Faster and shriller come the shouts. The Grand Stand is in convulsions. The bellowing is fearful to hear: the frantic commotion along the lines of coaches is frightful to see – as the horses, lying like a handful, sweep to the winning- post. Cheers and counter cheers, fluttering of handkerchiefs, waving of hats upon sticks, cries, fierce as though wild beasts had been let loose; all tend to a final crash of ten thousand voices, and – the Derby is won.[6]

Illegal Sports

In various secret locations across London, many in the slum districts, illegal sports such as prize fighting, dog, rat and cock fighting took place. The audiences were not only made up of poor people but also included people from higher up the social scale, who enjoyed watching such contests and betting on the result.

James Greenwood, a social investigative journalist, visited the scene of what he described as a 'dog-show' but was clearly a dog-fight, which he described in his book *Unsentimental Journeys Through Modern Babylon* (1867). The location was a foul-smelling room in the Duck Tavern in an East End slum street. The room, which was lit by gas and a roaring fire, contained stuffed dogs in cases around the walls. Greenwood did not describe the actual fight – he may not have stayed to watch it – but recorded a vivid picture of the menacing looking men and their fierce dogs, who were assembled ready for the fight to begin.

... there were shrill-voiced ratting dogs, and fighting terriers, and fighting bulldogs, struggling and straining their leashes to get at

> each other, with their red eyes starting from their heads, and their black lips curled back from their fangs, howling, yelping. barking shrilly and spitefully, or growling with a deeper rage from the bottom of their wide, red throats; while their masters, savages as themselves, roared out horrid blasphemy, and staked their eyes and limbs on the swaggering lies they uttered, and struck their great fists on the table to show they were in earnest in the wagers they offered to lay, and clapped hands together when the wager was made; while others, who had come on purpose to make a match and found a difficulty in "getting-on" with any one, sat apart, stirring up their dogs to show their mettle, or clenching their muzzles and holding still their writhing limbs when for business reasons it was desirable that their tremendous courage should not be made too public.[7]

The interest in animal fighting, which had been illegal since 1835, declined as the century progressed and society became more civilised.

Gentlemen's Clubs

The gentlemen's clubs in the West End of London provided a place for upper-class men to meet, enjoy good food and conversation. These private members clubs proliferated in London during the nineteenth century. The Carlton Club, founded in 1832, and the Reform Club, founded in 1834, were the private headquarters of the Tory and Liberal parties. They were both located in Pall Mall. These clubs provided a number of facilities for members, including libraries, cardrooms, and reading rooms.

Francis Wey, a French writer, came to London in the 1850s and later described a visit to the luxurious and well-appointed Reform Club in *A Frenchman Sees the English in the Fifties* (1935).

> The Reform Club is a majestic building, practically square and reminiscent of the Farnese Palace in Rome ... The interior hall is surrounded by colonnades supporting a large gallery. The floor is tessellated in imitation of Roman mosaic. The pillars are made

> of stucco of the colour of Siennese marble; the dome which lights the hall is of diapered flint glass and is supported by twenty Ionic columns; their red porphyry basements breaking the line of a stone balustrade rest on the gallery, which is reached by a broad white marble stairway. This gallery, where one can stroll as in a covered cloister, is fitted with easy chairs, mirrors, pictures and a thick carpet. It is a kind of general sitting-room from which you can observe the hall below into which visitors are ushered. A drawing-room so large that it must be intended for dancing, a card-room, reading-room, and private reception-rooms open into this gallery, as do also the two important libraries; the one containing literary works, the other legal and political ones. There are two librarians on the staff of the club. On the upper floor there are a considerable number of bedrooms. London is so vast, time so precious, that large sums of money are spent on saving minutes. If a member happens to have business appointments for the next morning, or expects to be kept late in the evening, instead of going home he brings or sends his things to the club and spends the night there.

After being shown around the club Wey went to the coffee room,

> a large high room giving on to a charming garden. Twenty servants in dress clothes wait on a number of small tables noiselessly and with extreme promptitude. They tread with felt soles on the thick pile of expensive carpets; plates and dishes, instead of being piled up on top of one another, are brought and removed singly. The sound of footsteps, creaky shoes, the clatter of crockery and knives and forks are vexations unknown to the fortunate mortals who dine in clubs.[8]

High Society

During the London season upper-class women enjoyed the capital's many attractions and the busy social round including visits, soirees, receptions, balls and events attended by royalty. These occasions provided opportunities for upper-class mothers to look for suitable husbands for their unmarried daughters. Mary MacCarthy, who was born into an upper- class family, recalled a ball she attended as a young woman. The following extract, taken from her memoirs *A Nineteenth Century Childhood* (1924), presents a vivid snapshot of a high society event in Victorian London:

> And now we are trip-clip-clopping, trip-clip-clopping up through the leafy bowers of Campden Hill, and stop at a tall Norman-Shaw architected house – alight, and pass through marble, up marble, through a close conglomeration of Italian shrines, caskets, cabinets, marqueterie; against the tangled background of William Morris's pomegranates; past the pictures by Rosetti, Sir Frederic Leighton, Burne-Jones, Holman Hunt, and Mr Watts, ofwhich the host is the renowned possessor. On and across the parquet floor to the fascinating, artistic, gracious hostess, and to the massive, comfortable chaperones in their rich waisted velvets and long trains, seated in formidable yet customary array.
>
> We have dance programmes given us, on which is printed only one word, 'Valse,' all the way down, interspersed twice with the word 'Lancers.' Soon, in our shimmering white or pink satins, with our long white kid gloves, elegant waists and sprays of flowers on the left side of our bodices, our hair coiled on the nape of our necks or on the top of our heads, our trains first swirling about our feet, then gracefully caught up and managed, we fall with our partners into the swinging rhythm of that old 'Blue Danube' Valse.[9]

Opera

Only the well-off could afford to attend the opera, as tickets were very expensive and the wearing of evening dress was obligatory. The two main opera houses were Her Majesty's Opera House in Covent Garden and the Royal Opera House in Drury Lane. The French visitor Hippolyte Taine likened these venues to 'luxurious and exotic hot house flowers'.[10] Opera was also performed occasionally at other theatres.

At the end of the century the comedy operas of Gilbert and Sullivan became popular. The impresario Richard D'Oyly Carte became very rich due to their success.

Music

There were a number of venues in Victorian London where classical music was performed. Concerts were held regularly in halls in Hanover Square and Langham Place, at Exeter Hall in the Strand, and, after 1854, at the rebuilt Crystal Palace at Sydenham. At the Foundling Hospital in Coram Fields the children performed choral music on Sundays.

Pleasure Gardens

Pleasure gardens had their heyday in the eighteenth century, but several of the gardens in London survived into the Victorian era. These were Vauxhall Gardens, Bagnigge Wells near Kings Cross, Cremorne Gardens in Chelsea, Surrey Gardens in Walworth and the Eagle Tavern Gardens in City Road. These landscaped gardens included such features as covered walkways, arbours, pagodas, rotundas and statues. The entertainment they offered included dancing, music, theatrical productions, pantomimes, balloon ascents, juggling, acrobats and circuses. As well as attracting respectable people these gardens also became a haunt for prostitutes.

Cremorne Gardens opened in 1845 on a 12-acre site close to the river in Chelsea. It was the most famous of the pleasure gardens still open in the nineteenth century. Edmund Yates described Cremorne Gardens in his *Recollections and Experiences*.

> The gardens were large and well laid out; some of the grand old trees had been left standing, and afforded pleasant relief to the town eyes which had been staring all day at brick and stucco, while their murmuring rustle was pleasant to the ears aching with the echo of city traffic. There were plenty of amusements – a circular dancing platform, with a capital band in a large kiosk in the middle; a lot of *jeux innocens,* such as you find at a French fair; once a week a balloon ascent, and a very good firework display. The admission-fee was one shilling; there was a hot dinner for half-a-crown, a cold supper for the same money; and it was not considered necessary, as at Vauxhall, to go in for expense; on the contrary, beer flowed

> freely and it was about this time, I think, and at Cremorne, that the insidious 'long' drinks – soda and 'something' – now so popular, first made their appearance. Occasionally there were big banquets organised by certain 'swells,' and held there, when there would be heavy drinking, and sometimes a row – on Derby night, once, when there was a free fight, which lasted for hours, involving the complete smash of everything smashable; and I mind me of another occasion, when a gigantic Irishman, now a popular M.P., sent scores of waiters flying by the force of his own unaided fists. But, on the whole, the place was well and quietly conducted, and five minutes after the bell for closing rang – just before midnight – the gardens were deserted. There was a general rush for the omnibuses and cabs, which were in great demand, and for one or two seasons there was a steamboat which left the adjacent Cadogan pier at the close of the entertainment, and carried passengers to Hungerford Bridge, and which was very popular.[11]

The Eagle Tavern Pleasure Gardens are remembered in the nursery rhyme *Half a Pound of Tuppenny Rice*, which includes the lines 'Up and down the City Road, In and out the Eagle'. Its attractions were listed in the following advertisement:

> **Royal Eagle Coronation Pleasure**
> Grounds and Grecian Saloon
> City Road
>
> Proprietor, Mr T. Rouse – Unrivalled Galas, with brilliant fireworks, and splendid illuminations, and a series of superior amusements, every Monday and Wednesday. To attempt a description of the numerous and varied sources of entertainment at this unrivalled establishment would be vain. Concerts in the open air, dancing and vaudeville in the Saloon, set paintings, cosmoramas, fountains, grottos, elegant buildings, arcade, colonnade, grounds, statuary, singing, music, & c.; render it a fairy scene, of which a due estimate can only be formed by inspection. Open every evening. On Thursday a Benefit, for the Laudable Pension Society, Bethnal Green. See bills.

The whole under the direction of Mr Raymond. Brilliant Discharge of Fireworks, By the inimitable British Artist Thomas Brock.

A Band will be stationed in the Temples, to play during the Evening.

Admission 2s.

The Doors will open at Five o'clock.[12]

London's pleasure gardens declined later in the century as indoor attractions became increasingly popular. They had all closed by the mid-1880s.

Penny Gaffs

The poorest Londoners had their own theatres known as 'penny gaffs'. These were makeshift theatres located in former shops and the backrooms of public houses in the slum districts. Alcohol was freely available and some of these venues were very disreputable places. The content of the shows they put on was often indecent and violent.

J. Ewing Ritchie, a journalist and writer, went to see a show at a penny gaff in Shoreditch, which he described as follows:

> But let us pass on to the penny theatre ... We climb up a primitive staircase, and find ourselves in a gallery of the rudest description, a privilege for which we have to pay a penny extra. Here we have an ample view of the stage and the pit, the latter chiefly filled with boys, very dirty, and full of fun, with the usual proportion of mothers with excited babies. The performance commences with a panorama of American scenery, with some very stale American criticisms, about the man who was so tall that he had to go up a ladder to shave himself, and so on; all, however, exciting much mirth amongst the youthful and apple-eating audience. Then a young lady, with very short petticoats and very thick ankles, dances, and takes all hearts by storm. To her succeeds one who sings about true love, but not in a manner which the Shoreditch youthdom affects. Then a fool comes upon the stage, and keeps

> the pit in a roar, especially when he directs his wit to the three musicians who form the orchestra, and says ironically to one of them, 'You could not drink a quartern of gin, could you?' and the way in which the allusion was received evidently implied that the enlightened but juvenile audience around me evidently had a very low opinion of a man who could not toss off his quartern of gin ... But the treat of the evening was a screaming farce, in one act, in which the old tale of 'Taming the Shrew' was set forth in the most approved Shoreditch fashion. A husband comes upon the stage, whose wife – I would not be ungallant, but conscientious regard to truth compels me sorrowfully to declare – is an unmitigated shrew. She lords it over her husband as no good woman ever did or wishes to do. The poor man obeys till he can stand it no longer. At length all his manhood is aroused. Armed with what he calls a persuader – a cudgel of most formidable pretensions – he astonishes his wife with his unexpected resistance. She tries to regain the mastery, but in vain; and great is the delight of all as the husband, holding his formidable instrument over his cowed and trembling wife, compels her to obey his every word. All the unwashed little urchins around me were furious with delight. There was no need for the husband to tell the audience, as he did, as the moral of the piece, that the best remedy for a bad wife was to get such another cudgel for her as that he held in his hand. It was quite clear the little Britons around me had resolved how they would act; and I fear, as they passed out to the number of about 200, few of them did not resolve, as soon as they had the chance, to drink their quartern of gin and to whop their wives.[13]

At another penny gaff in the New Cut, off Waterloo Road, Ritchie found 'the company and entertainment were of a much lower character'. He described the content of the show as 'indecent and disgusting'.[14]

Music Halls and Theatres

In the 1850s and '60s Penny Gaffs were replaced by music halls. They developed from the song and supper rooms found in some public houses. Two of the earliest music halls were Canterbury Hall in Upper Marsh, Lambeth, which was opened in 1852, enlarged in 1854 and again in the 1870s, and the Oxford Music Hall in Oxford Street, which opened in 1861. The most famous music hall was the Alhambra in Leicester Square, which was elaborately decorated in the Moorish style. As well as music, the entertainment on offer included dancing, acrobats and operatic selections. By the end of the century the music hall had created many famous stars such as Marie Lloyd, Dan Leno and Albert Chevalier.

In the early part of Victoria's reign two London theatres – Drury Lane and Covent Garden – enjoyed a monopoly of theatrical rights. The easing of these restrictions following the passing of the Theatres Act in 1843 permitted the performance of plays in all licensed theatres. Nearly forty new theatres opened in London and theatre going became a popular pastime. Queen Victoria and Prince Albert became regular theatre goers. In the 1860s theatres enjoyed another surge in popularity.

The Shakespearian actors Henry Irving and W. L Macready were much admired. Popular theatres included the Lyceum, the Savoy and the Royal Victoria, which had seats for 1,200 people.

Street Entertainers

There was an amazing array of entertainments and diversions for people of all classes to enjoy on the streets of the Victorian capital. Entertainers included musicians, dancers, jugglers, clowns, acrobats, puppeteers, tightrope and stilt walkers, strolling actors, reciters and performing animals. Certain locations were well known for particular forms of entertainment. Leicester Square and Regent Street were renowned for Punch and Judy shows, Oxford Street and Tottenham Court Road for puppeteers, and Gray's Inn Road for fire-eaters.

One of the largest groups of street entertainers were musicians. It was estimated that there were around 250 bands and 1,000 musicians on London's streets.[15]

Adults and children worked as street entertainers either alone, in groups, or in families. Some travelled around the shopping and residential districts in search of an audience. Their audiences were people of all classes and ages, including workers and tourists as well as residents.

One of the favourite entertainments for children was the one-man-band, as Frederick Willis recalled in his memoir of his London childhood.

> The best musical entertainment on the streets (with the exception of the piano organ) was that provided by the ingenious soul who called himself 'The one-man band.' He had a large drum strapped to his shoulders and resting on his stomach. On the drum were fitted cymbals and triangle, to his chin was fastened a set of Pan's pipes. He produced his music by blowing a tune out of his pipes, beating the drum with one hand and the triangle with the other, and operating the cymbals with his feet by means of a string attachment. He presented a figure that might have stepped straight out of a children's fairy-story book. The music was novel and striking.[16]

Alfred Rosling Bennett recalled the numerous and varied street amusements of the 1850s and 60s. One of his favourites was the 'ever-popular' Punch and Judy show.

> The presentation itself has varied but little except in the dress of the policeman, but in those days the manipulator of the puppets was always accompanied by a comrade who usually wore a pot-hat, not infrequently a white one, had a mouth-organ stuck in his stock or neckerchief, and carried a drum. The noise of the instruments was quite characteristic and children a street or two off could tell when a Punch was in the vicinity. The musician also acted as collector. In these degenerate days I notice no such picturesque collaborator, the artist's adjunct being often a music-mute youth or woman who looks after the ha'pence and nothing more.[17]

Art

The National Gallery, which was originally located in Pall Mall, moved to Trafalgar Square in 1838. It was very popular as the

Victorians loved looking at paintings. The building was altered and enlarged in 1860 and 1869, and a further wing was added in 1876. In his *Handbook of London* Peter Cunningham described the National Gallery as 'a highly important collection, containing, as it does, some of the best examples of the greatest painters'.[18]

George Augustus Sala recorded a visit to the gallery in his book *London Up to Date* (1895).

> I entered the building and delight to record that the halls of the National Gallery this particular Saturday afternoon were full; and that large numbers of the visitors were of the working class, and were not stolidly tramping from gallery to gallery, just glancing with listless gaze at the glorious works of art on the walls; but that they were steadily passing from room to room and scanning long and lovingly the marvellous collection of paintings which have grown up in Trafalgar Square from the nucleus of the Angerstein Gallery of thirty-eight pictures, purchased in 1824 by the Government, at the trifling price of fifty-seven thousand pounds, and which, were England bankrupt, and forced to sell her art treasures, would now fetch possibly half a million of money, to say nothing of the prodigious additions which have been made to the collection during the last fifty years.[19]

The Royal Academy

The Royal Academy, based in Burlington House, Piccadilly, held annual exhibitions from the beginning of May to the end of July, and a winter exhibition of loaned artwork. On becoming an Academician, artists presented their 'diploma' picture to the Academy and these were on view to the public all-year round. Charles Dickens Junior described the exhibition of these pictures as 'one of the largest picture shows in the world'.[20]

One of the most popular exhibits in the Royal Academy was William Powell Frith's huge painting *The Railway Station* depicting a busy scene at Paddington station. Frith also painted two other famous panoramic pictures of Victorian life – *The Derby Day* and *Ramsgate Sands*.

Dulwich Picture Gallery

Dulwich Picture Gallery was one of a number of small galleries in the Victorian capital. Opened in 1817, it was the oldest public art gallery in England. The gallery was housed in a building designed by the Regency architect Sir John Soane. It contained a number of works by great masters including Gainsborough and Lawrence. In Dickens' novel *Pickwick Papers* the character Samuel Pickwick visits this gallery.

Museums

In keeping with Samuel Smiles' ethic of self-help there were plenty of learning and cultural opportunities in Victorian London. These included many museums – some long-established and others newly founded. Many of these museums were free.

The British Museum

The British Museum, which was founded in 1753, was the first national public museum in the world. It originally comprised the huge collection of Sir Hans Sloane, a physician and President of the Royal Society. His collection included natural rarities, books, manuscripts, coins and medals. At one time tickets to the museum had to be applied for and only a few well-connected people gained admittance. In the 1850s, by which time the collection had grown considerably to include Assyrian, Egyptian and Medieval galleries, the museum became accessible to all people 'of decent apparel'.

The museum, which was originally housed in Montagu House, on the site of the current building, was rebuilt between 1823 and 1852. After the new Greek Revival-style building was opened there was a huge increase in the number of visitors.

A library and reading room, with a huge dome, were opened in 1857. Letters of introduction and a pass were needed to get into the reading room. Hippolyte Taine, having gained the necessary means to enter, visited the reading room and wrote the following description of it:

> The library contains 600,000 books; there is a huge Reading Room, circular and topped by a cupola, so arranged that no reader

is far from the central bureau or has the light in his eyes. The surrounding shelves are filled with reference books, dictionaries, biographical collections, classics in every field, very well arranged and which one can consult on the spot. Moreover, on every table there is a small map or plan to show the order and position of these books. Each desk is isolated, you have nothing but the wood of your desk under your eyes and are not disturbed or bothered by the stares of a neighbour. The chairs are of leather and the desks are covered with leather too; all very neat and clean. Two pens to each desk, one quill and one steel. There is a small book-rest so that you can have a second book conveniently to hand, or the book you are copying from.

To get a book you write the title on a form which you hand in at the central bureau: a library clerk brings it to your own desk, and that very quickly; I tried this out and proved it, even with very rare books.[21]

The South Kensington Museums

Further cultural opportunities were offered by the museums built on an area of land in south Kensington, which became known as 'Albertopolis', bought with the profits of the Great Exhibition. The first to be built was the Museum of Manufacture, which opened in 1857. A lot of exhibits from the Great Exhibition were shown there. It later became known as the South Kensington Museum. A new building was erected after Queen Victoria laid the foundation stone in 1899. The museum was then renamed the Victoria and Albert Museum.

Scientific exhibits from the South Kensington Museum were moved to a building which had housed an international exhibition in 1862. This became the Science Museum. In 1881 the Natural History Museum was opened nearby and the natural history and geological exhibits at the British Museum were moved there.

The Soane Museum and the Wallace Collection

There were a number of small museums and collections in London, such as the Soane Museum in Lincoln's Inn Fields and the Wallace

Collection in Manchester Square, near Oxford Street. Both of these museums still exist.

The Soane museum houses the collection of Sir John Soane, a famous architect of the late Georgian and Regency period. The museum was described in the following entry from *Mogg's New Guide to London and Visitors' Guide to its Sights*:

> The Soane Museum, in Lincoln's Inn Fields, is a splendid suite of rooms, ornamented with paintings by Canaletto and Hogarth, and many eminent modern masters, and with designs by J. Soane himself. They are likewise enriched with a choice selection of Roman and Grecian specimens of architecture, Etruscan vases, Egyptian antiquities, & c; particularly the alabaster sarcophagus, brought by the late enterprising traveller Belzoni from the ruins of Thebes. This unique collection was presented to the nation by the proprietor, in 1833, an act of Parliament having sanctioned the disposal of this valuable museum in its present form.[22]

The Wallace collection of paintings, armour and decorative artefacts was left to the nation by Lady Wallace in 1897. It is located in Hertford House, Manchester Square, near Baker Street, the former townhouse of the Seymour family, the Marquesses of Hertford. It was opened to the public in 1900, the last year of Victoria's reign.

New Attractions

A number of new attractions appeared in London for residents with the time and money to spend on entertainment, as well as for day visitors and tourists. They helped to satisfy the thirst for knowledge and curiosity about other countries, the natural world and dramatic events.

Regent's Park Zoo

London Zoo, or the London Zoological Gardens to give it its full title, was founded by the Zoological Society in 1826. It was founded 'for the advancement of zoology and the introduction and exhibition of the animal kingdom alive or properly preserved'.

The zoo, which was housed in Regent's Park, was opened to the public in 1828. The Parrot Walk and Jumbo the elephant were popular attractions. Peter Cunningham made the following entry in his 1849 guidebook:

> These Gardens are among the best of our London sights, and should be seen by the stranger in London. The number of visitors in the year 1849 was 168,895. The collection on the 31st December 1849 contained 1352 living animals viz. 354 mammalia, 853 birds and 145 reptiles. The giraffes and rattle snakes are very rare and fine.[23]

Astley's Amphitheatre

Another well-patronised animal attraction was Astley's Amphitheatre, a theatre with a circus ring which was used for equestrian displays and occasionally for performing elephants. By 1879, when Charles Dickens Junior wrote the following entry in his *Dictionary of Victorian London,* Astley's had changed hands:

> A theatre and hippodrome on the Surrey Side, about a hundred yards from Westminster Br.; formerly known as Astley's, now in the hands of Messrs. Sanger, who have introduced a large menagerie element into the performances.[24]

Wyld's Monster Globe

Wyld's Monster Globe, a gigantic model of the earth, was opened in Leicester Square in 1851. The hollow globe was 60 feet in diameter, with a staircase inside for visitors to climb and view the physical features of the earth from below.

The globe was built to attract the crowds who had flocked to London for the Great Exhibition. It was intended that the attraction would be closed when the Great Exhibition ended but it was so successful that it remained open for another decade. It was finally demolished in 1861.

Panoramas and Dioramas

Panoramas and dioramas were very popular in the Victorian era. Panoramas gave a 360-degree view of a scene and dioramas were models with three-dimensional figures. At the Colosseum in Regent's Park there was a famous panorama of London viewed from St Paul's Cathedral. This attraction survived until the 1870s. Another much-visited panorama was *Mr Burford's Panorama of Sebastopol* in Leicester Square depicting events in the Crimean War. The following paragraph is taken from *Mogg's Guide*:

> Burford's Panorama – Among the various attractive exhibitions of London, is that belonging to Mr Burford, situated at the Eastern corner of Leicester Square, where a series of unrivalled productions, from the pencil of that distinguished painter, afford a truly gratifying treat to the curious in topographical delineation. There are, generally, two views of celebrated places; admission to each view, 1s., and catalogues 6d.[25]

The *London Diorama*, which opened in 1813, was near Regent's Park. The audience sat on a rotating platform to view such scenes as the interior of Canterbury Cathedral, the Royal Castle of Stolzenfels on the Rhine, and events such as the eruption of Mount Etna. Lightning and other effects were used to enhance the scenes.

Madame Tussaud's Waxworks

One of the most visited attractions in London was Madame Tussaud's waxworks in Baker Street. Madame Tussaud, who learnt her skills by making death masks of people executed during the French Revolution, opened her exhibition in 1835. It contained waxworks of the monarchs of Europe, historical figures, famous actors and other celebrities. One of its main attractions was the Chamber of Horrors with its blood-stained figures of murderers and victims of the French Revolution. The exhibition was open daily and the entrance fee was one shilling.

The Polytechnic Institution

The Polytechnic Institution in Regent Street showcased 'popular science' and was also an entertainment venue. It was a good place to see optical devices such as the microscope, stereoscope and magic lantern, an early type of slide projector. There were also two rooms where lectures were delivered and scientific experiments were performed.

In an article published in *Punch* in 1843 'people of weak nerves' were advised to 'venture very cautiously into the Polytechnic Institution':

> For, at first entrance, there is such a whirlwind of machinery in full action – wonderful things going up, and coming down, and turning round all at once, that the mere view of them acting through the retina, might well addle the brains of ordinary visitors.[26]

Eating Out

In the early Victorian period there were very few places in London to eat out. Later on the Great Exhibition and the popularity of the theatre led to a growth in the habit of eating out and more eating places were opened. Around this time it became respectable for women to eat out, something hitherto considered unacceptable.

The cheapest establishments were the 'cookshop' or 'soup house' which sold cheap, plain food such as soup and baked potatoes. Dining rooms in and around the City provided basic meals at lunchtime for men who worked there. The quality of food was superior to that of the cookshop. There were also beef and chop houses, with limited menus, which also catered for this trade. Alfred Rosling Bennet recalled the chop houses of the 1850s.

> I once or twice in the 1850s had experience of a City chop-house, with its sanded floor, straight-backed wooden seats, and primitive arrangements. Pewter plates and dishes were said to have been discarded quite recently by some of them. The things supplied were excellent – chops and steaks, of English meat of course – and an air of good-fellowship prevailed, room being made for a stranger with

> the greatest readiness. The Head Waiter was always addressed by his Christian name, and was often a man of parts and character – wealth also sometimes – apt at repartee and free from the servility to which in later years the German waiter accustomed us.[27]

The grand hotels built near the main railway termini had restaurants selling excellent food.

The most famous Victorian chef was the Frenchman Alexis Soyer, whose 'Gastronomic Symposium of All Nations' was located in Kensington Gore. It enjoyed much custom at the time of the Great Exhibition, but its popularity then waned until it went out of business.

The lower classes patronised what came to be called song and supper rooms attached to public houses, where they could enjoy a cheap meal and be entertained at the same time. Well-known song and supper rooms included The Coal Hole in the Strand and Evan's in King Street, near Covent Garden. Many of these establishments later became music halls.

Public Houses and Gin Palaces

By the middle of the nineteenth century public houses, which had previously been patronised by men of all classes, became the preserve of the poor. This was partly due to the influence of the Temperance Movement, which made the drinking of alcohol less respectable. The pub was a popular place for poor Londoners to relax and enjoy a sing-song.

Gin palaces, which competed with pubs for customers, could be found in nearly every street in the slum districts. These gaudy establishments, with their long counters and large open-plan interiors, were less cosy than pubs. Max Schlesinger described the gin palaces which he came across as he walked through the slums near Drury Lane.

> But the gin-palaces are the lions of Drury Lane; they stand in conspicuous positions, at the corners and crossings of the various intersecting streets. They may be seen from afar, and are

> lighthouses which guide the thirsty 'sweater' on the road to ruin. For they are resplendent with plate glass and gilt cornices, and a variety of many-coloured inscriptions. One of the windows displays the portrait of the 'Norfolk Giant,' who acts as barman to this particular house; the walls of another establishment inform you, in green letters, that they sell 'The Only Real Brandy in London,' and a set of scarlet letters announces to the world, that in this house they sell 'The Famous Cordial Medicated Gin, which is so strongly recommended by the Faculty.' Cream Gin, Honey Gin, Sparkling Ale, Genuine Porter, and other words calculated utterly to confound a tee-totaller, are painted up in conspicuous characters, even so that they cover the door-posts.[28]

Drunkenness was rife in the capital. A number of temperance societies were set up to deal with the problem. Hippolyte Taine was shocked at the number of drunken people he came across in London, as described in this extract from *Notes on England*:

> ... drunkenness among the people is terrible. During the last few days I have twice been down to Chelsea and both times came across men lying dead drunk on the pavement. My friend who lives in that district often finds working girls and women in the same condition. A philanthropic clergyman of my acquaintance tells me that eight out of ten working men are drunkards ... Thirty thousand people are arrested every year in the London streets for being drunk. It is reckoned that the fourteen principal gin-palaces are patronised by two hundred and seventy thousand customers every week.[29]

For many members of the poorer classes, drink was the only way to find some temporary relief from their harsh lives and the struggle to survive in the Victorian capital.

Opium Dens

A small Chinese community lived in the East End of London, near the docks. They introduced the habit of smoking opium. Opium dens, where opium was sold and smoked, appeared in the area in the 1860s. Most of their customers were sailors who had become addicted to opium while abroad. Opium was not illegal in Victorian England – it was easily obtained in the form of laudanum for the treatment of minor ailments.

The following paragraph about opium dens comes from *Dickens's Dictionary of London*:

> Opium Smoking Dens. – The best known of these justly-named 'dens' is that of one Johnstone, who lives in a garret off Ratcliff-highway, and for a consideration allows visitors to smoke a pipe which has been used by many crowned heads in common with poor Chinese sailors who seek their native pleasure in Johnstone's garret ... A similar establishment of a slightly superior – or it might be more correct to say a shade less nauseating – class is that of Johnny Chang, at the London and St Katharine Coffee-house, in the Highway itself.[30]

8

THE GREAT EXHIBITION

In 1849 Henry Cole, Chairman of the Society of Arts (later the Royal Society of Arts), suggested that an international trade exhibition be staged in London, inspired by his visit to the French International Exhibition held in Paris that year.

A Special Commission was set up with Prince Albert as its President. In the Victorian period Britain was known as the 'Workshop of the World' because it was the most advanced industrial nation and led the world in inventions and ideas. The exhibition would show the best in British raw materials, industrial designs and new inventions and it would also display exhibits from around the world. It was hoped that the exhibition would boost trade for Britain and contribute towards improved understanding and peace between nations. It would also symbolise London's place at the centre of a growing empire.

When the idea of an exhibition was first discussed there was opposition both inside and outside the House of Commons. The *Times*, for example, expressed fears about the undesirable people who might be attracted to Hyde Park, the proposed site of the exhibition. It predicted:

> The whole of Hyde Park and, we venture to predict, the whole of Kensington Gardens, will be turned into a camp of all the

> vagabonds of London so long as the Exhibition shall continue. The annoyance inflicted upon the neighbourhood will be indescribable.[1]

The Crystal Palace

Despite the opposition the plans went ahead. A competition was held for a design for the building to house the exhibition but it did not produce an acceptable one. The design that was eventually used was the work of Joseph Paxton, head gardener to the Duke of Devonshire, the owner of the magnificent Chatsworth House in Derbyshire. Paxton had designed a glass and iron lily house at Chatsworth and the building he designed for the Great Exhibition was based on this revolutionary structure. It was to be a temporary, prefabricated building with a framework of cast iron and a roof and walls made of sheet glass.

The building, which was a cruciform shape, was over 1,800 feet long, over 400 feet wide and its transept was 108 feet high. It covered 19 acres and took 2,000 workmen twenty-seven weeks to erect and another sixteen weeks to fit out. The building had a domed roof so that some very large trees could be incorporated. A 27-foot high crystal fountain was erected in the central section. *Punch* magazine christened the building 'The Crystal Palace'. In the words of the official guidebook to the exhibition,

> Never before has a piece of glass-work been executed involving the treatment, in casting, cutting and polishing of a block of glass of a size so large, and of a purity so uniformly faultless.

Queen Victoria visited the building more than once as it was being erected. One of these visits, which took place on 18 February, was described in her journal.

> After breakfast we drove with the five children to look at the Crystal Palace which was not finished when we last went, and really now is one of the wonders of the world, which we English may indeed be proud of. The Galleries are finished and from the top of them the effect is quite wonderful. The sun shining in

> through the Transept gave a fairy-like appearance. The building is so light and graceful, in spite of its immense size. Many of the exhibits have arrived and some from Germany were being unpacked ... We were again cheered loudly by the two thousand workmen, as we came away. It made me feel proud and happy.[2]

Opening Day

'The Great Exhibition of the Works of Industry of All Nations' opened on 1 May 1851. There was a twenty-one-gun salute in Hyde Park as the Queen, dressed in a pale pink gown brocaded with silver, with diamonds in her hair and wearing the Garter ribbon, arrived accompanied by her two eldest children, Vicky and Bertie. Twenty-five thousand people were there for the opening ceremony during which the Archbishop of Canterbury said prayers and a choir sang the Hallelujah Chorus to the accompaniment of an orchestra. The Queen walked around the exhibition with the organisers, foreign commissioners and diplomats, representatives of the royal families of other nations and various other VIPs She then returned to sit on her throne under a canopy and declared the exhibition open. While the opening ceremony was in progress business throughout London was suspended and, apart from the streets around Hyde Park, the capital was deserted.

That evening the Queen sat down to record the day's events and her feelings in her journal. She described her reaction on arriving at the Crystal Palace in the following paragraphs:

> The park presented a wonderful spectacle, crowds streaming through it, – carriages and troops passing, quite like the Coronation Day, and for me, the same anxiety. The day was bright, and all bustle and excitement. At half-past eleven the whole procession in nine state carriages was set in motion ... The Green Park and Hyde Park were one mass of densely crowded human beings, in the highest good humour and most enthusiastic. I never saw Hyde Park look as it did, being filled with crowds as far as the eye could reach. A little rain fell, just as we started, but before we reached the Crystal Palace, the sun shone and gleamed upon

> the gigantic edifice, upon which the flags of every nation were flying. We drove up Rotten Row and got out of our carriages at the entrance in that side. The glimpse through the iron gates of the Transept, the waving palms and flowers, the myriads of people filling the galleries and seats around, together with the flourish of trumpets as we entered the building, gave a sensation I shall never forget, and I felt much moved.[3]

The Exhibition

The exhibits, which totalled 100,000, were divided into five categories – raw materials, machinery, manufactures (textiles), manufactures (metallic, ceramic, etc.) and miscellaneous works of art.

In the British section the steam engines were a great attraction as well as a scale model of the Liverpool docks, made from wood and paper, with 16,000 fully-rigged miniature ships. Large cities such as Sheffield and Birmingham had their own sections. Artworks included stained glass and statues, one of which was a statue of Prince Albert as a Greek shepherd. Among the many interesting items on display were the famous Koh-i-noor diamond lent by the Queen, stuffed elephants and an ornate carved ivory chair from India, a penknife with eighty blades and a group of stuffed frogs from Germany.

The exhibition attracted visitors from all over the world. Tickets were available at various prices to enable people of all social classes to attend and season tickets were also available. Excursion trains were run with inclusive tickets costing five shillings so that people could attend from all parts of the country. The company of Thomas Cook, the pioneering travel agent, sold 165,000 excursion tickets.[4] There were over six million visitors to the exhibition and vast quantities of food and drink were sold.

Charlotte Bronté visited the exhibition twice during a trip to London to see her publisher. Her description of her second visit gives some idea of the distinctive and magical atmosphere of the Crystal Palace.

> Yesterday I went for the second time to the Crystal Palace. We remained in it about three hours, and I must say I was more

> struck with it on this occasion than at my first visit. It is a wonderful place – vast, strange, new, and impossible to describe. Its grandeur does not consist in one thing, but in the unique assemblage of all things. Whatever human industry has created you find there, from the great compartments filled with railway engines and boilers, with mill machinery in full work, with splendid carriages of all kinds, with harness of every description, to the glass-covered and velvet spread stands loaded with the most gorgeous work of the goldsmith and silversmith, and the carefully guarded caskets full of real diamonds and pearls worth hundreds of thousands of pounds. It may be called a bazaar or a fair, but it is such a bazaar or fair as Eastern genii might have created. It seems as if only magic could have gathered this mass of wealth from all the ends of the earth – as if none but supernatural hands could have arranged it thus, with such a blaze and contrast of colours and marvellous power of effect. The multitude filling the great aisles seems ruled and subdued by some invisible influence. Amongst the thirty thousand souls that peopled it the day I was there not one loud noise was to be heard, not one irregular movement seen; the living tide rolls on quietly, with a deep hum like the sea heard from the distance.[5]

During the five months in which the Great Exhibition was open the streets of London were crowded. Many people made profits from the visitors including street vendors, hoteliers, railway and bus companies, and cab drivers. Sellers of souvenirs, guidebooks and maps of London also profited.

Queen Victoria, who was immensely proud of her husband's role in the Great Exhibition, visited the Crystal Palace no less than forty-four times between February and October 1851, when the exhibition closed. Another distinguished and frequent visitor was the Duke of Wellington, who lived nearby at Hyde Park Corner.

The Great Exhibition was a resounding success. In the five-and-a-half months during which it was open over six million people attended. It had come to symbolise London's place at the centre of a great empire.

The Closing Ceremony

The exhibition closed on 11 October in a solemn and dignified ceremony, which included a loud rendition of the National Anthem. David Bartlett, an American visitor to London who was in the watching crowd, recorded his impressions of the ceremony.

> On a somewhat cheerless day of October, with few ceremonies and little circumstance, the Great Exhibition was closed. The trees in Hyde Park had begun to shed their leaves, and there were approaching signs in every direction of the coming gloom of winter. The interior of the great Palace looked sad; the very branches of the old trees there, which, during the summer, had been blessed with such royal society, looked forlorn. The Royal Commissioners were there, surrounded by about ten thousand people. Prince Albert read a report; the Earl of Granville ditto; the white-haired Archbishop of Canterbury murmured a prayer in a faint voice; the great organs thundered forth one final Hallelujah; and the wondrous Exhibition, which had attracted the world together, which for many months had been the theme of converse in all cities and countries, from Tahiti to Hindostan, was brought to an end.
>
> There was no pageantry, no pomp – and no one of all the thousands there seemed to desire it. Upon every countenance there was a shade of solemn sadness, as if the moral of that day's scenic had found its way to the heart; that all in this world of ours, however gorgeous, however costly and beautiful, must come to an end. Yes, the scene was a striking one, but not more so than the moral which every one could not fail to draw from it. The world had tried its utmost, and built a palace of wondrous beauty, and filled it with its grandest, its proudest achievements. The summer passed away in gloryings, and rejoicings, in splendid revelry – and yet here was the end.[6]

Joseph Paxton, the designer of the Crystal Palace, was knighted. The exhibition raised the huge sum of £186,437. With the profits a large area of land was bought in south Kensington on which were built a number of educational establishments, including the museums which are still flourishing today.

As a tribute to Prince Albert, who played such an important part in the success of the Great Exhibition, the Royal Albert Hall was built nearby, using some of the exhibition profits. This grand Italian Renaissance-style building opened in 1871, ten years after the Prince's death, and was used for organ recitals, concerts and occasional public meetings, because of its excellent acoustics. The Albert Memorial, designed by Sir Gilbert Scott, was built in Kensington Gardens opposite. A huge bronze-gilt statue of the Prince was placed under Scott's ornate Gothic canopy. Marble statues representing Agriculture, Manufacture, Commerce and Engineering adorn the pedestals of four granite columns and around the base are marble figures of poets, painters, sculptors and architects – all reflecting the Prince's wide-ranging interests and a reminder of his enormous contribution to the Great Exhibition.

Sydenham

Following the closure of the exhibition the prefabricated Crystal Palace was dismantled and taken to Sydenham in south-east London, where it was re-erected, but not quite in its original form. The re-erected palace housed a museum and other recreational facilities, as described by Hippolyte Taine.

> Inside are: a Museum of Classical Antiquity – plaster facsimiles of all the Greek and Roman Statues in Europe; a Museum of the Middle Ages; a Museum of the Renaissance; an Egyptology Museum; a Ninevite Museum; an Indian Museum; a reproduction of a house in Pompeii; a reproduction of the Alhambra…
>
> There is a gigantic tropical hot-house, with ponds, fountains, swimming tortoises, large aquatic plants in flower, sphinxes and Egyptian statues sixty feet tall, specimens of colossal or otherwise strange trees, among others the bark of a Californian sequoia four hundred and fifty feet tall and one hundred and sixteen feet round the base; the bark is mounted upon an interior scaffolding so as to give some idea of the tree.

> There is a concert hall with the floor sloped about a centre so that the seats are in tiers, making it look like a Coliseum.
>
> Out in the gardens, latterly, they had life-sized models of antediluvian monsters, megatheriums, dinotheriums and others. Blondin [a famous tightrope-walker] goes through his performance there, at one hundred feet from the ground.[7]

Balloon ascents and firework displays were also held in the landscaped gardens.

The re-erected Crystal Palace was sadly burnt down in 1936 and all that remains are a few relics in the grounds.

9

HEALTH AND MEDICINE

Victorian London was an extremely unhealthy place in which to live and work. The mortality rate of London's inhabitants was high, especially among children, who were lucky if they survived until the age of five.

The major health hazards were the notorious London smog, bad drains, polluted rivers and drinking water, an inadequate sewage system, dirty streets and dangerously overcrowded graveyards and burial grounds.

Fog

London's famous pea-souper fogs (or 'smogs') were caused by fog mixing with smoke from coal fires and vapour from defective drains and the polluted River Thames. Often the fog hung around all day long and was so invasive at times that it insinuated itself into buildings. Its colour varied from white to yellow to dark green, depending on the temperature, and it was particularly bad in winter. Sometimes the fog was so dense that it was impossible to see the fingers of an outstretched hand. Not only was it dangerous to breathe in the noxious foggy atmosphere but obscured vision led to road and other accidents.

Fog helped to create the mysterious, menacing atmosphere of night-time London so vividly evoked by contemporary writers and artists. It made it easier for muggers and pickpockets to creep up on unsuspecting victims and to disappear quickly into the fog once they had achieved their objective.

The following description of London fog comes from the first chapter of Charles Dickens' novel *Bleak House*:

> Fog everywhere. Fog up the river, where it flows among green aits and meadows; fog down the river, where it rolls defiled among the tiers of shipping and the waterside pollutions of a great (and dirty) city. Fog on the Essex marshes, fog on the Kentish heights. Fog creeping into the cabooses [kitchens on deck] of collier-brigs; fog lying out on the yards, and hovering in the rigging of great ships; fog drooping on the gunwhales of barges and small boats. Fog in the eyes and throats of ancient Greenwich pensioners, wheezing by the firesides of their wards; fog in the stem and bowl of the afternoon pipe of the wrathful skipper, down in his close cabin; fog cruelly pinching the toes and fingers of his shivering little 'prentice boy on deck. Chance people on the bridges peeping over the parapets into a nether sky of fog, with fog all round them, as if they were up in a balloon, and hanging in the misty clouds.

The fog was less toxic after pollution of the River Thames was dealt with, but remained a problem in the capital well into the twentieth century.

Doctors and Nurses

At the top of the medical hierarchy in the Victorian era were physicians, who administered drugs or 'physic'. They had to be licensed by the Royal College of Physicians. Formal medical training was not required, but it became more common in the nineteenth century for physicians to have a university education followed by training at medical school.

The status of surgeons was below that of physicians. They performed minor surgery, reset broken bones and dealt with other medical problems which did not come under the remit of the physician. Surgeons learned their profession by apprenticeship and were required to hold a licence. They were regulated by the College of Surgeons, later the Royal College of Surgeons.

The apothecary was lowest in the hierarchy of doctors. Originally their role was to make up and dispense prescriptions for physicians but, where there were no physicians, they began to give medical advice as well. Apothecaries also had to be licensed.

Doctors became better qualified and more respected as the century progressed. Entry to the profession was controlled and it became properly regulated after the foundation of the British Medical Association in 1855 and the General Medical Council in 1858.

Better-off Londoners who could afford to pay for medical care were visited by doctors and treated at home. The poor either consulted a quack doctor, an apothecary or, in the last resort, the parish doctor employed by the Board of Guardians at the local workhouse. To consult a parish doctor it was necessary to obtain a letter from the Relieving Officer.

Nurses were not properly trained until the middle of the nineteenth century. Standards improved after reforms were carried out by Sister Mary Jones of the Anglican Nursing Sisterhood, who led a team of nurses at King's College Hospital in London. Florence Nightingale, who was famous for her success in nursing soldiers during the Crimean War, set up a School of Nursing at St Thomas's Hospital in 1860. She revolutionised the nursing profession and nurses became highly trained and respected.

Hospitals

For most of the nineteenth century members of the middle and upper classes paid to be treated and cared for at home, even when seriously ill. There were a large number of 'voluntary' hospitals in London which had been founded for the poor. There were not enough, however, to cater for the capital's ever-growing population. Such hospitals were funded by donations and subscriptions from wealthy benefactors. To gain admittance it was usually necessary to obtain a letter of recommendation from a member of the committee of benefactors and subscribers. Some hospitals, such as

St Barthlomew's, did admit accident and urgent cases without a letter and at any time. While researching his book *Unsentimental Journeys Through Modern Babylon* (1867) James Greenwood sat near the entrance to St Bartholomew's, observing people waiting patiently to be admitted. There were people of all ages, including

> ... mothers cuddling to their bosoms sick infants, varying in age from the tiny creature ignorant of a want beyond to the languid little fellow of four or five whom affliction has once more reduced to babyhood.

Greenwood watched as several seriously injured people were rushed inside, bypassing the queue.

> The liveried porter, hearing the hasty wheels, has just peeped out to see a cab, with a policeman descending from the driving-seat, and the next moment makes his appearance with a companion, the two carrying a "stretcher." "Slater off a roof!" exclaims the policeman, shortly; and, gently handled by a dozen willing hands, as though he were a baby, the pallid man, with his great, dirty, labouring hands, and the slating-nails dropping from his jacket-pocket and tinkling on the pavement, is borne through the gate to have his shattered bones set and be brought to life again, if the ripest skill in the kingdom can accomplish the doubtful business.
>
> Shortly after the commotion (very slight it was) consequent on the slater's arrival had subsided, there came in succession two "run-overs" and an Irish person severely wounded on the head with a drinking-vessel.[1]

An alternative place for the poor to seek medical advice and drugs was at a charitable dispensary. To use some of these dispensaries, however, it was necessary to pay subscriptions.

Specialist Hospitals

Most London hospitals excluded children and those suffering from fevers, chronic conditions and infectious diseases. A number of specialist hospitals were therefore built in London during the nineteenth century, financed by endowments and donations, to treat people with conditions not catered for in general hospitals. As a result, knowledge of different diseases and the treatment and care of those suffering from them improved. These hospitals specialised in, for example, dental cases, cancer, fistulas, orthopaedics, chest diseases, skin diseases and eye and ear complaints. There were special institutions known as 'lock hospitals' for the treatment of fallen women with venereal disease.

In 1860 there were sixty-six specialist hospitals in London.[2] The many London guidebooks and handbooks included detailed information about the different hospitals in the capital. By the 1860s, when hospitals were safer and more efficiently run, it became more common for better-off Londoners to be treated in them.

Maternity Hospitals

Among the specialist hospitals were maternity or 'lying-in hospitals', which provided a safer alternative to home births. Mothers were cared for by trained male obstetricians, who could use instruments for deliveries. Some of these hospitals did not accept unmarried women. The following details of the British Lying-In Hospital is taken from *Dickens's Dictionary of London*:

> British Lying-In Hospital, Endell-st., St Giles; Secretary Fitz-Roy Gardner. – To provide proper nursing, medical attendance, and nourishment for poor married women at the time of childbirth. Out-patients visited at their own homes. Visitors admitted daily from 9 a.m. to 6 p.m. (except on Sundays). Admission of patients by letter of recommendation from governor.[3]

The Hospital for Sick Children

In 1852 the first specialist children's hospital in the United Kingdom opened in Great Ormond Street, with ten beds and two physicians. Twenty years later James Greenwood was shown around the much-enlarged hospital and described his visit in

The Wilds of London (1874), from which the following extract is taken:

> We passed from ward to ward, where the cheerful fires were burning, and the kind-faced nurses moved hither and thither, and some of the sick ones sat up at work on their basins of bread-and-milk or beef-tea, and others were contentedly busy at their play-boards, hooking gay railway carriages one to the other, or giving the animals of Noah's Ark an airing, or, as yet unequal to such active employment, with quiet interest turning the leaves of a painted picture-book. No crying to go home, no fretting or pining; all as happy under the circumstances not only as might be expected reasonably, but twenty times more so. All glad to see the doctor ... all grateful for his encouraging word, or a touch of his kind hand.[4]

Workhouse Infirmaries

The destitute poor could seek medical assistance at workhouse infirmaries. They were treated by medical officers and nursed by other paupers. These infirmaries were not always clean or well run, and their death rates were unacceptably high.

The state eventually accepted responsibility for providing hospitals for the poor. A system of public hospitals was established when the Metropolitan Asylum Board was established in 1867. These hospitals initially only treated paupers with scarlet fever and smallpox, but later they took patients who were not paupers and dealt with a wide range of illnesses. In 1877 there were five of these hospitals in London and by 1890 their number had risen by another 26.[5]

Dentistry

For most of the nineteenth century the usual treatment for toothache was removal of the tooth. Laudanum or a swig of whisky were used to dull the pain. The filling of dental cavities was rare. James Greenwood saw a number of people with their jaws bandaged waiting in the queue at St Bartholomew's Hospital.

Dentistry became a profession in the Victorian period. The London Dental Hospital was opened in Soho Square in 1858 and later moved to larger premises in Leicester Square. In the words of Charles Dickens Junior it was established to 'provide the poorer classes with gratuitous advice and surgical aid in diseases and irregularities of the teeth'.[6]

It was also responsible for regulating and improving standards in dental care. Innovations in dentistry at this time included the use of treadle drills and the introduction of chloroform and nitrous oxide as anaesthetics.

Homeopathy

Homeopathy is a holistic, natural approach to treating the sick, based on the use of highly diluted substances to help the body heal itself. It was introduced in England in the 1860s.

The London Homeopathic Hospital was founded in 1849. It was originally located in Golden Square, Soho before moving to Great Ormond Street in 1859. Admission was by recommendation of a subscriber.

Mental Health

There was little change in the knowledge and treatment of mental illness between the medieval and Victorian periods. In London patients were locked away in private asylums, if they could afford to pay for their care, or in charitable institutions if they were poor. Men and women were kept in separate wards and solitary confinement and straitjackets were in common use.

The most famous hospital in London for the mentally ill was Bethlehem Hospital, commonly known as 'Bedlam'. The following extract from *Cruchley's Handbook of London* shows how attitudes to mental illness and the care and treatment of patients improved during the nineteenth century:

> Bethlehem [Hospital], vulgarly called Bedlam, is situated in St George's Fields...[The hospital] removed to its present site in 1814. The new hospital was designed by James Lewis, and was

originally constructed for 198 patients; but was enlarged in 1838, by the addition of a new wing for 166 more patients. The entire pile now occupies fourteen acres. The method and regimen adopted are those which have been suggested by the wisdom and humanity of the present school of medicine. Love, and not fear, is the great principle of government, and the unhappy insane are watched over with the tenderest pity ... the average number of cases annually treated [is] 350. The hospital will accommodate 400 patients, but is seldom completely full. Criminal lunatics are confined here.[7]

In the late nineteenth century attempts were made to improve conditions in asylums as a result of pressure from William Wilberforce and other concerned people. An important change came about as a result of the passing of the Idiots Act in 1886. From then on a distinction was made between patients suffering from mental illness and those suffering from a mental disability or learning difficulties. From 1886 they were cared for in different institutions.

Street Doctors

Throughout the first half of the Victorian period there were numerous street doctors or 'quacks' selling their wares on the streets of London. It was not illegal for anyone to offer medical services so long as they did not claim to be doctors. Selling herbal concoctions, fever powder, pills and potions was a lucrative trade. Many of these street doctors were fakes and swindlers. The journalist Adolphe Smith interviewed several street doctors while researching his book *Victorian London Street Life*. He was told by one of them, 'If it [his remedy] don't lengthen the life of the buyer it lengthens the life of the seller.'[8]

This man told Smith about another street doctor:

Togged like a military swell, [he] scares the people into buying his pills. He has half-a-dozen bottles filled with different fluids he works with, turnin' one into t'other. He turns a clear fluid black, and says, 'Ladies and gentlemen, this is what happens to your

> blood when exposed to the fogs of London'. 'Without blood there is no life! You seem bloodless, my friends; look at each other.' They look, and almost believe him. 'Next to no blood is impure blood! This is your condition, I can describe your symptoms. I offer you the only safe, certain, and infallible remedy.' This style of 'patter' makes the pills fly, but it's not everyone can come it to perfection.[9]

Advertisements for remedies and other treatments were placed in newspapers and journals. Cures were offered for all sorts of complaints and even serious diseases such as tuberculosis, with some preposterous claims for their effectiveness. Many such cures contained dangerous ingredients which caused serious side effects. Godfrey's Cordial, which was sold as a remedy for babies' wind, contained opium and was widely used by professional baby minders to dope the infants in their care.

Two other popular, but dangerous, remedies were Morrison's Pills, which were known to have caused many deaths, and Fowler's Solution, which contained arsenic.

Later in the century, after the introduction of free hospitals and improvements in education which led to people being more informed, street doctors lost their appeal and eventually disappeared from the streets of the capital.

Disease

Disease was so rife in Victorian London, especially in the overcrowded slum districts, that it became known as the 'doomed city'. A lack of understanding about the cause of contagious diseases and how they spread made tackling the problem impossible. Diseases prevalent in the capital included cholera, typhus, typhoid fever, diphtheria, scurvy, consumption, rickets, venereal disease and smallpox. Vaccination was available against the last named from 1853 but this was not enforced until 1867.

Poor diet, squalid living conditions and a lack of both proper sanitation and clean drinking water all contributed to disease. The Victorian virtue of cleanliness had no chance of being observed in the slums.

Cholera

Probably the worst and most feared disease which plagued Victorian London was cholera. It entered England in 1830, having arrived from Asia via eastern Europe. There was no cure for this disease, which attacked suddenly and could kill within two hours.

There were serious outbreaks of the disease in 1832, 1848–49 and 1851. London became known as the 'capital of cholera'. The outbreak of 1849 led to 14,000 deaths and church services were held to pray for protection from the disease. These outbreaks caused serious alarm and calls for the authorities to tackle the problem.

It was believed that cholera and other diseases were caused either by direct contact or were carried in the air by bad smells, the so-called 'miasma theory'. According to Alfred Rosling Bennett,

> The fell disease was not understood, and in the prevailing ignorance all sorts of notions were current ... Remedies recommended were numberless. Acorns, mustard plasters, castor-oil, laughing-gas, cold mutton broth, and hot mint-tea each had its strenuous advocates.[10]

It was not until 1854 that it was discovered that cholera was caused by polluted water. An epidemic in Soho that year resulted in the death of over 500 people in ten days. Dr John Snow, a local doctor, worked out that all the victims had drunk water from a water pump in Broad Street, Soho. He also noticed that the workers at a nearby factory had not contracted the disease because they drank beer instead of water. After the pump handle was removed Dr Snow's theory was proved correct. The number of cholera cases decreased immediately. Despite Dr Snow's discovery, however, the miasma theory was not dismissed until 1858. The final outbreak of cholera was in 1866.

Polluted Rivers

The River Thames, its tributaries the Wallbrook and the Fleet, smaller streams, ditches and other bodies of water in London, including the Serpentine in Hyde Park and the ornamental lake in St James' Park, were all polluted and foul smelling. Industrial, municipal and human waste were all emptied into the Thames. The industrial waste included lime, fluid from slaughterhouses, refuse from tan yards, knackers yards and bone grinders. Even dead animals were thrown into the Thames and the river police regularly fished out the bodies of people who had committed suicide. The foul river water was then pumped out for household use, including half of London's drinking water. It is no wonder that waterborne diseases were rife in the capital. The following poem, published in Punch in 1848, neatly sums up the problem and suggests that the Lord Mayor was partly to blame.

Dirty Father Thames

Filthy river, filthy river,
Foul from London to the Nore
What art thou but one vast gutter,
One tremendous common shore?

All beside thy sludgy waters,
All beside thy reeking ooze,
Christian folks inhale mephitis,
Which thy bubbly bosom brews.

All her foul abominations
Into thee the City throws;
These pollutions ever churning,
To and fro thy current flows.

And from thee is brewed our porter –
Thee, thou guilty, puddle, sink!
Thou, vile cesspool, art the liquor
Whence is made the beer we drink!

Thou, too, hast a Conservator,
He who fills the civic chair;
Well does he conserve thee, truly,
Does not, my good Lord Mayor?[11]

Agitation for Reform

Public health and sanitation increasingly became matters for public concern and debate in the 1840s. They were highlighted in a number of published articles, the most important of which were written by Edwin Chadwick, a Poor Law Commissioner, and Hector Gavin, a doctor at Charing Cross Hospital. Chadwick's *Sanitary Conditions of the Labouring Population of Great Britain* was published in 1842 and Gavin's *The Unhealthiness of London* and *Sanitary Ramblings* were published in 1847 and 1848.

Both of these campaigners drew attention to the link between filthy, overcrowded living conditions and infectious disease, and concluded that poverty was the result of environmental factors. This flew in the face of the prevailing belief that the poor were responsible for their own misfortunes due to their laziness, vices and bad habits. Gavin pointed out that poverty bred disease and disease spread poverty as it resulted in the poor being unable to work.

Adding to the campaign for sanitary reform was a fear among the better-off classes, who were disturbed by the graphic revelations of journalists and others, that disease-carrying air might waft from the slums to the areas where they lived. As a result of the campaign Public Health and Sewers Acts and the Nuisances and Diseases Prevention Act were passed. A General Board of Health was established in London which appointed a Medical Officer for Health to investigate the cause of infectious diseases. A Metropolitan Commissioner of Sewers was also established for London to co-ordinate the removal of health hazards, or 'nuisances' as they were called. These 'nuisances' included overflowing cesspools, factory waste, slaughterhouses and rubbish heaps. The Commission was also given the task of creating a proper sewage and drainage system in the capital. Some progress was made with regard to sewage when cesspools were replaced by 50 miles of drains. Progress was halted, however, by a lack of money and insufficient powers to carry out plans for a proper sewage system. Feuds between vested interests also made progress difficult.

The Great Stink

In the summer of 1858 the foul stench of the sewage-filled River Thames, combined with a heatwave, resulted in a smell so bad that it affected proceedings in the Houses of Parliament. One day that summer Queen Victoria and Prince Albert set off for a pleasure cruise on the river but had to turn back hastily because of the foul stench. The following description by Charles Dickens of 'The Great Stink', as it was called, is one of many written at the time:

> You will have read in the papers that the Thames in London is most horrible. I have to cross Waterloo or London Bridge to get to the railroad when I come down here, and I can certify that the offensive smells, even in that short whiff, have been of a most head-and-stomach-distending nature. Nobody knows what is to be done; at least everybody knows a plan, and everybody else knows it won't do; in the meantime cartloads of chloride of lime are shot into the filthy stream, and do something I hope.[12]

The curtains in the Houses of Parliament had to be soaked in chloride of lime to mask the overpowering stench. Once the problem began to affect the Members of Parliament they were forced to take action. A bill was rushed through instructing the Metropolitan Board of Works, which had replaced the Sewage Commission, to build a capital-wide system of sewers. Sir Joseph Bazalgette, the Chief Engineer of the Board of Works, oversaw the construction of a new sewage system which cost £2 million.

Under this system sewage was directed through over 80 miles of underground tunnels to pumping stations in the East End. These stations, like the tunnels, were remarkable feats of engineering. Crossness and Abbey Mills Pumping Stations, which were opened in 1867 and 1868, were housed in ornate Gothic-style buildings.

The work, which was completed by the late 1860s, ended the outbreaks of cholera and other waterborne diseases. The health of London's inhabitants, who now had a safe, clean water supply, was improved greatly. In the 1880s new storm relief sewers were built to deal with surface rainwater.

Public Disinfectors

Under new sanitary legislation people suffering from infectious diseases had to be removed to hospital or isolated in one room, which was disinfected by public disinfectors after the death or recovery of the victim. In *Victorian London Street Life*, Adolphe Smith described these officials arriving with their handcarts.

> Alone and unseen, they remove, one by one, all the clothes, bedding, carpets, curtains, in fact all textile materials they can find in the room, carefully place them in the handcart, and drag them off to the disinfecting oven.[13]

The room itself was then disinfected. These measures led to a reduction in the death rate from infectious diseases.

Churchyards

Another serious health hazard in London were the ancient churchyards, where most of the capital's dead were buried. London was just as overcrowded below ground as it was above ground. These churchyards, from which a foul smell emanated, had been crammed full for many years. Bodies were buried on top of one another and were perilously close to the surface. Rotting corpses were regularly dug up by gravediggers. According to Dr John Simon, the Medical Officer for Health, 'every dead body buried within our walls receives its accommodation at the expense of the living'.[14]

In addition to the churchyards there were a few small burial grounds, such as Bunhill Fields in City Road, which were also full to overflowing. The following extract taken from *London by Day and Night* (1852) by David Bartlett graphically describes the problem of overcrowded churchyards:

> St Martin's Church, measuring 295 feet by 379, in the course of ten years received 14,000 bodies. St Mary's, in the region of the Strand, and covering only half an acre, has by fair computation during fifty years received 20,000 bodies. Was ever anything heard of more frightful? But hear this: two men built, as a *mere speculation*, a Methodist Church in New Kent Road, and in a mammoth vault beneath the floor of that church, 40 yards long, 25 wide, and 20 feet high, 2000 bodies were found, *not buried*, but piled up in coffins of wood one upon the other. This in all conscience is horrible enough, but seems quite tolerable in comparison with another case.
>
> A church, called Enon Chapel, was built some twenty years ago, *by a minister*, as a speculation, in Clement's Lane in the Strand, close on to that busiest thoroughfare in the world. He opened the upper part for the worship of God, and devoted the lower – separated from the upper merely by a board floor – to the burial of the dead. *In this place, 60 feet by 29 and 6 deep, 12,000 bodies have been interred!* It was dangerous to sit in the church; faintings occurred every day in it, and sickness, and for some distance about it, life was not safe. And yet people not really knowing the state of things, never thought of laying anything to the vault under the chapel.[15]

Private Cemeteries

One solution to this problem was to copy the continental practice of burying the dead in purpose-built cemeteries. These spacious designated burial grounds provided a safe alternative to London's churchyards and small burial grounds. The first cemetery in London, Kensal Green Cemetery, was built by the General Cemetery Company, a commercial enterprise which was formed in 1832 with government support. It is described in this entry from *Mogg's Guide*:

> Cemeteries. The General Cemetery, Kensal Green, Harrow Road. A cemetery for the interment of persons of all religious persuasions has been lately established here, under the sanction of an Act of Parliament, on an elevated and beautiful site, at a

> distance of three miles from Oxford Street. It contains nearly fifty acres of ground, surrounded on three sides by a high and massive wall and, on the remaining side, in order to admit a view of the scenery of the adjoining country, by a handsome iron railing, of equal height with the wall, the enclosed area being planted, and laid out in walks, after the manner of Père la Chaise at Paris. The greater part has been consecrated, and a small chapel has been erected for the performance of the burial service, according to the forms of the established church, to which office a clergyman of the Church of England has been appointed. In the unconsecrated part, which is appropriated to the use of such persons as object to the burial service of the established church, an elegant Doric chapel has been erected, where the burial rites of every religious sect may be solemnised. This was the first mortuary of its kind established in the vicinity of the metropolis, and its success has led to the formation of five others viz., one at Highgate; another at Norwood, in Surrey; Abney Park Cemetery, Stoke Newington; the Tower Hamlets Cemetery, Mile End Road; and the London Cemetery, Nunhead, near Peckham. The Dissenters' Cemetery, better known as Bunhill Fields Burying-ground, is wholly appropriated to the reception of Dissenters, and is situated north of the Artillery Ground in Bunhill Row.[16]

Highgate Cemetery, where a number of famous people are buried including Karl Marx and the novelist George Eliot, was built in 1839. It became the most fashionable cemetery in London and was so popular that it had to be extended in 1854.

Private cemeteries were mainly used by the middle classes, but some included a few acres for the burial of paupers.

Public Cemeteries

The commercial cemeteries did not help those who could not afford to pay the costs of burial. In 1848 a General Board of Health was created with powers to build new cemeteries, buy private cemeteries and run them and, if necessary, to forbid burials in overcrowded churchyards and burial grounds.

Apart from buying Brompton Cemetery, however, it did not achieve much.

Real change was brought about by the passing of the Metropolitan Burials Act of 1852. This empowered local authorities to open cemeteries, run by parish Burial Boards, if their burial grounds were inadequate or a danger to health. Although a number of authorities used these powers more still needed to be done. The introduction of cremation in the 1870s went some way towards solving the problem. Eventually with the creation of public cemeteries and cremation London's commercial cemeteries declined.

Brookwood Cemetery

To take some of the pressure off London cemeteries the London Necropolis and National Mausoleum Company opened a cemetery in 1854 on a 2,000-acre site in Brookwood, near Woking in Surrey. A special train was provided to take bodies and mourners to a private station near the cemetery. The train service was run from the Necropolis station near Waterloo station. The company placed the following advertisement in the *Times* on 6 June 1856:

> NECROPOLIS – Established by Parliament – WOKING CEMETERY – The Company act also as Undertakers – FUNERALS PROVIDED complete, including private grave. Statuary work, and every expense, as follows:-
>
> First Class £21 0s.0d. Second Class £18 0s. 0d. Third Class £14 0s.0d. Fourth Class £11 0s.0d. Fifth Class £4 0s.0d. Sixth Class £3.5s.0d.
>
> The above charges include the performance of the funeral from the house, with the usual furniture and attendants, but they may be considerably reduced by dispensing with the funeral cortege through the streets of London, and the Necropolis Company think it right to state that the arrangements of meeting at their private station in the Westminster-road has been introduced by them to

relieve the public from unnecessary and costly display, and that it is now daily adopted and gives complete satisfaction.

Apply personally or by latter to the Secretary, 2, Lancaster-place, Strand, or any agent of the Company, either of whom will wait on the parties and undertake all the arrangements. The train leaves the Westminster Station daily at 11.20. Separate waiting rooms.

10

RELIGION

Most people in Victorian Britain were Christians whose faith was very important to them. The majority of the higher social classes were God-fearing people who attended church or chapel regularly and held family prayers at home. There was some religious diversity, however, as Britain was home to people of other faiths such as Hindus, Muslims and Jews.

Despite the importance of Christianity, the Bible and Christian beliefs were questioned by some as a result of scientific progress and Charles Darwin's Theory of Evolution, as set out in his book *On the Origin of Species*, published in 1859.

The Church of England, or Anglican Church, was made up of various factions loosely labelled Low, High and Broad Church. The Low Church was another name for the Evangelicals, who believed in the literal truth of the Bible and whose services were simple. The High Church, whose services were elaborate, shared some of the practices and rituals of the Roman Catholic Church. The Broad Church, as the label indicates, had broad-minded principles.

Those churches which had broken away from the Church of England were collectively known as Nonconformists or Dissenters. This group comprised a wide range of denominations including Methodists, Congregationalists, Baptists and Quakers.

Many new Christian churches, of all denominations, were built in London in the nineteenth century to provide places of worship for the ever-increasing population. Some churches were privately built while others were paid for by the government to encourage church building. The building of new churches and the restoration of existing ones continued throughout the Victorian era. Some of these new churches were designed by eminent architects in a variety of styles, adding to the architectural beauty of London.

According to Charles Dickens Junior there were 263 places of worship in London in 1888, in addition to St Pauls' Cathedral and Westminster Abbey. This number included Anglican, Methodist, Roman Catholic, Congregational, Presbyterian, Unitarian and Quaker churches and chapels as well as Jewish synagogues.[1]

Among the new Nonconformist and Catholic churches were Lyndhurst Road Chapel and the Catholic Apostolic Church in Gordon Square. These churches are both described in *The Queen's London.*

> Lyndhurst Road Chapel stands at the corner of Lyndhurst Road and Rosslyn Hill, in the prosperous suburb of Hampstead. It was built for the Rev. Robert F. Horton, M.A. D.D., one of the most eminent of Congregationalist ministers, whose works on Biblical criticism have won for him no little distinction. Dr Horton is a graduate of New College, Oxford, of which he was elected a Fellow in 1879. The Lyndhurst Road church was founded in the following year, and is active in good works. The chapel, which seats 1,200 persons nominally, though the congregation is often much larger, is octagonal in shape and constructed of red brick, and is richly decorated within. Dr Horton has a co-pastor, the Rev. A, Hamilton, M.A., who settled in 1894.[2]
>
> If the Catholic Apostolic Church at the corner of Gordon Square were only finished it would be one of the finest as it already is one of the largest modern churches in London. Built in 1850-54, it is the cathedral of the Catholic Apostolic body founded by the richly-gifted but erratic Edward Irving. It is cruciform in shape, and its interior is an admirable specimen of the Early English style, with

> a graceful triforium in the aisle roof, and two richly-decorated chapels, one of them containing the altar at which Irving was wont to officiate. There is some fine stained glass in the windows, and the music is a great feature of the frequent services. The architect was Raphael Brandon.[3]

The Church Census

Despite the large number of new churches in the capital, a census held in England and Wales on Sunday 30 March 1851, the results of which were published with the 1851 Census, revealed that nearly two thirds of the population of London did not attend church or chapel on that day. Horace Mann, the author of the report on the findings, declared that 'a sadly formidable portion of the English people are habitually neglectful of the public ordinances of religion'.

The census showed that of those who did attend on that day less than half attended an Anglican church. It also indicated that the highest proportion of absentees were members of the working class. Their absence is understandable considering that they worked long hours, often in physically demanding jobs throughout the week and Saturday mornings as well. They needed Sundays as a day of rest. Another reason for their absence was that they were made to feel unwelcome in some, mainly Anglican, churches. While the better-off classes occupied pews, for which they paid rent (which covered the clergyman's stipend) at the front of the church, poor people were relegated to the 'free' seating at the back or in the upstairs gallery. Class divisions were strictly observed.

Joseph Arch, founder of the National Agricultural Labourers Union and a preacher in the Primitive Methodist Church, remembered his childhood experience of this class segregation in a parish church and how it affected him.

> I never took communion in the parish church in my life. When I was seven years old I saw something which prevented me once and for all ... First, up walked the squire to the communion rails; the farmers went up next; then up went the tradesmen, the

> shopkeepers, the wheelwright, and the blacksmith; and then, the very last of all, went the poor agricultural labourers in their smock frocks. They walked up by themselves; nobody else knelt with them; it was as if they were unclean … I said to myself, 'If that's what goes on – never for me.'[4]

St Paul's Cathedral

Divine service was held in the cathedral on Sundays at 8 a.m. and 10.30 a.m. in the morning and at 3.15 p.m. and 7 p.m. in the afternoon and evening. Short services were also held on weekdays.[5]

Molly Hughes, the daughter of a London stockbroker, regularly attended Sunday services at St Paul's Cathedral. She and her brothers learned the collect for the day at breakfast and then walked with their parents from their home in Canonbury to the cathedral. She recorded her memories of attending the services and alleviating the boredom of the long sermons in *A London Family 1870-1900* (1946).

> How cool and vast the cathedral seemed after the dusty streets! We walked with precision to our special seats, for the vergers knew us well. My father had a stall, my brothers sat in a pew beyond the choir, my mother and I sat in the reserved front row under the dome. The cathedral seemed to belong to us, and little took place that escaped the notice of one or other of us.
>
> My back still aches in memory of those long services. Nothing was spared us – the whole of the 'Dearly Beloved,' never an omission of the Litany, always the full ante-Communion Service, involving a sermon of unbelievable length. The seats and kneeling boards were constructed for grown-ups (and not too comfortable for them), and a child had the greatest difficulty in keeping an upright kneeling position all through the long intoned Litany. We found some alleviations even here. How would the officiating priest take the fence in intoning 'uncharitableness'? Canon Milman was our delight over this, because he used to quaver forth '- table' all by itself and leave a long pause of suspense before he could reach the high note of '-ness.' After this we looked forward to beating down

Satan under our feet, partly because it seemed a nice final thing to do, and partly because it was the half-way mark. Some energetic clergymen put in extra prayers at the end, even the thanksgiving – always associated with my blackest thoughts.

Like all children I put some kind of workable meaning into the strange Prayer Book phrases. 'The Scripture moveth us in Sundry places' must mean that it pokes us in various parts of our body – a spiritual dig in the ribs: 'Come now, own up.'

Molly enjoyed the 'inspiring music' that 'burst' from the 'organ'.

It was worth all the endurance, even of the Litany. No footling sentimental hymns, but Te Deums, Psalms, Creeds, Introits and Kyries that intoxicated us.

The long sermons were the worst part of the service for Molly.

Sermons, of course, were on the endurance side, but had some alleviations. I had a nice long sit-down, and as I was always seated close to the pulpit I enjoyed the colours of the marble pillars, and could weave fancies round the Punjaub, a funny name to have on a pulpit. If the preacher grew fierce I looked at the statue of Samveli Johnson, whom I vaguely connected with Sam Weller [character in Dickens' novel *The Pickwick Papers*], and if he were gentle I looked at the one of Howard [John Howard, prison reformer] with his keys, a satisfying face and figure ... The sermons were seldom less than three quarters of an hour ... [and] were usually stiff with learning and far over our heads.[6]

Westminster Abbey

Services were held in the abbey on Sundays at 10 o'clock in the morning and 3 o'clock in the afternoon, and in the evenings at 7 o'clock, during Advent and Lent, and from Easter to the end of July. Services were also held on weekdays.[7]

Hippolyte Taine described a visit to Westminster Abbey in his *Notes on* England.

Westminster Abbey: superb nave, admirable Gothic architecture – the only style which suits the climate; the jumble of shapes, the sinuous and roaring bones of the building, the profusion of fine sculpture are required to fill this sombre atmosphere, and people the vast formlessness of dark interiors. I spent some time there, looking at monuments to the dead, a great number of graceful 18th century sculptures, others, cold and pedantic, belonging to our own time. Suddenly, voices were raised in song, not the monotonous psalmody of our own vespers, not a rude and monkish plain-chant; not the lines and responses uttered in what always seem to be the voices of sick monks, but beautiful songs, in parts, grave and noble recitatives, round and full, melodious, a style and harmony redolent of the best epoch. Then, after a reading on Sisera, the organ and choir, both boys' voices and bass voices, resumed – a motet, full and rich. All this music is a worthy accompaniment to the psalms and prayers I had just been reading.[8]

After attending morning service at Westminster Abbey, Taine went on to two other, unnamed churches where he compared the congregations and clergymen with their French counterparts.

Visit to two other churches in the afternoon. Here, too, the hymns were fine, and the buildings were filled by people of the comfortable middle-class. The tall, closed pews and all the galleries were full of well-dressed worshippers; as many men as women, and many of them 'gentlemen.' Very different from our own congregations of women, aged dyspeptics, servants, working-class people. Of the three ministers I saw, one, a polite, worthy man who talked to me, seemed, by his air and bearing, half-professor, half-magistrate. Another, bland and well-groomed, resembled a Paris notary, the sort of man who assumes a soft voice and a sentimental air at the signing of a marriage contract. I met others, last year, in London and in the country. With their white bands and black gowns, and the tone they take in the pulpit, one might take them for judges. They are, by education, marriage, mores and function, laymen, a little graver in bearing than the rest; their attire, outside church, is the same excepting for the eternal white tie; nor is the moral difference much greater than the physical one. The essential point is this: priest and laymen are on an equal footing; or separated at most by a single step: such was the principal achievement of the Reformation.[9]

St George's Church, Camberwell

St George's Church in Camberwell was one of the new churches built in the early nineteenth century to cater for the rapidly increasing population of the area. Alfred Rosling Bennett attended the church as a boy and described it in his memoir.

St George's Grecian portico gave entrance and exit to a numerous congregation. There were two pulpits, one containing a lower stage with a seat for the parish clerk, who gave out the hymns, always prefacing the number with the exhortation, 'Let us sing to the praise and glory of God'; led the responses; said Amen to every prayer; proclaimed banns of marriage and other necessary announcements. The minister above him conducted the service, reading the prayers and also the lessons, a separate lectern for the latter purpose being then unusual. A much higher pulpit was reserved entirely for sermonising. An awe-inspiring beadle of the type already described kept order by force of personal magnetism or majesty or something, no child of either sex daring to meet his imperious glance. To see him standing with his wand of office, cocket hat and calves on the top of the steps leading to the classic portico as we filed into church banished all ideas of naughtiness; he prevailed more mightily than many sermons.

We sat about half-way down the main aisle, to the left, somewhat in advance of the churchwardens' pews, which were marked by two black staves, about six feet long, one surmounted by a gilded crown, the other by a crimson mitre. They were kept upright by being passed through holes in the seats upon which the wardens sat in solemn awfulness. We understood that the beadle sometimes handled these staves; that they were used for beating the bounds. Being loose, they might obviously also be employed for beating boys.

... The vicar, the Rev. Samuel Smith, was a middle-aged gentleman about whom I can remember nothing definite except that he wore a white surplice, was particular in enunciating his texts and talked of matters beyond our comprehension. Of all the sermons preached in my presence – I cannot say listened to – not one phrase has survived. But that must not be taken as a reflection on him. Strange, but true, I remember the clerk and beadle much better than the vicar. But I learnt to find my places in the Prayerbook – indeed, came to know the morning service almost by heart.[10]

A Fashionable Church

In 1836, the year before Victoria came to the throne, Charles Dickens published a pamphlet entitled *Sunday Under Three Heads*, using the pseudonym Timothy Sparks. The object of the pamphlet was to defend the right of people, especially members of the working class, to enjoy a much-needed day off on Sunday. While researching this article he visited a 'fashionable church' in London and questioned the motives of the middle-class congregation. He concluded that they went to church just to be seen there and to demonstrate their superiority to those who did not attend.

Here is a fashionable church, where the service commences at a late hour, for the accommodation of such members of the congregation – and they are not a few – as may happen to have lingered at the Opera far into the morning of the Sabbath; an excellent contrivance for poising the balance between God and Mammon, and illustrating the ease with which a man's duties to both, may be accommodated and adjusted. How the carriages rattle up, and deposit their richly-dressed burdens beneath the lofty portico! The powdered footmen glide along the aisle, place the richly-bound prayer-books on the pew desks, slam the doors, and hurry away, leaving the fashionable members of the congregation to inspect each other through their glasses, and to dazzle and glitter in the eyes of the few shabby people in the free seats. The organ peals forth, the hired singers commence a short hymn, and the congregation condescendingly rise, stare about them, and converse in whispers. The clergyman enters the reading-desk – a young man of noble family and elegant demeanour, notorious at Cambridge for his knowledge of horse-flesh and dancers, and celebrated at Eton for his hopeless stupidity. The service commences. Mark the soft voice in which he reads, and the impressive manner in which he applies his white hand, studded with brilliants, to his perfumed hair. Observe the graceful emphasis with which he offers up the prayers for the King, the Royal Family, and all the Nobility; and the nonchalance with which he hurries over the more uncomfortable portions of the service, the seventh commandment for instance, with a studied regard for the taste and feeling of his auditors, only to be equalled by that displayed by the sleek divine who succeeds him, who murmurs, in a voice kept down by rich feeding, most comfortable doctrines for exactly twelve minutes, and then arrives at the anxiously expected 'Now to God,' which is the signal for the dismissal of the congregation. The organ is again heard; those who have been asleep wake up, and those who have kept awake, smile and seem greatly relieved; bows and congratulations are exchanged, the livery servants are all bustle and commotion, bang go the steps, up jump the footmen, and off rattle the carriages: the inmates discoursing on the dresses of the congregation, and congratulating themselves on having set so excellent an example to the community in general, and Sunday-pleasurers in particular.[11]

Roman Catholics

According to Charles Dickens Junior's list of principal London churches, there were twenty Roman Catholic churches in the capital in 1879. The Catholic Church, unlike some other denominations, welcomed the poor.

The most important Catholic church in London was the Church of Our Lady of Victories in Newland Terrace, Kensington, which was also known as the Pro-Cathedral. This was an Early English Gothic-style building with an ornate interior. It was superseded by

Westminster Cathedral which was built between 1892 and 1903. The architect of the new cathedral was John Francis Bentley.

There was another Catholic cathedral in Southwark – the seat of the Roman Catholic Archbishop of Southwark. St George's Cathedral was completed in 1848, following eight years of construction, to replace a smaller building. This was necessary because of the influx of Irish Catholic immigrants. The cathedral was designed by the famous architect Augustus Pugin. The Gothic-style building contained a handsome pulpit made from Caen stone. According to *The Queen's London*, 'While the chancel and some parts of the cathedral compel admiration, the general effect of the interior is undeniably bare.'[12]

Nonconformist Services

Another church visited by Hippolyte Taine was a nonconformist church in the Strand (he does not specify the particular denomination). He noted that the congregation were all members of the middle class and there was no sign of the 'common people'.

> Next for the church.
>
> I visit four, and hear two sermons, the first in a Nonconformist church in the Strand. The nave bare, cold, without ornament, excepting for two allegorical figures at the far end. Tall, wooden pews, in which one is shut in up to the neck. These are not filled by the common people, but by respectable middle-class people very correctly dressed, and with serious, sensible faces. They are here for moral advice and to refurbish their principles. The preacher chose as his text, "Of one mind and one soul", and on its basis advised his congregation to be firm in their principles, but conciliatory towards all men. A good sermon, a little commonplace, but solid. It is quite obvious, from the numerous essays in English literature and, today, the "little morals" in the *Saturday Review* that commonplaces do not bore them. Apparently they consider morality not an object of curiosity, but of use – a tool in daily requisition, so that on Sundays, it needs sharpening.

> Books set out on the rests in the pews: they are the *Psalms*, and the *Book of Common Prayer*, the Mass-book of England. A great deal of wordiness and a certain Hebraic grandiloquence in the style of Milton. No tenderness, no ecstasy, as in the *Imitation*. No flowers of rhetoric or gentle sentimentalities, as in our own pious tracts, but a tone which is imposing, passionate, and sometimes lyrical. The liturgy was composed during the Renaissance, and the accent of that period has been retained. A thing worth noting: the date and origin of each passage are given in a note; one piece may be from the sixth century, another, a prayer, was taken from the Apocrypha, but has been retained because of its elevated sentiments. By means of these notes, the faithful are educated, informed, in the criticism and history (of their religion).[13]

Methodism

Methodists were the largest nonconformist denomination in Victorian London. According to *Dickens's Dictionary of London* in 1888 there were more than fifty 'Wesleyan' chapels, three 'Primitive Methodist' chapels and two 'Primitive Methodist Connection' chapels. Various factions had emerged in the Methodist Church following the death of its founder John Wesley in 1791.

The most famous Methodist chapel in Victorian London was the City Road Chapel, which was built to replace an earlier chapel, under the direction of John Wesley himself. The architect was Charles Dance, the surveyor of the City of London. Next door was the house in which John Wesley lived for the last ten years of his life and in which he died.

The chapel was described by the author 'Uncle Jonathan' in his book *Walks In and Around London* (1895).

> The outside of the chapel ... has a quaint, pleasant, classical appearance; and Mr Wesley did not exceed the truth when, at its opening, he pronounced it 'perfectly neat, but not fine.' Passing through the Doric portico, we enter the venerable building, and are pleased with its light, cheerful aspect. There is the old pulpit, in which so many great preachers have stood; and behind

it the semicircular recess in which the communion table stands is lighted by three windows, and has its right and left walls covered with tablets in memory of the Wesleys, Fletcher, Clarke, Benson, and Coke, while in the centre we can read the Lord's Prayer, the Commandments, and the Creed. A deep gallery runs round three sides of the chapel; numerous tablets on the lower walls commemorate the names and the worth of several eminent ministers and laymen and devout ladies; and a fine granite pillar stands as a son's memorial to Dr Waddy.[14]

Synagogues

There was a considerable Jewish population in Victorian London, mainly living in the East End. Many of these people had fled from persecution in Europe. There were two main groups within the Jewish community – the Ashkenazic Jews and the Sephardic Jews, who had different cultures and traditions. The vast majority of the Jewish population in London were Ashkenazic Jews.

There were more than a dozen synagogues in London including the Bevis Marks Synagogue near Aldgate and the Central Synagogue. The latter was described in *The Queen's London.*

> The great Central Synagogue of the Jews, in Great Portland Street, is a fine specimen of Oriental architecture, with Moorish columns and arches ... the Ark, which in synagogues is always placed at the end nearest Jerusalem; and for the moment the gold-embroidered curtain which hides it is drawn back. Above the Ark are tables of stone, on which the two first words of each of the Ten Commandments are engraved; and through the small circular window, higher still, shines the light that is never allowed to go out. The galleries are occupied by women, the body of the synagogue by men, who, according to Jewish custom, worship with covered heads. This synagogue is one of those under the superintendence of Chief Rabbi Adler.[15]

David Bartlett accompanied a friend on a visit to St Helen's Synagogue which he described in *London By Day and Night* as 'the best synagogue in London, and perhaps in Europe'. It was situated in a 'dirty quarter of London' and Bartlett was, therefore, surprised when he saw the inside of the synagogue. He stayed for the service and described his experience in detail.

> The place was crowded – the lower part was devoted to males, and the galleries to females. Every man wore his hat and the taled, a white, embroidered scarf. The interior is of no great extent, and yet it wore an air of spaciousness and elegance which surprised us. It is said to be one of the finest specimens of interior architecture to be found in London. The upper portion of the place – where the altar usually stands in churches – the 'ark,' consists of a beautiful recess a little elevated from the floor of the rest of the building, and is built of fine Italian marble. A splendid velvet curtain, in red, hangs over the lower part of the alcove, fringed with gold, and emblazoned with a crown. In this recess are kept the books of the Law. Between rich Doric and Corinthian columns are three arched windows, with stained, arabesque glass. Upon the centre one is the name of Jehovah, in Hebrew, and the tables of the Law and this sentence
>
> 'KNOW IN WHOSE PRESENCE THOU STANDEST'
>
> The appearance of this recess from where we stood was exquisitely beautiful. The lower portion of it was the 'Ark,' or 'a *shadow* of that in the Temple.' The decorations were gorgeous, and as the sunlight from the beautiful eastern windows fell upon it, we could almost unite with the Jews present in their feelings of reverence for that holy spot. As the worship proceeded, we listened with intense interest, for it was our first visit to such a place, and to us the Jews have always seemed a melancholy, interesting, class of religionists. It seemed as if we were living in David's or Abraham's days, and were mingling with them in worship ... While we were there, they sang some Hebrew melodies, and they were exceedingly plaintive. There was a wild sorrowfulness in them which it was touching to hear. The women in the galleries sang with excellent skill but the gentle mournfulness of their songs reminded us of when – 'By the rivers of Babylon there we sat down, yea, we wept, when we remembered Zion.'[16]

Hyde Park Preachers

Preachers surrounded by a small crowd of listeners were a regular feature on Sundays in Hyde Park, as described in the following paragraphs by Hippolyte Taine:

> Last Sunday and the Sunday before that, there were open-air preachers in Hyde Park, each with a Bible and an umbrella. They were private persons who felt the need to communicate their religious ideas to the public...
>
> The Hyde Park preachers had long, thin faces, nasal voices, and they kept casting their eyes up to Heaven, they had an audience of about a score, sharing in the edification. Zeal is very lively, especially in the case of 'dissenters'; their young men are recruited for the work. One will take up a position at a certain cross-roads every Sunday and give away pious tracts; another gathers together a dozen or so lightermen every Thursday and lectures them on the Bible.[17]

Sabbatarianism

Many Victorians regarded Sunday as the Lord's Day and a day of rest. Sabbatarianism, as this was termed, was particularly practised by members of the better-off classes. Some people took the observation of the Sabbath to extreme lengths. Sabbath observers wore special clothes on Sunday and children were only allowed to read religious books and play with religious toys such as Noah's Arks.

Molly Hughes described her childhood experiences of Sunday observance in her memoir.

> The mere word 'Sunday' is apt to give a mental shiver to people of long memories. The outer world closed down. It was wrong to travel except for dire necessity, and then very difficult. It was wrong to work and wrong to play...
>
> The afternoons hung heavy. It seemed to be always three o'clock. All amusements, as well as work, were forbidden. It was a real privation not to be allowed to draw and paint. However, an

> exception was made in favour of illuminated texts, and we rivalled the old monks in our zeal for copying Scripture, with the same kind of worldly decorations that they devised.[18]

Molly's reading was limited 'by mother's notions of what was appropriate for Sundays'. She recalled that *Tom Brown's Schooldays, Robinson Crusoe, Hans Christian Anderson's Tales* and *Pride and Prejudice* were all permitted but *The Arabian Nights* and the novels of Walter Scott were forbidden. 'We had to fall back on bound volumes of *Good Words for the Young,* which were not so bad as the title suggests, and contained plenty of stories.'[19]

Frederick Willis also recalled the Sundays of his Victorian childhood.

> Sunday clothes were absolutely essential. Anyone who appeared on Sunday in work-a-day clothes was beyond the pale. The ritual of Sunday clothes was sacrosanct, to the labourer, in his respectable black suit, black choker and bowler hat, as much as to the Balham bank clerk in his silk hat and frock coat. Working people who were accustomed to easy clothes all the week looked as comfortable as Joe Gargery [a character in Dickens' novel *Great Expectations*] when he discarded his picturesque blacksmith's dress for the funereal garb of Sunday. Little children, with strict instructions to 'Take care of your best clothes,' walked the streets like badly-made puppets, especially the boys. The girls were more adaptable and appeared to enjoy the experience. For those who were not in the habit of walking about in fine feathers this business of Sunday clothes cast a certain amount of gloom over what was otherwise a very welcome day of rest. There was a dreadful predilection for black and sombre colours among this class, as they considered this gave them an air of respectability.[20]

East End Missions

In the later Victorian period mission churches of all denominations began to appear in the East End of London, to minister to the poor and provide them with pastoral help. Charles Booth wrote of the difficulties of such work in his study *Life and Labour of the People of London* (1887).

> Thus is the seemingly hopeless task of Evangelising the masses shared between the Church and the Nonconformists. The methods employed are usually the same in every case. The mothers' meetings and its adjuncts; the Sunday-school and all that goes with it; these form the staple work of every mission, whatever the denomination, and there is a good deal of overlapping; for where the poor are, there the missions are crowded together. We meet here the first specimen of an independent 'Medical Mission', though there are branches of this work connected with several of the larger Missions in East London. Those who seek medical advice have first to sit through a half-hour's religious service. They make no objection to this. It is very kindly meant and is doubtless better than sitting in sadness and silence as they might have to do anywhere else, but I conceive it to be absolutely futile as a means of 'spreading the Gospel'.[21]

The Salvation Army

In 1865 the Whitechapel Christian Mission was founded by William Booth (no relation to Charles Booth) and his wife Catherine. Booth was a Methodist minister who arrived in London in 1849. The Booths, both gifted preachers, decided to take God's word to the poor of London who did not attend church. They preached on street corners and outside public houses in the slums of the East End.

The Mission became known as the Salvation Army because it was run in a regimented fashion. William Booth became known as General Booth. His officers lived among the poor and offered them practical help as well as spiritual guidance and comfort. They ran soup kitchens, homeless shelters and safe houses for women fleeing domestic abuse and prostitution.

The Salvation Army also established the first free labour exchange. Catherine Booth started the army's women's work in 1878 and became known as the 'Mother of the Army'.

Charles Booth described the Salvation Army and its good work as follows:

> No-one who has attended the services, studied the faces, and listened to the spoken words, can doubt the earnest and genuine character of the enthusiasm which finds in them its expression. The Army claims to be, and is, 'a force of converted men and women, who intend to make all men yield or at least listen to the claims of God to their love and service.'[22]

Church Army

The Church Army was founded in 1882 by the Reverend William Carlile, an Anglican clergyman. Its purpose was to evangelise outcasts and criminals in the slums of Westminster. Like the Salvation Army, their trained officers worked directly with some of London's poorest people; they provided practical help as well as spreading the gospel.

The Church Army opened hostels for homeless men and women, and homes for children. Their horse-drawn mission caravans travelled around the metropolis and beyond.

Charles Haddon Spurgeon

Charles Haddon Spurgeon was a famous Baptist preacher, and was appointed pastor of New Park Street Chapel, Southwark, in 1853. He was such a charismatic preacher that his congregation grew too large for the chapel. It moved, first to Exeter Hall in the Strand, and then to the Surrey Gardens Music Hall in Walworth, for more space. Spurgeon frequently preached to a crowd of 10,000.

In 1861 the Metropolitan Tabernacle, a purpose-built church with seating for 6,000, was opened near the Elephant and Castle in Southwark. In the words of a contemporary observer,

> The crowd was so immense that seat holders could not get to their seats. Half an hour before time the aisles were solid blocks and many stood throughout the service, wedged in by their fellows and prevented from escaping by the crowd outside who sealed up the

> doors and filled up the yard in front and stood in throngs as far as the sound could reach.[23]

The largest ever congregation Spurgeon preached to was nearly 24,000 at the Crystal Palace in Sydenham in April 1857. Tens of thousands were converted as a result of his preaching.

Spurgeon helped the poor of London by founding an orphanage in Stockwell and building almshouses for the elderly. He also founded a college for training Baptist preachers.

The Metropolitan Tabernacle burnt down in 1898 and had to be rebuilt.

11

CRIME

Crime was a serious problem in Victorian London. Some parts of the capital were so steeped in crime that they were beyond the control of the police. There was a particularly worrying increase in juvenile crime (which will be covered in depth in the next chapter).

The crime rate fluctuated; it went up, not surprisingly, when wages fell and the price of bread rose. There was a strong link between crime and poverty. The appalling conditions in the slums provided the perfect breeding ground for crime. Children who were not brought up in criminal families came into contact with crime in the slums, especially in the low lodging houses, and many were dragged into it. Once a career in crime was started it was very difficult to break away from it and many juvenile criminals became hardened adult criminals. There was also a link between crime and alcohol. Many crimes were fuelled by alcohol and the proceeds of crime were often spent on drink. A lot of debauchery and violence was centred on the public houses and gin palaces in the slums, especially on Saturday nights. In 1868, for example, 100,000 cases of drunkenness were dealt with in the London courts.[1]

Almost as bad as crime itself was the fear of crime, in particular of violent crime. A few cases reported sensationally and graphically in newspapers added to this fear. Smogs and gas street lighting made London a spooky and frightening place after dark, adding to the tension.

Despite the widespread fear of crime, by the 1880s, London was in fact the safest capital for life and property in the world. In 1831, 378 people per 100,000 were taken into custody for violent crimes but sixty years later this figure had dropped to 216 per 100,000, so the crime rate in London actually improved as Victoria's reign progressed.[2] This was partly due to the work of an increasingly efficient and professional police force. The extension of street lighting and the introduction of electric street lights also helped.

Theft

Pickpockets

Pickpocketing was rife in London. Handbooks and guidebooks for visitors gave advice on how to avoid becoming a victim of this crime. The following advice comes from *Routledge's Popular Guide to London*:

> In walking through the streets, avoid lingering in crowded thoroughfares, and keep on the right-hand side of the footway.
>
> Never enter into conversation with men who wish to show you the way, offer to sell 'smuggled cigars' or invite you to a glass of ale or play a game at skittles.
>
> If in doubt about the direction of any street or building, inquire at a respectable shop or of the nearest policeman...
>
> Do not relieve street-beggars, and avoid bye-ways and poor neighbourhoods after dark.
>
> Carry no more money about you than is necessary for the day's expenses. Look after your watch and chain, and take care of your pockets at the entrance to theatres, exhibitions, churches, and in the omnibuses and the streets.[3]

Pickpockets often worked in pairs – one person would cause a disturbance while the other stole valuables when their victim was distracted. The items usually stolen were handkerchiefs, watches, wallets and pocketbooks (which contained banknotes). It was easier to steal from the outside pocket in a gentleman's coat tails, known as 'dipping', than it was to steal from the pocket of a lady's dress. Stealing handkerchiefs was known as 'clouting'. Boy thieves often worked in gangs controlled by a 'kidsman', like Fagin in *Oliver Twist*.

'Sneak Thieves'

Thieves targeted a number of different places and people in London. They could be divided into different categories. 'Sneak' or 'common' thieves stole from street stalls, tills, the doors and windows of shops, vehicles, hotel lobbies and railway station waiting rooms. They also stole clothes from washing lines, lead from roofs and, probably the most heartless of all, from children.

Carriage Thieves

Charles Dickens Junior considered thieves who stole from vehicles as particularly despicable and he advised his readers to be careful.

> Carriage Thieves – Among the many thieves who infest the London streets none are more artful or more active than the carriage thieves. No vehicle should ever be left with open windows; and valuable rugs in victorias &c. should always be secured to the carriage by a strap or other fastening. Ladies should be especially careful of officious persons volunteering to open or close carriage doors. In nine cases out of ten these men and boys are expert pickpockets.[4]

Omnibus Thieves

Omnibus pickpockets were mostly well-dressed women working in twos or threes. Henry Mayhew described how they operated.

> They generally manage to get to the farthest seats in the interior of the omnibus, on opposite sides of the vehicle, next to the horses.

As the lady passengers come in, they eye them carefully, and one of them seats herself on the right side of the lady they intend to plunder. She generally manages to throw the bottom of her cape or shawl over the lap of the lady, and works with her hand under it, so as to cover her movement.

Her confederate is generally sitting opposite to see that no-one is noticing. In abstracting from a lady's pocket, the female thief has often to cut through the dress and pocket, which she does with a pocket-knife, pair of scissors, or other sharp instrument. So soon as she has secured her purse, or other booty, she and her companion leave the omnibus on the earliest opportunity.[5]

Not even omnibus horses were safe from thieves, as the following report from the *Daily News* of 8 November 1884 illustrates:

Robbing Omnibus Horses of Their Tails. Wm. Thos. Ferray, 35, of Northwold-road, Clapton, and Edward Rist, 19, of Defoe-road, Stoke Newington, horse keepers, were charged with stealing during the past fortnight a quantity of hair from the manes and tails of horses in the omnibus yard of the London General Omnibus Company at Church-street, Stoke Newington. Evidence was given on behalf of the company that the prisoners were horse keepers, who each had daily charge of eleven horses in the omnibus yard. There are 122 horses kept in the yard. It was discovered that the prisoners had been in the habit of pulling hairs from the horses' tails and selling them to a marine store dealer's nearby. The dealer, Jacob Ludkin, who said that he had not known that the prisoners were acting wrongly, proved having purchased horse hair from them at a rate of 10d a pound. It was stated that the foreman of the horse keepers was the only employee in the yard who was allowed certain small perquisites, and the amount of hair that would be combed out of the horses' tails and manes in a legitimate manner would be very small. The company did not prosecute on account of the value of the horsehair, but because the prisoners had disfigured the horses' tails – Mr Hannay sentenced both the prisoners to 21 days hard labour.

'The Swell Mob'

Another group of thieves to look out for was the 'swell mob' – thieves who dressed fashionably and appeared to be respectable, as described by John Murray, author of *The World of London.*

> Who would suppose, for example, that those young men at the corner, dressed in the height of the Cockney fashion, bedizened with mosaic jewellery, and puffing their cigars, are members of the swell mob – thieves, in short, and pickpockets? They are exchanging cards: truly so they are; but, if you observe, the cards are pawn-brokers' duplicates of the plunder of the preceding day – yet you say it is impossible: they are young, of genteel address, and look like gentlemen; how is it you can detect their dishonest calling? At this moment a policeman is turning the corner – mark with what instinct of self-preservation the crumpled duplicates are crammed into their respective pockets.[6]

Stealing from Children

Stealing from children out alone in London was a particularly nasty crime. The following report of a case of 'child plundering' was published in the *Times* on 2 June 1866:

> At the Thames Police-court, Elizabeth Brewer of 1, James-place, North-street, Poplar, was charged on remand with stealing a pair of boots, valued at 5s., from the feet of a child named John Spencer, whose parents are living at 50, Stainsby-road, Bromley. On the 25th of last month the child, who is only six years old, was passing along Narrow-street, Limehouse, when the prisoner bribed him with a penny to allow her to pull off his boots, with which she immediately decamped. A young man named Joseph Hirons of No. 15, Sidney-place, Commercial-road, saw the boy crying, ascertained what had happened and which way the woman had gone, and immediately pursued her with the

boy in his arms, came up with her, and found the boots under her shawl. He gave her into custody. On her way to the station-house with a police constable named Hart, No.154 K, she tore up three pawnbrokers' tickets and threw the fragments away. She stated on her first examination that she was in want of food, and had applied for admission to Poplar workhouse and been refused. She must either rob or starve. It was now stated by Inspector Beare, of the K division, that there was not a word of truth in the prisoner's statement, and that she was an incorrigible thief. There were several summary convictions recorded against her and she was once convicted at the sessions and sentenced to nine months' imprisonment and hard labour. Several children had been very recently robbed of their clothes in the same locality as the child Spencer, and by a woman answering the appearance of the prisoner, but he could not bring the children because they were so young. Mr. Paget committed the prisoner for trial.

Shoplifting

Most shoplifters were women. Working in twos or threes, they went into shops at busy times, usually wearing large cloaks or shawls. While one distracted the shopkeeper, the others slipped something under their cloaks, inside their baskets or secreted it inside a large pocket sewn into the lining of their crinoline dresses. Large items were hidden under their arms. While in the crowded shop, they often took the opportunity to pick the pockets of lady shoppers. Reports of the trials of people charged with shoplifting, such as this one published in the *Times* on 4 June 1901, appeared regularly in the press:

> At Westminster, Mary Shadgett, 59, a well-dressed woman, who after felony convictions, was under police supervision until March last, was placed in the dock on remand before Mr. Sheil, charged with robberies at the Army and Navy Stores, Gorringe's, and other premises. Mr. Warburton, who prosecuted, said that the prisoner had been trapped in a really clever way by two young women – Miss Payne and Miss Lange – employed in the

detective department of the stores. They followed the prisoner on several occasions, and patiently waiting caught her red-handed with stolen goods about her. It was proved that the prisoner was systematically watched and followed on several occasions to public houses, pawn-brokers, and to Gorringe's Bazaar, where she was seen to commit a robbery. The prisoner was arrested with a packet of 36 pawntickets in her possession, and several of the tickets related to silver-mounted pocket-books, a fur-trimmed mantle and other articles identified as stolen. Mr. Sheil complimented the young ladies who followed the prisoner, and committed her for trial.

Housebreaking and Burglary

The fashionable and expensive townhouses of west London were often targeted by burglars, mostly working in twos or threes, in search of valuable items like silver plate. Access was usually obtained through the basement kitchen window, another back window or through the attic. Sometimes access was gained by bribing servants or lodgers. False keys were also used. Boys who could climb through small windows were often involved.

According to Henry Mayhew, attic or garret thieves were

> generally the most expert thieves in the metropolis ... These attic robberies are generally effected through unoccupied houses – perhaps by the house next door, or some other on the same side of the street. They pass through the attic to the roof and proceed along the gutters and coping to the attic window of the house to be robbed. They unfasten the attic window by taking the pane of glass out, or pushing the fastening back, and enter the dwelling.[7]

These burglaries often took place in the early evening when the family were at dinner and the servants were busy. In one such burglary in Lowndes Square in 1861 £3,000 worth of valuables were stolen.[8]

Thieves' Dens

Some of the worst criminals in London were to be found in the low lodging houses; it was in such places that they plotted their crimes and disposed of their ill-gotten gains.

Several social investigative journalists visited these 'thieves' kitchens' or 'flash houses', accompanied by police officers, as it would have been too dangerous to go alone. In 1851 Charles Dickens met Inspector Field of the Metropolitan Police and went with him to Rats' Castle in the foul slums of St Giles parish, near Holborn.

> Inspector Field is the bustling speaker, Inspector Field's eye is the roving eye that searches every corner of the cellar as he talks. Inspector Field's hand is the well-known hand that has collared half the people here, and motioned their brothers, sisters, fathers, mothers, male and female friends, inexorably to New South Wales. Yet Inspector Field stands in this den, the Sultan of the place. Every thief here cowers before him, like a schoolboy before his schoolmaster. All watch him, all answer when addressed, all laugh at his jokes, all seek to propitiate him. This cellar company alone – to say nothing of the crowd surrounding the entrance from the street above, and making the steps shine with eyes – is strong enough to murder us all, and willing enough to do it; but let Inspector Field have a mind to pick out one thief here, and take him; let him produce that ghostly truncheon from his pocket, and say, with his business-air, 'My lad, I want you' and all Rats' Castle shall be stricken with paralysis, and not a finger move against him, as he fits the handcuffs on.[9]

When they left Inspector Field gave some money to the lodging house keeper to buy coffee the next morning for all those living there. Dickens noticed the warmth with which the Inspector was received in the lodging houses, public houses, 'lairs and holes' which they visited that night.[10]

Over twenty-five years later Blanchard Jerrold was shown around a similar thieves' kitchen in a ghastly lodging house in the

East End. His police guides explained how many criminal careers were started in such places.

> 'Once they come here,' said one of our police guides, 'the best of them are lost. They can't help it. Some will struggle for a long time; but unless they are fortunate enough to get away, they are done for. You see, they come into the kitchen early, to cook their supper; and thus they fall in with all sorts – except those who could do them any good. That's how it begins with many of them. The rest are born in it.
>
> 'And God knows,' said another guide, 'how hard some of 'em – decent creatures who have got into trouble – fight to leave it all. But you see, there's no place for them as cheap as this.'[11]

'Thieves' Latin' was the slang used by thieves among themselves. James Greenwood, in *The Seven Curses of London* (1869), explained it to his readers as follows:

> It will be seen that the prime essential of 'thieves' Latin' is brevity. By its use, much may in one or two words be conveyed to a comrade while rapidly passing him in the street, or, should opportunity serve, during a visit to him while in prison.
>
> The following are some of the examples of 'Thieves' Latin' given by Greenwood.
>
> The treadmill – *shin scraper.*
> Breaking a square of glass – *starring the glaze*
> To commit burglary – *crack a case, or break a drum*
> Trainer of young thieves – *kidsman*
> Three years' imprisonment – *a stretch*
> Three months' imprisonment – *a tail piece*
> To rob a till – *pinch a bob*
> A person marked for plunder – *a plant*
> Going out to steal linen in process of drying in gardens – *going snowing*

Stealing lead from the roof of houses – *flying the blue pigeon*

Coiners of bad money – *bit fakers*

Hidden from the police – *in lavender*

The condemned cell – *the salt box*

The prison chaplain – *Lady Green*[12]

Receiving Stolen Goods

Disposing of stolen goods was easy in Victorian London. They could be taken to marine stores located near the river, licensed pawnbrokers' shops, unlicensed pawnbrokers' shops known as 'dolly' or 'leaving shops', and second-hand shops. Many keepers of low lodging houses were willing to receive stolen goods and dispose of them with no questions asked.

There were also many private houses, pretending to be shops, which received stolen goods at any time. They had furnaces in backrooms where silver could be melted down quickly. Receivers were often given advance notice of a burglary, and were ready and waiting to receive the booty. The receiving houses were watched by members of criminal gangs as well as the house being burgled. They were always aware of the policeman on the beat.

There was a brisk trade in stolen silk handkerchiefs, as Flora Tristan described in her journal.

> Quite close to Newgate, in a little alley off Holborn Hill called Field Lane, which is too narrow for vehicles to use, there is absolutely nothing to be seen but dealers in second-hand silk handkerchiefs...
>
> The shops are in fact stalls which project into the street, and this is where the handkerchiefs are displayed: they hang on rails so that intending purchasers can recognise at a glance the property they have had stolen from them! The men and women dealers, whose looks are in perfect harmony with their trade, stand in their doorways and hector the customers who come under cover of the night to buy dirt cheap the spoils of the day. There is a bustle of activity in the streets as prostitutes, children, and rogues of every age and condition come to sell their handkerchiefs. They are taken into

> the back of the shop to haggle over the price, then the handkerchiefs are given to a servant whose sole and constant occupation is to unpick any identifying marks and then to wash them. On the pretext of searching for two handkerchiefs we had had stolen, and by which we claimed to set great store, we went into four or five shops where we were shown all the handkerchiefs brought in over the past five days – a total of over a thousand! Now, as there are more than twenty shops in Field Lane, one may safely conclude that between four and five thousand handkerchiefs are brought each week to this repository of stolen goods. There I saw really superb handkerchiefs selling for two or three shillings. The trade in Field Lane is as brisk as any in the City, and it looks as if fortunes are made there.[13]

Cheats, Swindlers and Tricksters

Among those trying to earn an honest living on the streets of Victorian London lurked many whose intentions were to cheat, swindle or trick the unwary. Alfred Rosling Bennett described some of the tricks he remembered from the 1860s.

> Sleight-of-hand came in, too, in the three-card trick, in which the victim was invited to pick out the Queen amongst three cards shuffled in his sight, and then thrown face downwards, which he never could do unless it pleased the operator to let him. I watched some respectable-looking men, reasonable beings seemingly, badly robbed in this way at Ealing races in the mid 1860s. And the purse trick I saw effectively worked at Croydon races some years later. The prestigiator pretended to rain half-crowns into a purse, and then sold it for a quarter of its apparent value. But the purchaser would find only a penny or perhaps two to represent the silver. Instead of complaining he would usually swallow his wrath and slink away, unable to face the derision of the crowd; so that a new purse and a new softy usually materialised in a few minutes.[14]

Food Adulteration

The adulteration and mis-selling of food was a common way of cheating unsuspecting customers. James Greenwood was angered by this because it was poor people struggling to survive who often fell victim to such fraud.

> You simply palm off on the unwary customer burnt beans instead of coffee, and ground rice instead of arrowroot, and a mixture of lard and turmeric instead of butter. You poison the poor man's bread. He is a drunkard, and you are not even satisfied to delude him of his earnings for so long a time as he may haply live as a wallower in beer and gin, that is beer and gin as originally manufactured; you must, in order to screw a few halfpence extra and daily out of the poor wretch, put grains of paradise in his gin and coculus indicus in his malt liquor! And, more insatiable than the leech, you are not content with cheating him to the extent of twenty-five per cent by means of abominable mixtures and adulteration, you must pass him through the mill, and cut him yet a little finer when he comes to scale! You must file your weights and dab lumps of grease under the beam, and steal an ounce or so out of his pound of bacon.[15]

Violent Robberies

Robberies involving violence were not as common as theft and pickpocketing. According to Henry Mayhew these crimes were 'generally done in the dusk, and rarely during the day'. Violent robberies were usually carried out by more than one person and sometimes involved a woman, as described by Mayhew.

> Other robberies are perpetrated by brutal violence with a life-preserver or bludgeon. It is usually done by one or more brutal men following a woman. The men are generally from thirty to forty years of age – some older – carrying a life-preserver or bludgeon. This is termed 'swinging the stick,' or the 'bludgeon business'. The woman walks forward, or loiters about, followed by the men, who are hanging in the rear. She walks as if she was a common prostitute, and is often about twenty-six to thirty years of age. She picks up a man in the street, possibly the worse of liquor; she enters into conversation, and decoys him to some quiet, secluded place, and may there allow him to take liberties with her person, but not

> to have carnal connection. Meanwhile she robs him of his watch, money, or other property, and at once makes off.[16]

The men remained in the background to use the bludgeon if necessary. These criminals were often well known to the police and when convicted were punished with transportation.

Garrotting

Garrotting, or 'stringing someone up' in street slang, was a form of brutal mugging. It involved strangling someone with an arm, or a length of rope or wire, and stealing from them while they were being strangled. Two criminals were usually involved. Sometimes the attack was so brutal that the victim was killed.

In the 1850s and '60s fears about garrotting increased, especially after a Member of Parliament named Hugh Pilkington was attacked in this way in 1862. This led to the passing of the Security from Violence Act in 1863. Under the terms of the Act anyone convicted of garrotting faced a punishment of fifty lashes in addition to a heavy prison sentence.

Murders

Newspaper reports of murders added to the fears of Londoners about crime. Alfred Rosling Bennett remembered a murder which was reported in the press in July 1844.

> Late one Saturday evening, Mr Thomas Briggs, over sixty years of age, chief clerk in a Lombard Street bank, a season-ticket holder on the North London Railway, took a train at Fenchurch Street – then the terminus of that line – where he was recognised by the officials, to proceed to his home at Hackney. A little later the driver of a light engine saw something dark between the tracks – 'in the 6-foot', as railwaymen phrase it – near the canal bridge between Bow and Hackney Wick Stations. He stopped and found the body of Mr Briggs battered and gashed, and lying where it had evidently fallen from a train. The deceased's watch, chain, ring and hat were missing and an examination of the carriages disclosed

a bloodstained first-class compartment presenting evidence of a desperate struggle. Murder had without doubt been committed; but by whom?

At first the detectives were baffled, but a Mr Death, jeweller, of Cheapside, gave information that a short foreigner had exchanged a gold chain for another chain and a ring at his shop, while a hatter detailed how a top-hat had been brought to him by a similar personage for whom he had altered and shortened it. A cabman likewise came forward, and their combined testimony directed suspicion to a young German tailor named Muller, who, however, had disappeared from his usual haunts. Ultimately it was found that he had embarked for New York on the sailing-ship *Victoria* – we are writing of times when wind and canvas still claimed no small proportion of the Atlantic passenger traffic. Detectives, with Death, the Jehu and other witnesses, followed in hot pursuit by the next mail-steamer, *City of York,* and before *Victoria* arrived in the offing had obtained a warrant of arrest.

Muller was arrested on board ship where the victim's hat and watch were found in his luggage. The suspect was taken back to London, where he was tried, found guilty and executed. Bennett added that – 'The low flat-crowned hats which were coming into vogue about the time of the murder became popularly known as 'Muller-cut-downs.'[17]

The Whitechapel Murders

Between August and November 1888 six women, all prostitutes, were brutally murdered in the slums of Whitechapel, one of the most dangerous and lawless districts of London. The victims' throats were cut and their bodies were mutilated.

The killer became known as Jack the Ripper, this being the name used by a person claiming to be the murderer in a letter sent to a news agency. The sadistic Whitechapel murderer caused great terror and people all over London became afraid to venture out after dark. The murders were never solved and the killer's identity is still a mystery, despite various theories as to who he was.

The Baby Farming Case

Baby farmers were women paid to look after babies, often the illegitimate offspring of single women who needed to work. Many of these babies were neglected and, in some cases, 'adopted' for a one-off payment, giving the baby farmers little incentive to take care of them.

Margaret Waters was a thirty-five-year-old widow who lived in Brixton. She drugged the babies in her care with opiates which suppressed their appetites, leading to starvation. Waters was sentenced to death for the murder of John Walter Cowan and indicted for the murder of four more unknown infants. It is believed that she was responsible for the deaths of nineteen babies in all. Waters was hung in Horsemonger Lane Gaol in October 1870.

In 1872 the Infant Life Protection Act was passed to regulate foster parents and end abuse.

Crimes on the River Thames

Theft by people working on the River Thames was common. As well as thefts by mudlarks, dredgermen, lightermen, fishermen and labourers working on ships there was also the smuggling of contraband goods by seamen arriving from other countries. According to Henry Mayhew,

> There are a great number of robberies of various descriptions committed on the Thames by different parties. These depredations differ in value, from the little ragged mudlark stealing a piece of rope or a few handfuls of coal from a barge, to the lighterman carrying off bales of silk several hundred pounds in value. When we look to the long lines of shipping along each side of the river, and the crowds of barges and steamers that daily ply along its bosom, and the dense shipping in its docks, laden with untold wealth, we are surprised at the comparatively small aggregate amount of these felonies.[18]

Debtors

To be in debt was a crime in the Victorian period. Debtors were put in specials prisons until their assets had been sold to settle their debts or their debts had been paid for them. The two London prisons which were mainly used to house debtors were Marshalsea and Fleet Prisons. Debtors were allowed to have visits from their families and, in some cases, their families could stay in prison with them. Charles Dickens' father John was imprisoned for debt in Marshalsea Prison.

In 1837 there were over 30,000 bankrupts and debtors in prison in London.[19] Fleet Prison was closed in 1842 and debtors' prisons eventually ceased to exist once individuals were allowed to declare themselves bankrupt.

Begging

Begging was an offence under the 1824 Vagrancy Act but this had little deterrent effect. There were many beggars of all ages and nationalities on the streets of London. Some did not disguise the fact that they were beggars, while others pretended to be street sellers or tried to get sympathy and money by pretending, for example, to be disabled, the victim of a disaster, or a gentleman or tradesman who had fallen on hard times. A common way to beg was by sending begging letters.

Charles Dickens met a begging letter-writer when he visited Rat's Castle with Inspector Field.

> 'So, you are here, too, are you,' [said Inspector Field] 'you tall, grey soldierly-looking, grave man, standing by the fire? – Yes, Sir, Good evening, Mr Field! – Let us see. You lived servant to a nobleman once? – Yes, Mr Field. – And what is it you do now; I forget? – Well, Mr Field, I job about as well as I can. I left my employment on account of delicate health. The family is still kind to me. Mr Wix of Piccadilly is also very kind to me when I am hard up. Likewise Mr Nix of Oxford Street. I get a trifle from them occasionally, and rub on as well as I can, Mr Field. Mr Field's eye rolls enjoyingly, for this man is a notorious begging-letter writer. – Good night, my lads! – Good night, Mr Field, and thank'ee, Sir![20]

Prostitution

Prostitution was a problem because it was associated with crime. Prostitutes were often thieves as well and many lived in the same slum lodging houses as criminals. Some areas were well known for being the haunts of prostitutes, and these included the riverside districts of the East End, the theatre districts of the West End and Cremorne Gardens in Chelsea.

The presence of so many prostitutes on the streets of the world's richest city was shocking and embarrassing, as shown by this extract from *Notes on London* by Hippolyte Taine, who blamed poverty for the problem. After walking along the Strand and in the Haymarket Taine wrote,

> Every hundred steps one jostles twenty harlots; some of them ask for a glass of gin; others say, 'Sir, it is to pay my lodging.' This is not debauchery which flaunts itself, but destitution – and such destitution! The deplorable procession in the shade of the monumental streets is sickening; it seems to me a march of the dead. That is a plague-spot – the real plague-spot of English society.[21]

Although prostitution was not against the law, pimping and keeping a brothel were. Henry Mayhew investigated the brothels of London, which he referred to as 'accommodation houses'. According to him brothel-keepers were 'generally worn out prostitutes' and in certain areas of London 'an enormous amount of money is made by these people'.[22]

'Procuress' was the name Mayhew gave to the keepers of 'introducing houses', which were brothels in all but name. According to him,

> Procuresses are women who in most cases possess houses of their own, where they procure girls for men who employ them. These establishments are called 'Introducing Houses,' and are extremely lucrative to the proprietors. There are also men who go about for these people, finding out girls, and bringing them to the houses, where they may meet with men. The procuresses who keep introducing houses often take in women to lodge and board. But they are quite independent, and must be well-known about town,

> and kept by someone, or the procuress, if she is, comparatively speaking, in any position, will not receive them.[23]

Male prostitution was much less of a problem than female prostitution. In Holywell Street, off the Strand, male homosexual pornographic literature was sold. Details of male brothels and suggestions for places where homosexual men could meet were also obtainable there.

The co-existence of hideous brothels, where moral depravity and wicked exploitation flourished, with the beauty and elegance of the grand new buildings was an example of the extremes to be found in Victorian London.

The Police

The visible presence of the Metropolitan Police made a noticeable difference to the safety of the streets. According to Thomas Burke the police soon 'lived down' the hostility they faced when the force was first introduced and 'proved themselves useful public servants'.[24]

Max Schlesinger noticed the effectiveness of the constables on the beat.

> The London policeman ... knows every nook and corner, every house, man, woman and child on his beat. He knows their occupations, habits and circumstances. This knowledge he derives from his constantly being employed in the same quarter and the same street...His position on his beat is analogous to that of the porter of a very large house; it is a point of honour with him, that nothing shall escape his observation.[25]

The next stop following arrest was the police station, which was often very busy. Police cells were, in the words of James Grant, author of *Sketches in London* (1838), 'the most miserable receptacles into which a human being could be put, short of burying him alive'.[26] When his turn came the accused appeared before the Inspector on duty to be released or detained in custody.

George Augustus Sala was present at Bow Street Police Station at three o'clock one morning to witness the proceedings.

> In a commodious gas-lit box, surrounded by books and papers, and with a mighty folio of loose leaves open before him – a book of Fate, in truth – sits a Rhadamanthine man [stern judge in the underworld], buttoned up in a greatcoat often; for be it blazing July or frigid December, it is always cold at three o'clock in the morning ... Rhadamanthine man in greatcoat being but the Inspector of police on night duty, sitting here at his grim task for some fifty or sixty shillings a week...
>
> He has had a busy time since nine last evening. One by one the 'charges' were brought in, and hour after hour, and set before him in that little iron-railed dock. Some were felonious charges; scowling, beetle-browed, under-hung charged, who had been there many times before, and were likely to come there many times again. A multiplicity of Irish charges, too; beggars, brawlers, pavement obstructors – all terribly voluble and abusive of tongue; many with squalid babies in their arms. One or two such charges are lying now, contentedly drunken heaps of rags, in the women's cells. Plenty of juvenile charges, mere children. God help them! swept in and swept out; sometimes shot into cells – their boxes of fusees, or jagged broom -stumps, taken from them. A wife-beating charge; ruffianly carver, who has been beating his wife with the leg of a pianoforte ... There was a swell-mob charge, too, a dandy *de premiere force*, who swaggered and twisted his eye-glass, and sucked his diamond ring while in the dock, and declared he knew nothing of the gentleman's watch, he was 'shaw' ... As the night grew older, the drunk and disorderly and drunk and incapable charges began to drop in; but one by one they have been disposed of in a calm, business-like manner, and the charges are either released or, if sufficient cause were apparent for their detention, are sleeping off their liquor, or chewing the cud of sweet and bitter fancies, in the adjacent cells.[27]

If not released the next stage for the accused was an appearance before a magistrate, who decided his fate. The most serious cases were dealt with by a higher court, such as the Middlesex Sessions House or the Old Bailey, where members of the public were allowed to watch the proceedings.

Prisons

On Census Day in 1851 there were 6,188 inmates in London's prisons.[28] It was estimated that over a period of twelve months 20,000 individuals passed through the capital's prisons.

There were three categories of prison in London. Detentional prisons, such as Newgate and Clerkenwell, held those who had been charged by a magistrate and were awaiting trial. Houses of Correction held prisoners with short sentences – these included Coldbath Fields, Tothill Fields, Westminster and Brixton. Prisoners with long sentences were sent to convict prisons such as Pentonville, Millbank (until 1890) and the prison hulks for those awaiting transportation.

Newgate Prison

Newgate Prison was a gloomy granite building with very few windows, dating back to 1782. It held both men and women who had received the death sentence in the Central Criminal Court (Old Bailey), next door to the prison.

The forbidding interior of Newgate Prison is illustrated by this description taken from *A Story Teller; Forty Years in London* (1923) by William Pett Ridge:

> To enter Newgate you went up four steps to a narrow door with two rows of iron teeth at the top. You pulled a bell. In the entrance hall was a desk, with a gas-jet burning near; a high-backed chair with green cushions. As you went along, each door was locked behind you; the consulting room (for solicitors) was at the end of the passage, and the interview room. A whipping-post and birch were at hand, and you were shown handcuffs and heavy ankle chains; and the axe made for the Cato Street conspirators. In the chapel, you noticed a grill on one side for the concealment of women prisoners; the inscription overhead

> was 'Dieu et mon Droit'. In the burying passage, where the bodies of the hanged, set in lime, were put away, there stood initials on the wall.
>
> 'That,' said the warder, pointing, 'is Milsom and Fowler, and that's Fougeron, and that's Mrs Dyer, and that's the Flowery pirates, and –'
>
> In the condemned cell was the notice, 'God will Supply.'[29]

Any prisoners who persistently misbehaved at Newgate Prison were punished by a diet of bread and water or, in the worst cases, by a spell in the 'dark cell'. When being shown around the prison Thomas Archer was allowed to spend a few minutes in this cell to experience it for himself.

> The doors (for there are two) are about a foot apart; and that which renders the darkness more terrible and oppressive is that not a sound made by the prisoner can be heard outside, and that he is acquainted with this fact. A few minutes, during which I suffer myself to be incarcerated in this cell, convince me that only the most dogged and brute-like prisoners can submit for any length of time to this punishment ... My own sensations were, first, the utter blankness of everything, including my own identity; then an intolerable feeling that one might lose count of time, be forgotten, and yet never lose a horrible consciousness. A few hours are frequently enough to bring a stubborn rebel to submission, but the punishment is continued until there is reason to believe that this effect is produced.[30]

Coldbath Fields House of Correction

Coldbath Fields was a 'model Institution', which improved following a number of reforms and the adoption of the 'silent system', forbidding prisoners from communicating with one another. The prisoners worked at various tasks in their cells or in workshops.

When Thomas Archer visited this prison he found a busy, well-run institution.

> I come upon the yards where the workshops are in full swing. Carpenters' workshops, where the whiz of saw and plane sounds cheerfully after the dread monotony of the cells; coopers' workshops, where tubs and casks are being set upon the frames and hoops are being driven in a workmanlike manner; smiths' workshops, where the hammers clink upon the anvils beside the forges; wire-workers' shops and brushmakers' shops, where everybody is busily engaged; these are a part of the more recent discipline which has superseded the old useless labour to which the prisoners were once consigned almost without exception.[31]

There was also a printing room where prisoners were employed in printing religious texts, which were hung on the prison walls, police bills and other forms and documents used in the administration of the law. The prisoners also did all the laundry for the prison.

Pentonville Prison

Pentonville Prison, which was also described as a 'model prison', opened in 1842. Prisoners were trained there for two years before being sent to another prison to 'labour at public work'.

Pentonville was built to the panopticon design invented by philosopher Jeremy Bentham. It consisted of five wings of cells radiating from a central hub, where the warders were positioned with a view of the whole building.

Prisoners were provided with education and training for a trade. They were allowed daily exercise. The 'separate system' was operated in which prisoners had separate cells and separate compartments in the chapel. The 'silent system' was also practised 'to prevent contamination' and to encourage prisoners to think about their crime and resolve to mend their ways. Prisoners wore face masks to conceal their identities.

Archer was impressed with the way the prisoners were looked after at Pentonville and concluded,

> I may say without prejudice that the health and physical comfort of the British felon is better cared for than that of the ordinary British

pauper, and receives far more earnest attention than that of the British soldier or the British sailor.[32]

Hard Labour

Prisoners sentenced to carrying out hard labour could be set the boring task of picking oakum. This involved pulling apart lengths of tarred rope so that the fibres (the oakum) could be reused. The demand for oakum appeared to be insatiable; it was used to plug gaps in ship and boat building and for making mats. Picking oakum made the hands so sore that they bled.

Other forms of hard labour included working the treadmill or turning the crank. The treadmill was a large wooden wheel with steps on the outside. Prisoners had to cling onto a ledge at shoulder height and climb the steps to turn the wheel. Some treadmills ground corn but, quite often, all they ground was empty air. Shifts on the treadmill were usually eight hours with rest breaks.

The crank was a large handle in his cell which the prisoner turned for up to eight hours a day. The warder could adjust the crank from outside the cell to make turning more difficult. This, like grinding the air with a treadmill, was a totally futile exercise other than to punish the prisoner.

Prison Hulks

Prison hulks, old warships adapted to house prisoners, were used to ease pressure on London's overcrowded prisons. Many of the prisoners were awaiting transportation. The hulks – the *Defiance*, the *Warrior* and the *Sulphur* – were moored at Woolwich. These ships, which were insanitary, wet, dark and rat-infested, were very difficult to escape from. Prisoners on the hulks worked at repairing the riverbanks or dredging the riverbed. The hulks were used until 1858.

Escaped Convicts

Occasionally convicts managed to escape from London prisons. Such escapes were reported in the press, adding to the fears and anxieties of Londoners. Two escapes occurred within weeks of each other in 1862. The later escape, from Newgate Prison, was a particularly daring and astonishing feat. It was reported by the *Penny Illustrated Paper* on 10 May 1862.

> An Escape from Newgate. – Early on Tuesday morning Philip Krause, a sailor, awaiting his trial on a charge of robbery in the gaol of Newgate, made his escape, and for the present he remains at large, 'with the world before him where to choose.' Such a feat had scarcely been supposed by anyone familiar with the prison and its present arrangements within the range of possibility. At all events, under any circumstances it would be fraught with imminent peril to life and limbs, and has always been of rare occurrence there. Krause is a native of Hamburg and about twenty-four years of age. He is a little above the average height, with light hair and complexion, and rather stout. He had been committed from the Thames Police Court. By a series of ingenious expedients and great daring he regained his liberty. He was confined, it is said, in a new wing of the prison, and he effected his escape by cutting a panel out of his cell door. He had previously taken down from the interior of his dormitory about ten feet of gas piping, with which, and his blankets, he appears to have made a sort of ladder. Then eluding the 'vigilance,' as the phrase goes, of the night watchman, he passed on to one of the airing yards, and, scaling a wall, clambered over the roof of an adjacent building to one of the lower level, and by degrees worked his way down to the open street, landing in the Old Bailey, near the governor's private entrance, and getting clear off. After escaping from his cell he had torn down another piece of gas piping of considerable length, breaking it off near an angular joint and making thus a sort of crook, which he afterwards used with great effect in scaling the wall and letting himself down on the further side. A reward has been offered for his recapture.

The press also reported the recapture of convicts. This report appeared in the *Penny Illustrated Paper* on 5 July 1862.

> Recapture of a Convict – On Friday fortnight, three notorious convicts effected their escape from the county gaol,

> Horsemonger-lane. On Thursday week, two detective officers of the M division, whilst looking after a thief, espied one of the escaped convicts, named G. Brunell, emerging from a small gardener's cottage in a gentleman's garden at Highbury. The detectives pounced upon him, but they met with a desperate resistance; for the man being armed with a life-preserver, made a desperate attack upon the two policemen, but they succeeded in securing him, and handed him over to the governor of the gaol. When the convict found he was in the hands of the police, he coolly remarked, 'If you had come five yards nearer the cottage I would have settled both of you.' Upon searching the cottage, a pistol loaded with ball was found therein, which, if the detectives had entered, would no doubt have been discharged at them.

Transportation

Transportation with hard labour was a common punishment, even for minor crimes such as petty theft. Not only was this a way of banishing criminals but it was also cheaper than keeping them in prison. The sentence was usually for seven years but in some cases it was longer. Most criminals were transported to Australia and a few to other colonies. After 1853 transportation was only used for criminals sentenced to more than fourteen years. If any transported convicts escaped and returned, they faced the death penalty. Once transportation ended in 1867 more prisons had to be built.

Executions

Executions, by hanging, were held in public until 1868. They took place outside the prison in which the criminal was held – in London these were Newgate Prison or Horsemonger Lane Prison. After 1861 the only crimes punishable by death were murder and treason.

Public hangings were a great attraction. Huge crowds turned up to watch and made a day of it by taking food and drink with them, as described by Max Schlesinger.

> Go to Newgate on a hanging day, or to Horsemonger Lane, or to any other open space in front of a prison; there you will find

shouting, and joking, and junketting, from early dawn until the hangman has made his appearance and performed his office. The windows are let out, stands are erected, eating and drinking booths surround the scaffold; there is an enormous consumption of beer and brandy. They come on foot, on horseback, and in carriages, from a distance of many miles, to see a spectacle which is a disgrace to humanity; and foremost are the women – my countrywomen – not only the females of low degree, but also ladies, 'by birth and education.' It is a shame but, nevertheless, it is true. And our newspapers are afterwards compelled to chronicle the last death-struggles of the wretched criminal! [33]

12

STREET CHILDREN

The many visitors to Victorian London could not fail to notice the vast number of poor children who spent most of their time working, and in some cases, living on the streets of the capital. This was largely due to the government's 'laissez faire' policy on social issues and its harsh poor law, which left the most vulnerable to look after themselves in the overcrowded metropolis.

Henry Mayhew, who is the best source of information about the street children, drew attention to their plight in his letters to the *Morning Chronicle*. According to him,

> There are thousands of neglected children loitering about the low neighbourhoods of the metropolis, and prowling about the streets, begging and stealing for their daily bread. They are to be found in Westminster, Whitechapel, Shoreditch, St Giles's, New Cut, Lambeth, the Borough and other localities. Hundreds of them may be seen leaving their parents' homes and low lodging-houses every morning sallying forth in search of food and plunder.[1]

No one was quite sure at the time exactly how many street children there were in London. Estimates varied from 30,000 to 100,000.

In 1852 William Locke, Secretary to the London Ragged School Union, wrote this description of the street children:

> Many of them are quite homeless; many of them are entirely neglected by their parents; many are orphans, outcasts, street beggars, crossing-sweepers, and little hawkers of things about the streets; they are generally very ignorant, although in some points very quick and cunning.[2]

The majority of these children were boys who came from a variety of backgrounds. They included indigenous Londoners, children from other parts of Britain, and from the English countryside. Some had arrived in London with families or alone, in search of work and others were children of foreigners, including Irish and Jewish settlers.

The street children could be divided into two categories – those with some kind of family support and those without. A number of these children belonged to the respectable 'industrious poor' class – otherwise known as the 'deserving poor'. The majority, however, were members of the underclass, referred to as 'outcast London'.

There was a contemporary stereotype of the London street child, which they did not all fit. This stereotype, and the general attitude towards them, are illustrated by the derogatory names used to describe them, such as 'guttersnipe', 'street Arab', and 'ragamuffin'. Henry Mayhew wrote the following paragraph about the feral street children:

> Parental instruction; the comforts of a home, however humble – the great moral truths upon which society itself rests; – the influence of proper example; the power of education; the effect of useful amusement; are all denied to them, or come to them so greatly vitiated, that they rather tend to increase, than to repress, the very evils they were intended to remedy.[3]

There were, however, many street children who were generally honest, law-abiding, respectful, polite and articulate.

The children who spent so much of their lives on London's streets lived, or at least sought shelter in, many different places. These included slum tenements, jerry-built back-to-back houses, common lodging houses, night shelters, refuges, casual wards and, in the absence of any alternative, on the streets themselves.

The maze of arches under the Adelphi Terrace in the Strand, the dry arches of bridges over the Thames and railway arches were popular shelters for street children. Thomas Archer described the sight of children sleeping under the arches in *The Terrible Sights of London*.

> It is to the arches of the railway – those great bare blank walls of bricks which are sometimes supposed to have made a clean sweep in a whole neighbourhood of evil repute, but which in reality build the traffic of foot passengers out of the slums which crouch behind them – that the homeless children go for shelter, happy if an empty van, a cart, a wagon, a pile of timber is lying there to keep them from the bitter wind. Is there a carpenter's shop, a smith's shop, a nook of brickwork, or any sort of projection that can hide a dog; there you may find a child for whom the law has done no more than to teach them that practically everybody is supposed to be guilty till he can prove himself innocent, and for whom the Gospel has done nothing, for he has heard no part of it. The glad tidings of greatest joy to him would be to learn where to find food, a fire and a bed this piercing night, without being 'jawed at' and 'knocked about', and treated like – well no! there is a Society for the Prevention of Cruelty to Animals, which would protect the dog.[4]

One of the street children interviewed by Henry Mayhew explained the difficulties he and his comrades faced each night and how they often had to choose between paying for a night's shelter or buying food.

> In the winter we has to be out in the cold, and then in summer we have to sleep out all night, or go asleep on the church steps, reg'lar tired out.

'One of us'll say at night – 'Oh, I'm sleepy now, who's game for a doss? I'm for a doss' – and when we go eight or ten of us into a doorway of the church, where they keep the dead in a kind of airy-like underneath, and there we go to sleep. The most of the boys has got no homes. Perhaps they've got the price of a lodging, but they're hungry, and they eats the money, and then they must lay out. There's some of 'em will stop out in the wet for perhaps the sake of a halfpenny, and get themselves sopping wet. I think all our chaps would like to get out of the work if they could...[5]

Occupations of the Street Children

Children were employed in the same four categories of street occupations as adults – selling, finding, entertaining, and providing services.

Child street sellers worked alone or with other children. They sold easy to carry items which required small start-up costs, such as matches, fly papers, shoe and stay laces, nuts, oranges, watercress and flowers. They worked long hours exposed to the elements in inadequate clothing, often with no shoes. Some walked miles every day to sell their wares.

Not all of these children were honest; some used selling as a cover for begging and for picking the pockets of unwary shoppers. Others cheated customers with short weights and imperfect goods.

Among the children interviewed by Henry Mayhew were two orphan flower sellers. They did not fit the stereotype of the feral street child as they were polite, respectful, intelligent and articulate, and they had received a little education. The girls were half-sisters aged fifteen and eleven. Mayhew described them in detail.

Both were clad in old, but not torn, dark print frocks, hanging so closely, and yet so loosely, about them as to show the deficiency of under-clothing; they wore old broken black chip bonnets. The older sister (or rather half-sister) had a pair of old worn-out shoes on her feet, the younger was barefoot, but trotted along, in a gait at once quick and feeble – as if the soles of her little feet were impervious, like horn, to the roughness of the road.[6]

The girls lived with their brother and their landlady in the slums off Drury Lane. Their meagre earnings barely covered their rent and starvation diet of tea, bread and the occasional herring.

Mayhew was impressed by the resilience of the flower girls in the face of adversity. Desperate though their situation was, they were better off than many other street children because of the kindness of their landlady, who helped them as much as she could.

Street Finders

Child street finders collected anything they could sell, including dog faeces to sell to the tanneries of Bermondsey, cigarette ends to dry and sell to the poor, and rags and bones. Some worked as sewer scavengers.

Mudlarks

Many children, mainly boys, worked as mudlarks. They mostly lived in rooms and lodging houses in the slums by the river. The areas in which they mainly worked were the Pool of London, near the Tower of London, the places where vessels were built or repaired, and around the coal wharves.

The mudlarks barely communicated with each other while they raked the mud. They carried baskets or tin kettles for their finds, or used their hats or caps. The young mudlarks spent six or seven hours at a stretch looking for items, such as coal, rope, driftwood, metal, copper nails, animal bones and bottles. Occasionally they found something valuable, but most finds only fetched a few pennies.

When the tide came in the mudlarks went into the streets near the river to sell their finds in the rag and bone shops and marine stores. Some scraped the mud off their clothes and used the time between tides to do odd jobs in the streets, such as opening cab doors and holding horses.

Henry Mayhew met a group of twelve boy mudlarks gathered by one of the staircases down to the river, waiting for the tide to recede so that they could start work. These children, whose ages ranged from six to twelve years, were huddled together. Mayhew described the sorry sight.

> It would be almost impossible to describe the wretched group, so motley was their appearance, so extraordinary their dress, and so stolid and inexpressive their countenances. Some carried baskets, filed with the produce of their morning's work, and others old tin kettles with iron handles. Some, for want of these articles, had old hats filled with the bones and coals they had picked up; and others, more needy still, had actually taken the caps from their own heads, and filled them with what they had happened to find. The muddy slush was dripping from their clothes and utensils, and forming a puddle in which they stood. There did not appear to be among the whole group as many filthy cotton rags to their backs as, when stitched together, would have been sufficient to form the material of one shirt. There were the remnants of one or two jackets among them, but so begrimed and tattered that it would have been difficult to have determined either the original material or make of the garment.[7]

One of the boys, the son of a deceased coal-backer, told Mayhew that

> he had been three years mud-larking, and supposed he should remain a mud-lark all his life. What else could he do? for there was nothing else that he knew how to do.
>
> Like so many street children this boy had received very little education and his knowledge was limited to just what was necessary for survival. He gave his mother all the money he made and 'she bought bread with it, and when they had no money they lived the best way they could'.[8]

Street Entertainers

Some children worked as street entertainers to scrape a living. Playing musical instruments, singing, dancing, and performing acrobatics were popular forms of entertainment they provided. They either worked in the same place every day or travelled around the streets alone, with other children, or as part of a family troupe.

Another boy Mayhew met on the streets was an eleven-year-old who worked as a street acrobat or 'tumbler' and also swept crossings around St Martin's Church in Trafalgar Square. Johnny was an orphan who lived with his grandmother in the slums. He gave her all his takings of up to a shilling a day. He had earned his nickname of 'The King' due to his superior ability in performing 'cat'en wheels' (Catherine wheels). Mayhew described Johnny as

> a pretty-looking boy ... with a pair of grey eyes that were as bright and clear as drops of sea-water. He was clad in a style in no way agreeing with his royal title; for he had on a kind of dirt-coloured shooting-coat of tweed, which was fraying into a kind of cobweb at the edges and elbows. His trousers, too, were rather faulty, for there was a pink-wrinkled dot of flesh at one of the knees; while their length was too great for his majesty's short legs, so that they had to be rolled up at the end like a washer-woman's sleeves.
>
> ... He could bend his little legs round till they curved like the long German sausages we see in the ham-and-beef shops; and when he turned head over heels, he curled up his tiny body as closely as a wood-louse and then rolled along, wabbling (sic) like an egg.[9]

Often all the boy tumblers received for their efforts was a kick or a blow. They also had to contend with hostile policemen who attacked them with their tunic belt buckles.

The services provided by street children included running errands, carrying parcels, sweeping crossings and guiding people through the foggy streets.

Crossing-sweepers

Sweeping a path across the dirty London streets was a popular way for children to earn money. The only equipment needed was a broom, although these wore out quickly and needed to be changed frequently.

Some children worked alone and others worked in gangs. The number of child crossing-sweepers increased in 1851, when the Great Exhibition attracted crowds of people to London.

Ellen, a fourteen-year-old crossing-sweeper who worked in Trafalgar Square, was interviewed by Mayhew. She was a 'clean washed girl with a pretty expressive countenance' dressed in ragged, inadequate clothing. She lived with her grandmother in the slums of Holborn – a district later cleared to make way for the railway to be extended.

Ellen had joined a gang of crossing-sweepers after she failed to make money by selling laces. She told Mayhew,

> 'It's a capital crossing, but there's so many of us, it spiles it. I seldom gets more than sevenpence a day, which I always takes home to grandmother.
>
> 'I've been on that crossing about three months. They [her fellow gang members] always calls me Ellen, my regular name, and behaves very well to me. If I see anybody coming, I call them out as the boys does, and then they are mine.
>
> 'There's a boy and myself, and another strange girl, works on our side of the statey [statue], and another lot of boys and girls on the other.
>
> 'I like Saturdays the best day of the week, because that's the time as gentlemen as has been at work has their money, and then they are more generous. I gets more then, perhaps ninepence, but not quite a shilling, on the Saturday.
>
> 'I've had a threepenny-bit give to me, but never sixpence. It was a gentleman, and I should know him again. Ladies gives me less than gentlemen. I foller 'em, saying, "If you please, Sir, give a poor girl a halfpenny;" but if the police are looking, I stop still.
>
> 'I never goes out on Sunday, but stops at home with grandmother. I don't stop out at nights, like the boys, but I gets home by ten at latest.[10]

Link Boys

A useful service provided by children, usually boys, was guiding people by torchlight through Victorian London's smogs. They were known as 'link boys'. An American visitor to London in 1862 likened the smogs to a 'solid wall constantly opposing our further progress'. He wrote the following description of the ragged link boys:

> It was an amusing sight to see scores of ragged boys, carrying about torches for sale. The cry of 'Links, links', resounded on all sides. 'Light you home for sixpence, sir,' said one of them, as I stood watching their operations. 'If 'tan't far,' he added presently, 'I'll light you for a joey [3 pence].'[11]

As with other street occupations, not all who worked as link boys were honest. Anyone who made the mistake of paying up front risked losing their money, as some rogues pocketed the money and slipped away into the smog without providing a service.

Competition on the Streets

Children working on the streets faced fierce competition from other child street workers and adults. Many children struggled to make enough money to survive. William Booth met one such child and recorded what he told him in *In Darkest England and the Way Out*.

> I've been walking the streets almost day and night these two weeks and can't get work. I've got the strength, though I shan't have it long at this rate. I only want a job. This is the third night running that I've walked the streets all night; the only money I get is by minding blacking-boys' [shoe cleaners] boxes while they go into Lockhart's for their dinner. I got a penny yesterday at it, and twopence for carrying a parcel, and today I've had a penny. Bought a ha'porth of bread and a ha'penny mug of tea.[12]

Little Mothers

Another group of street children were the 'little mothers' – older children, usually girls, who looked after their younger siblings while their parents worked, or to help their over-burdened mothers. Some looked after the babies and young children of neighbours for a few pennies a week.

The 'little mothers' were to be found in the courtyards, alleys and streets of the slums. They spent their days watching over little children as they played in the filthy gutters. The journalist and author known as 'Uncle Jonathan' noticed that the 'little mothers' he saw in the East End looked after their charges 'with as much care and anxiety as though they were real mothers'.[13]

Child Criminals

Many street children resorted to crime in order to survive. The majority of child criminals were boys and their most common crimes were theft and pickpocketing. These included children who were born into criminal families and knew no other way to acquire the necessities of life. James Greenwood described these children, who had never been taught the difference between right and wrong, in *The Seven Curses of London.*

> ... if in the benighted den in which he is born, and in which his childish intellect dawns, no ray of light and truth ever penetrates, and he grows into the use of his limbs and as much brains as his brutish breeding affords him, and with no other occupation before him than to follow in the footsteps of his father the thief – how much more hopeless is his case?[14]

Some children turned to crime because of the difficulties of earning a living honestly. Others were actively encouraged by parents who forced them into crime and by parents who did not care how their children obtained money, as long as they did so. Another group of child criminals was those who started off as beggars and then turned to crime – there was a strong link between vagrancy and crime.

A significant factor in juvenile crime was the influence on children of 'gutter' or 'gallows' literature which glorified violence and crime. 'Penny dreadful' magazines, which were sold in vast numbers in London every day, contained stories with such titles as *Tyburn Dick* and *The Boy Burglar*. These luridly illustrated stories were read by children who could read to those who could not.

Acts of crime, violence and depravity were also enacted in the popular Penny Gaff theatres in the slums.

Pickpockets

Henry Mayhew met many young pickpockets on the London streets. One pickpocket he interviewed was the son of a Wesleyan minister who had rebelled against his strict upbringing and ran away from home at the age of ten. He joined a gang of pickpockets who stole handkerchiefs from the back pockets of male passengers alighting from boats at the Adelphi Stairs. He told Mayhew,

> At this time there was a prison-van in the Adelphi arches, without wheels, which was constructed different from the present prison-van, as it had no boxes in the interior. The boys used to take me with them into the prison-van. There we used to meet a man my companions called 'Larry.' I knew him by no other name for the time. He used to give almost what price he liked for the handkerchiefs. If they refused to give them at the price he named, he would threaten them in several ways. He said he would get the other boys to drive them away, and not allow them to get any more handkerchiefs there. If this did not intimidate them, he would threaten to give them in charge [get them arrested], so that at last they were compelled to take whatever price he liked to give them.[15]

By the age of thirteen this boy was well on his way to becoming a hardened criminal. He was in and out of prison for years and each time he was released he was met by his fellow gang members and began stealing again. His criminality finally ended when he narrowly escaped transportation after committing a burglary. When he met Mayhew he was making an honest living as a patterer – selling goods on the streets by using verbal patter. He was just about able to survive but had broken free of crime.

Thieving Mudlarks

Henry Mayhew came across a group of boy mudlarks who stole from vessels moored on the river. One of the boys spoke to Mayhew, who described him as a 'strong and healthy thirteen-year-old'. He was wearing 'a brown fustian coat, greasy patched trousers and a striped shirt and cap'. In his own words,

> We are often chased by the Thames Police, and the watermen, as the mudlarks are generally known to be thieves. I take what I can get as well as the rest when I get an opportunity.
>
> We often go on board of coal barges and knock or throw pieces of coal over into the mud, and afterwards come and take them away. We also carry off pieces of rope, or iron, or anything we can lay our hands on and easily carry off. We often take a boat and row on board of empty barges and steal small articles, such as pieces of canvas or iron, and go down into the cabins of the barges for this purpose, and are frequently driven off by the police and bargemen. The Thames police often come upon us and carry off our bags and baskets and the contents.[16]

When Mayhew met him, this boy had so far avoided being tried in court for any felony.

Girl Criminals

The few girl criminals on the streets of London usually committed less serious crimes than the boys, but were likely to become more hardened criminals. Society viewed them more harshly due to the belief in the moral superiority of the female sex. It was considered more shameful for a girl to turn to crime.

Girls often acted as accessories and lookouts for boys. They disposed of the boys' ill-gotten gains. Sometimes they committed crimes themselves, usually theft. Some combined theft with prostitution, by stealing from their clients.

Punishment

For the first half of the nineteenth century prison was the only punishment for juvenile crime. Up to the age of seven children could not be held responsible for any criminal action, between the ages of seven and fourteen years the prosecution had to prove a child's ability to tell the difference between good and evil, and children over the age of fourteen were deemed fully responsible for their actions. Even minor offences were punishable by imprisonment and repeat offenders could be transported. In prison, children received the same harsh punishments as adults, including the silent system, the treadmill and flogging. Prison failed juveniles because they learned from the adult prisoners they were incarcerated with, they became hardened by their harsh treatment and, for many children, a criminal record was considered a badge of honour.

Charles Dickens saw for himself how prison failed juveniles when he visited Newgate Prison. He described this visit in *Sketches by Boz*.

> The whole number, without an exception, we believe, had been committed for trial on charges of pocket-picking; and fourteen such terrible little faces we never beheld. There was not one redeeming feature among them – not a glance of honesty – not a wink expressive of anything but the gallows and the hulks, in the whole collection. As to anything like shame or contrition, that was entirely out of the question.[17]

State Intervention

The revelations of Henry Mayhew, Charles Dickens and other journalists added to the fear and alarm about juvenile crime. With the passing of the Juvenile Offenders Act in 1842 child criminals began to be treated differently to adults. Special courts were set up for them and there was a move towards reforming young criminals instead of punishing them.

The Young Offenders Act of 1854 led to the establishment of the first reform schools for under seventeen-year-olds, when they had finished their prison sentences. A number of these schools were opened in London and a reformatory ship, the *Cornwall*, which was moored on the Thames. Industrial schools were also opened to provide moral and industrial training to help young criminals break the cycle of crime. The following information about the

Cornwall is taken from Charles Dickens Junior's *Dictionary of the Thames*:

> This reformatory training ship of the School-Ship Society is anchored off Purfleet. As a general rule the committee do not admit boys unless the three following conditions are satisfied:
>
> 1 That the boy be sentenced to not less than three years' detention.
> 2 That he be not less than 13 years of age nor more than 15.
> 3 That he be certified as sound and healthy.
>
> Visitors were allowed to go on board the ship, but not on Saturday, as it was cleaning day.[18]

The Reformatory and Refuge Union

In 1856 the Reformatory and Refuge Union, a charitable concern, was founded to help juvenile criminals. It established 'half-way houses' for children released on special licence and appointed a Boys' Beadle to investigate the circumstances of children found on the streets and return them to their parents, school, a place of safety, the police or a magistrate, as appropriate.

Child Prostitution

Scarcity of work and financial desperation led some children, mainly girls, into prostitution. Like other street children, child prostitutes were an embarrassment and a blight on the world's richest city.

The exact number of child prostitutes in Victorian London is unknown, as there was no clear definition of prostitution and only those known to the police were included in the official figures. The age of consent was twelve until 1871, when it was raised to thirteen. The fact that under-age sex was illegal did not offer much protection. There was a demand for young girls due to the lower risk of them having venereal disease.

A true story related by Charles Dickens shows how girls became prostitutes. Although the events occurred in 1835, many girls followed the same path in the Victorian period. Dickens was among a crowd of people watching newly convicted prisoners getting into a police van outside Bow Street police station. The first prisoners, handcuffed together, were two sisters aged around sixteen and fourteen named Ellen and Bella. Although their gaudy clothes revealed that they were prostitutes, it was not clear what offence they had committed, as prostitution was not illegal. The younger girl was

> weeping bitterly – not for display, or in the hope of producing effect, but for very shame; her face was buried in her handkerchief; and her whole manner was but too expressive of bitter and unavailing sorrow.

For the older girl, who had been sentenced to six months and labour, this was obviously not a new experience. She cheekily ordered the coachman to drop her off in 'Coldbath Fields – large house with a high garden wall in front, you can't mistake it'.

The younger sister had just received her first conviction, which accounted for her shame and distress. Dickens observed,

> These two girls had been thrown upon London streets, their vices and debauchery, by a sordid and rapacious mother. What the younger girl was then, the elder had been once; and what the elder then was, the younger must soon become. A melancholy prospect, but how surely to be realised; a tragic drama, but how often acted.[19]

For much of the Victorian period the government had a 'laissez-faire' attitude to prostitution, so the only help available came from charities and philanthropical individuals, who were often motivated by their religious beliefs. The London Society for the Protection of Young Females and Prevention of Juvenile Prostitution, established in 1835, and the Society for the Rescue of Young Women and Children, founded in 1853, did much to help child prostitutes by providing shelter, food, clothing, training and work placements.

The government eventually took action after a campaign against child prostitution led by W. T. Stead, editor of the *Pall Mall Gazette*. The Criminal Law Amendment Act of 1885 raised the age of consent to sixteen, punished those who permitted under-age sex on their premises, and made it a criminal offence to abduct a girl under eighteen for sexual purposes.

Not all young prostitutes wanted help, however, as prostitution was often a better option than the alternative ways of making a living. Some child prostitutes went on to become hardened adult prostitutes. For many others, however, prostitution was a transitory phase in their lives.

Helping the Street Children

Once the public became aware of the misery and suffering of London's street children there was an outpouring of help from concerned people, and a new, more humane and understanding attitude towards them.

Probably the most effective action taken on behalf of the street children was the establishment by charities and individuals of ragged schools (as described in Chapter 2.) The teachers who ran the early schools were mainly untrained volunteers. They looked after the physical, moral and spiritual welfare of their pupils by providing a warm shelter, food, clothing and a rudimentary education with a high religious content. Treats and outings were offered too. They succeeded in civilising some of the feral children whose presence on the streets was such a cause of concern.

Homes of the Later Street Children

Some street children lived in the slums in houses crammed from cellar to attic with the poorest of the poor, and in squalid lodging houses alongside criminals, prostitutes and other undesirables. These slums were worse in the second half of the century due to slum clearance, which resulted in more and more people being squashed into the remaining slum housing.

Refuges

Shelter and help were available in refuges across the metropolis. One of the largest in London was the Field Lane Refuge, which grew out of the Field Lane Ragged School. The institution soon outgrew its original buildings and in 1865 Lord Shaftesbury laid the foundation stone of new premises in Saffron Hill. In 1860 the boys offered three nights a week respite from the streets numbered between 70 and 200 per night, and girls numbered between 30 and 100.

In the last decades of the century more temporary shelters were provided by the Salvation Army, the Church Army and the Congregational Union.

There were a number of orphanages founded by philanthropists and charities in London but most only accepted children from respectable homes, or with a particular connection, such as the Soldiers' Daughters Home. In the 1870s and '80s homes were founded for destitute children and children whom no one else was prepared to help.

Thomas Barnardo opened his first children's home in Stepney Causeway in 1870. Barnardo went on regular night searches with Lord Shaftesbury to rescue homeless boys. He went on to found more homes where children were housed, fed, and given a basic education as well as moral and spiritual training. Children in the homes were given work to do, such as chopping wood and making brushes and tools to sell. There was much interest in Barnardo's work and donations poured in to help.

According to *Memoirs of Dr Barnardo* (1907), written by his widow and James Marchant,

> He helped during his lifetime, more or less permanently, a quarter of a million children, nearly sixty thousand of whom he maintained, educated, and started in life under his own roof.[20]

This number included countless London street children.

Around the same time as Barnardo began his rescue work, Charles Haddon Spurgeon, the popular Baptist preacher, was given

£20,000 to build an orphanage for poor fatherless boys. Thomas Archer visited his orphanage in Stockwell and described its aspect as 'bright and cheerful, the air clear and salubrious'.[21] Spurgeon went on to rescue many children from destitution and crime by giving them a safe home, a good education and training to enable them to find work.

Another man who made a significant contribution to helping London's destitute children was the Reverend Thomas Bowman Stephenson, a Methodist minister. In 1869 he converted a cottage near Waterloo Station into a home for boys; this was the start of the National Children's Home.

In 1895 the journalist 'Uncle Jonathan' described Stephenson's Children's Home at Victoria Park as

> one amongst many others engaged in giving a fresh start in life to many a destitute and friendless boy or girl ... In these Homes everything that can be done is done to enable the children to overcome their bad habits, and to fit them for some useful occupation when they leave the Home. Industry and intelligence, order and cleanliness, cheerfulness and activity, are encouraged; religion is inculcated; and the whole discipline through which the children pass cultivates and improves them so much, that it is difficult to recognise in these sturdy, active, intelligent boys and girls leaving the Home, the pale-faced, poor, neglected ones who entered it some years before. Many more lives would be brightened, if people, seeing how much we are all benefited by this work of rescue, would give of their charity. All can help by prayer and effort.[22]

Waifs and Strays Society

In 1882 the Church of England became involved in rescuing London's destitute children. Two brothers, Edward and Robert de Montjoie Rudolf, learned about the plight of these children through their work as Sunday School teachers. They founded the Church of England Central Society for Providing Homes for Waifs and Strays and opened their first home in Dulwich. By the end of Victoria's reign the society had 2,826 children in its care.[23]

Despite all the efforts of charities and churches, however, there were not enough places for all the children in need and some still had no choice but to sleep on the streets.

Legislation

The street children of the later Victorian period benefited greatly from the new compassionate attitude towards them and other suffering children. In 1884 the London Society for the Prevention of Cruelty to Children, which later became a national society, was founded.

The government also took action. In 1889 the Prevention of Cruelty to and Protection of Children Act was passed. This gave children rights for the first time and protection against abuse and mistreatment. It included restrictions on child employment and outlawed child begging. A further Act in 1894 placed additional restrictions on the employment of children and more safeguards to protect them.

Solving the Problem

The decline in the number of children on the streets of Victorian London began in the 1860s with the introduction of reformatory and industrial schools.

It was the arrival of a national system of state education which finally provided a solution to the problem of the street children. Education turned those children who had not had a good start in life into good citizens and prepared them for work fitting their station in life. Attendance was difficult to enforce at first because many families relied on the money their children earned. As time passed the authorities became stricter and Attendance Officers were appointed to seek out truants. Although some managed to slip through the new state safety net, the majority of poor children, including those who may have ended up on the streets, were at last cared for and protected. By the end of Victoria's reign large numbers of poor children spending most of their lives on the streets was a thing of the past.

Dr Barnardo described how the new state schools had 'brought education to the most neglected' and how it had contributed to the 'silent but profound revolution' which he noticed all around him in London in the last years of the century.

> As I walk through the streets I see no more the organised beggary, the universally ingrained ignorance, the systematic neglect, the vicious exploiting of homeless little victims of cruelty and greed which disgraced London in the sixties.
>
> Of course I speak broadly. Alas, however, all is not 'couleur de rose'. There are still many wrongs to right; there is much wickedness to combat; the cry of the children still rises to the God of Sabaoth. But, as compared with the time when I first began my work, the law had broken with its evil traditions, and the spirit of apathy and laissez-faire is beginning to die out. Behind the law is a rising level of public opinion and Christian sentiment, which means yet greater things in the future than in the past.[24]

The rise and growth of socialism, an increase in wages, better living standards, a fall in prices and a decline in the birth rate all contributed to the disappearance of destitute children from the streets of London.

13

THE IMPERIAL CITY

Prince Albert's Death

In December 1861 Prince Albert died of typhoid. Since their marriage he had helped the Queen with official business and had always been there to advise and support her. Victoria, needless to say, was utterly heartbroken and inconsolable at the death of her beloved 'Angel'.

At the age of forty-two Victoria had to face life, and her heavy official workload, alone. Her reaction was to withdraw completely from public life – she would not even attend the opening of Parliament. Initially there was sympathy for the Queen, but as time passed, public opinion turned against her. The Queen's subjects and the press began to criticize her and question what she was doing for her Civil List money. It was not long before the criticism turned into full-blown republicanism.

There were two men who helped to bring Victoria out of her seclusion – John Brown and Benjamin Disraeli. John Brown was her devoted personal assistant, or ghillie, at Balmoral, her home in Scotland. He had developed a close relationship with the Queen during her many family holidays at Balmoral. Brown was brought to London, at the suggestion of her doctors, to encourage the Queen to move on and face the world again. It was an excellent idea as Victoria was soon performing her public duties again and, wherever she went in London and elsewhere, she was greeted by cheering crowds. She had regained the love and respect of her people.

Benjamin Disraeli was Prime Minister briefly in 1868, and then from 1874 to 1880. Disraeli, like Melbourne in the 1830s, enjoyed a close personal relationship with the Queen, who described him as 'one of the kindest, truest and best friends, and wise counsellor'. Having a Prime Minister she liked and could depend on helped Victoria when she re-entered public life.

Empress of India

Queen Victoria had been interested in India for a long time and at Osborne House, her home on the Isle of Wight, she had a large room, the Durbar Room, full of Indian artefacts and treasures. By the 1870s the British Empire had grown to such an extent that nearly a quarter of the globe was ruled by Britain. Of all these colonies India was described as the 'Jewel in the Crown'. In 1876 Disraeli obtained the title of Empress of India for the Queen – a cause of great pride and pleasure for her.

By this time many of the improvements in London, described in previous chapters, were in place. London's transformation into a grand imperial city was well underway, but more still needed to be done.

London changed considerably between 1837, when Victoria became Queen, and 1887, when she celebrated her Golden Jubilee. The skyline and scenery of the capital had changed and continued to do so. Richard Rowe described these changes in *Life in the London Streets; or Struggles for Daily Bread.*

> London nowadays is being pulled down and built up again on so extensive a scale, and the new buildings are so unlike the old ones they supplant, that many parts pf the huge city we see are as identical with those places as we remember them, as the knife that had been rehandled and rebladed, and the gun that had received new lock, stock and barrel were with the original weapons.[1]

Roads and Transport

New roads, new bridges, the embankments and the removal of obstacles such as Temple Bar and bridge tolls had put an end to the chronic traffic congestion on London's streets. The extended railway network, both above and below ground, had also made moving around London quicker and easier. The congestion on pavements had been eased as fewer people were using them.

Horse-drawn transport existed for a long time after the arrival of the railway. The horse still had an important job to do transporting goods in wagons and people in omnibuses, cabs, carriages and, from the 1860s, in horse-drawn trams.

In the 1880s the bicycle first appeared on the capital's streets and became a popular form of transport. Cyclists could be a danger on the London streets because, unlike buses and cabs, they were not always visible. Thomas Burke remembered the evening paper boys, whom he described as the 'most reckless of cyclists' racing around the streets on their bicycles.

> On an ordinary bicycle of the period, with half a hundredweight of papers on his back, he shot into Fleet Street and through the traffic at scorching speed, weaving his way under horses' heads through any opening that offered. No tangle of traffic stopped him; he stopped for nothing but a policeman's arm; and he had hair's-breadth escapes every minute.[2]

The River Thames

The Thames was now a fast-flowing and cleaner river. The embankments had tidied up the riverside, and the new docks had put an end to ships and barges clogging up the river while they waited to be unloaded. River traffic flowed more easily. The construction of Tower Bridge helped with this and made access to London easier, as it enabled large ships to reach the Pool of London.

Housing

The population of London continued to grow in the later Victorian period, as more and more people arrived. New arrivals included

Jewish people fleeing persecution in Russia. They came in the 1880s and settled in the East End. London expanded to accommodate the rising population. It was now so vast and sprawling that the phrase 'greater London' was coined to describe it.

Speculative housebuilding continued, providing more villas and terraced homes, mainly for the middle classes, but also for better-off working-class people, especially after the introduction of cheap workmen's train fares.

The extended railways, both above and below ground, made it easy to get into central London from the suburbs. Some of the new homes were close enough to make commuting by foot possible. Living in the suburbs became so popular that in 1881 a guidebook called *The Suburban Homes of London* was published.

Some of the poorer Londoners were now living in flats built by philanthropists and charitable organisations, but not many could afford the rent. Although there were fewer slums by this time, those remaining were more overcrowded and appalling than ever. Under legislation passed in the 1880s developers were supposed to provide alternative accommodation for those displaced by slum clearance, but many companies failed to do so.

There was still great poverty and unemployment in London, with the worst deprivation found in the East End. As some parts of the capital were being transformed other parts, where the poorest people lived, became worse.

Public Services

Public services were better in the later Victorian period due to the improvements described earlier. There was now a safe sewage system, and cemeteries had replaced the overcrowded churchyards and burial grounds. Cholera outbreaks had come to an end. Clean drinking water was now available and drinking fountains had appeared on the streets. The first public conveniences were built in Trafalgar Square in the 1880s. The building of more general and specialised hospitals had also helped to improve the health of Londoners.

Another public service which had made life better was the provision of more street lighting. The streets were lit in some areas by electric lights while in others the old gas lights remained.

Crime and Street Life

It is difficult to be certain whether crime levels in later Victorian London were up or down on those of the earlier period, but the need for more prisons suggests that crime had not declined.

Comparing figures was difficult as new crimes had been added to the statute book and there had been an increase in arrests as policing had improved. Crime always increased during severe winters and when prices rose and wages fell – factors which distorted the figures. Improved street lighting and the discovery of fingerprinting helped to reduce crime. There were still dangerous areas in London, however, where violence was a daily occurrence. Drunkenness had declined a little but prostitution was still rife. Thomas Burke, who was born in London in the 1880s, described crime at that time in *The Streets of London*.

> It was the London of the Sherlock Holmes stories (the late eighties); a London in which the criminal, by then more alert than his predecessors, had a good run. Telephones were not in general use: no more than Sherlock Holmes detectives. The quickest communication was by telegram, and there were no mobile police in fast vehicles. The criminal who used his brains had a more than sporting chance against the authorities; they could move no faster than he could, and if he did not make the mistake of dashing away by train (which allowed them to head him off by telegram) but remained in London, he could move about in the knowledge that his feet or his hansom were as good as theirs. It took some time even for news of an affair to reach them, and arrests were seldom made on the day of a crime. It was usually many days later, and it was not the quiet affair it is now. Criminals were more desperate. There was in most cases a struggle, and the capture was seldom made single-handed. Handcuffs were more commonly used than they are today.[3]

The streets of later Victorian London were as noisy, lively and colourful as in the earlier period. Street markets and street sellers were as busy as ever, and music and entertainment added to the atmosphere.

As described in the previous chapter, the street children remained but there were fewer of them. Most of them were in the new state schools being educated and prepared for work suited to their station in life.

New Buildings

By the time of Queen Victoria's Golden Jubilee there were many important buildings in London, of various architectural styles, befitting the world's richest city and the capital of an expanding empire. In the words of Thomas Burke, 'The Empire was a mighty fact and London was its capital. In harmony with this Empire, the city and its buildings grew larger and larger.'[4]

These new buildings included the museums and other educational institutions, the Royal Albert Hall, the Albert Memorial, and the Imperial Institute paid for by the profits of the Great Exhibition. The last named was built to celebrate the Queen's jubilee and cement the British Empire. The Queen laid the foundation stone in 1887 and opened the building in 1893.

Gothic-style public buildings included the new Houses of Parliament, which were mostly completed by 1860, replacing the buildings destroyed by fire in 1834. The Public Record Office in Chancery Lane, completed in 1896, was also Gothic in style, as were the nearby Royal Courts of Justice, with a splendid Great Hall, designed by G. E. Street and opened in 1882. Even comparatively lowly buildings such as the Bow Street Police Court, completed in 1881, were impressive.

More government buildings were needed as the functions of government increased and the British Empire grew. The new London Board School Offices, housed in an early Renaissance-style building on the Victoria Embankment, were opened in 1870. A new building complex in Whitehall included the Foreign, Colonial, India and Home Offices. A good view of these offices, which were designed by George Gilbert Scott, could be seen from St James' Park. The new public buildings were added to the list of recommended sights for visitors and tourists, who continued to flock to London.

More large and impressive hotels were built in the later Victorian period, as described in this entry in Charles Dickens Junior's *Dictionary of London*:

> One of the latest and most remarkable enterprises for providing a large and attractive hotel is that of the Grand Hotel, Trafalgar-sq. – a large and sumptuously-fitted building in the very centre of London, and close to most of the chief public resorts. It is very splendidly appointed ... Still of later date are the large and commodious First Avenue Hotel, Holborn, and the splendid Hotels Metropole and Victoria in Northumberland-avenue. Almost every great railway has now a handsome hotel in connection with its terminus.[5]

By the 1880s London's wholesale markets had been extended or rebuilt. The West End department stores were growing larger. In 1872 Army and Navy Stores opened with a small grocery store in Victoria Street, one of the new streets built to ease traffic congestion. This was to become another large department store. Victoria Street was built on the site of a notorious slum.

The Queen's Golden Jubilee

Over two days in June 1887 the country celebrated the Queen's fifty years on the throne. On the first day, 20 June, the Queen wrote in her journal,

> I hurried my dressing this morning, in order to get down early to breakfast at Frogmore. Drove from there with Beatrice [her youngest daughter] and Liko [Prince Henry of Battenburg, Beatrice's husband], through the beautifully decorated town [Windsor] to the station. At Paddington we got into the open landau, with the usual escort. Enormous crowds and immense

> enthusiasm. Drove by Edgware Road into the Park and everywhere the crowds were enormous.

The following eyewitness account of the celebrations is taken from the diary of R. D. Blumenfeld, an American-born journalist and writer:

> Wonderful day for Queen Victoria's Golden Jubilee celebration. I spent most of last night wandering through the streets to observe the decorations and preliminary illuminations. The gas-lit streets looked brilliant. Holborn, which with great enterprise, has electric street lighting, particularly attractive; walking from the Inns of Court Hotel in Holborn at eight o'clock this morning in order to take up my place in the window at the foot of Haymarket, opposite her Majesty's Opera House (now Carton Hotel), but the crowd was so dense that I could get no further than Waterloo Place, facing my window, and I was stuck in the heat until long beyond noon after the procession had passed. I climbed up the statue of King George, but could not maintain myself and came down. But I got a good view of most of the procession. The Queen's face was hidden from me by a sun-shade...
>
> I thought the German Crown Prince [Emperor Frederick], in his silver helmet and shining cuirass, the most striking figure in the procession. The young Princes, Edward [Duke of Clarence] and George [later King George V], were a popular feature in their naval uniforms.[6]

Following the parade through the streets of London the Queen and her invited guests, including all the crowned heads of Europe, had lunch and dinner at Buckingham Palace. That night the Queen wrote in her journal 'this never to be forgotten day will always leave the most gratified and heart-glowing memories behind'.

A service of thanksgiving was held at Westminster Abbey on 22 June, followed by more feasting at Buckingham Palace.

On the second day of the celebrations a huge party was held in Hyde Park for 27,000 schoolchildren. This event was witnessed by

Edward Owen, a police officer at Hyde Park police station, who described it in his memoir *Select Narratives, Annual Events etc. During twenty years police service in Hyde Park* (1906).

> The great festival gathering in Hyde Park of London's School Children in celebration of the 50th year of the reign of Her Most Gracious Majesty the late Queen Victoria was a most notable day, and as far as the weather was concerned a most glorious one also. It will not be easily forgotten by old or young who were fortunate enough to be present at this event. It appeals more to the younger generation, considering about 30,000 were regaled and entertained in celebration of the above auspicious occasion. Ten enormous marquees, besides many other minor tents, were pitched on the 'Guards' Ground,' or the north-east portion of the Park, for the accommodation of this multitude of children, where, at a given time, accompanied by their teachers, they all assembled and partook of a substantial repast. This concluded, a host of attractions and games of the fair and fête description were provided out in the open. Numerous ladies and gentlemen also rendered every possible assistance for their amusement, and, to add to their enjoyment, a peal of bells occasionally rang out merrily, at least a mechanical arrangement that produced the sound of bells, kindly lent and supplied by Sir Henry Irving from the Lyceum Theatre, having been previously utilised there in one of his plays. The arrival of H.M. the Queen on the ground, and the singing by the children of *The Old Hundredth* hymn, *God Bless the Prince of Wales* and *God Save the Queen* accompanied by the Guards' and other regimental bands combined, under the conductorship of Lieut. Dan Godfrey, was a most impressive item in the day's programme.
>
> At the end of the day the children 'gaily marched' out of Hyde Park holding souvenir cups.[7]

The transformation of London continued with the construction of more impressive buildings, such as the New Scotland Yard building on the Thames Embankment, near the Houses of Parliament.

Nevertheless, areas of great poverty still remained. A dockers' strike in 1889 was a measure of the deprivation of 'outcast London'.

New entertainment venues opened at this time. The Earls Court Exhibition Centre and Olympia were both opened in the 1880s. A Great Wheel was one of the attractions at Earls Court.

In the 1890s the first motor cars, known as 'horseless carriages', and motor buses, appeared on London's streets.

London County Council

In 1889 London County Council was formed and assumed responsibility for the administration of the capital. It was housed in a building on the south bank of the Thames, just over Westminster Bridge from the Houses of Parliament. The following year the old vestries and district boards were replaced by twenty-eight new Metropolitan Borough Councils.

Among the early achievements of the new Council was the building of the Boundary Estate in the East End, the first council housing in London. It also built the Blackwall Tunnel, a road tunnel under the Thames, which opened in 1887. In 1900 the Council started work on the last of the roadway improvements of the Victorian era. It cleared 28 acres of land for the construction of Kingsway and the Aldwych, to connect the Strand with Holborn.

The Queen's Diamond Jubilee

The Queen's Diamond Jubilee celebrations were held in June 1897. The theme was Empire, at the suggestion of the Colonial Secretary, Joseph Chamberlain. The day was both a celebration for the Queen and a 'Festival of the British Empire'. The foreign guest list was restricted to the heads and representatives of countries in the British Empire. Being older and more frail than she was at her Golden Jubilee, the Queen was not involved in the arrangements this time. She recorded the day's events and her emotions in her journal – her excitement and pride are palpable.

> A never to be forgotten day. No-one ever I believe, has met with such an ovation as was given to me, passing through those 6 miles of streets, including Constitution Hill. The crowds were quite indescribable and their enthusiasm truly marvellous and deeply touching. The cheering was quite deafening, and every face seemed to be filled with great joy. I was much moved and gratified.[8]

The days' events were recorded by artists, cartoonists, newspapers, diarists and cinematographers.

The Queen became increasingly frail in the final years of the century, and was troubled with failing eyesight and rheumatism. She managed to struggle on until the end of 1900. At Osborne House, on New Year's Day, the Queen recorded that she felt weak and unwell. On 19 January the Queen's subjects were informed of her illness. Three days later Victoria died.

The Queen's coffin, covered with the royal standard, was placed on a gun carriage for the journey back to London. Sorrowing crowds lined the route to Paddington station. Among the crowds was Frederick Willis, who described the funeral procession in his memoir.

> The well-to-do people wore mourning clothes and never was such a display of mourning seen as in the shops at this time. The poorer people wore black ties and black crape armlets ... I have vivid recollections of how everyone went about as if they had suffered a great personal loss. The funeral took place on February 4th 1901 and passed through greater crowds than even the Diamond Jubilee attracted. Practically every civilised country was represented in the procession. I managed to get into Hyde Park in the early hours of a cold, drizzling morning, but saw nothing of the procession. I got wedged in the crowd in an obscure corner, but two impressions stand out in my memory; the solemn music and silence of the crowd, and the sudden breaking of that silence by waves of cheers, which were almost instantly hushed.[9]

The coffin was taken by train from Paddington station to Windsor, where the Queen was laid to rest beside her beloved husband in the mausoleum at Frogmore. It was the end of an era.

At the time of Victoria's death, although not all of London's problems had been solved, it was a city fit to be the capital of a great empire and fit to face the twentieth century under a new monarch.

NOTES

(victorianlondon.org is abbreviated to vl.org)

Introduction

1. digitalpanopticon.org/London

1. Housing

1. Charles Manby Smith, *The Little World of London, How London Grows* vl.org Publications – Social Investigation/ Journalism – *Curiosities of London Life*
2. Hippolyte Taine, *Notes on England*, 13-14
3. Max Schlesinger, *Saunterings In and Around London*, 13
4. Robert Kerr, *The Gentleman's House*, vl.org – Houses and Housing, – Housing of the Upper Classes, – *A London Town House.*
5. Taine, 14 and 16
6. Ibid, 14
7. Schlesinger, 6-7
8. Gustave Doré and Blanchard Jerrold, *London A Pilgrimage*, 99
9. Friedrich Engels, *The Condition of the Working Class in England* – Jon E. Lewis, *London The Autobiography*, 213

10. Steve Humphries and Gavin Weightman, *The Making of Modern London,* 113
11. https://citymonitor.ai/environment/its-been-housing-londoners-150-years-what-peabody-trust-2836
12. William Booth, *In Darkest England and the Way Out*, 32-3
13. Henry Mayhew, *London Labour and the London Poor*, 421-2
14. Thomas Archer, *The Terrible Sights of London,* 403-4
15. Mayhew, *London Labour and the London Poor,* 113-14
16. Charles Dickens, *On Duty With Inspector Field, Selected Journalism 1850-70*, 306-7
17. Stephen Porter, London, *A History in Paintings and Illustrations,* 107
18. James Greenwood, *A Night in the Workhouse* in Peter Keating, *Into Unknown England,* 37
19. Charles Dickens, *A Nightly Scene in London, Selected Journalism,* 361
20. Booth, 37-8
21. Ibid, 33
22. www.workhouses.org.uk, Salvation Army Establishment

2. *Education*

1. John Timbs, *Curiosities of London,* vl.org – Education – Schools – *Dulwich College*
2. Taine, 101 and 104
3. Edmund Yates, *His Recollections and Experiences,* vl.org – Education – Schools – *Highgate School*
4. Peter Cunningham, *Hand Book of London,* 414
5. Charles Dickens (Junior), *Dictionary of London 1888*, 36
6. Mayhew, *London Labour and the London Poor,* 211
7. Ethel Hogg, *Quintin Hogg, A Biography,* 55
8. Charles Dickens, *Crime and Education, Daily News* 4.2.1846, – Neil Philip and Victor Neuburg, *A December Vision and Other Thoughtful Writings,* 93
9. Mayhew, *The Morning Chronicle Survey, The Metropolitan Districts,* Vol. 4, 60
10. Archer, *The Terrible Sights of London,* 234

11. Ibid, 240
12. *The Queen's London*, 317
13. Ibid, 238
14. Ibid, 239
15. George Sims, *How the Poor Live* – Peter Keating, *Into Unknown England*, 82
16. *Cruchley's London in 1865, A Handbook for Strangers*, vl.org – Education – Professional/ Technical Colleges/ Institutions – *Mechanics Institutes*
17. Cunningham, 403
18. Dickens (Junior), *Dictionary of London, 1888*, 195

3. Work

1. Hannah Cullwick, *Diary*, quoted in Jon E. Lewis, *London, The Autobiography*, 248
2. Mayhew, *The Morning Chronicle Survey*, vol. 6, 53
3. George Augustus Sala, *Twice Round the Clock*, 35
4. Anon, *Toilers in London or Inquiries Concerning Female Labour in the Metropolis*, vl.org, 238-9
5. Timbs, vl.org – Professions and Trades – Food and Drink – *Brewers*
6. Doré and Jerrold, 130-2
7. Mayhew, *The Morning Chronicle Survey*, vol.1, 209-10
8. Mayhew, *London Labour and the London Poor*, 239
9. Ibid, 239
10. Ibid, 246-7
11. Alfred Rosling Bennett, *London and Londoners in the Eighteen-Fifties and Sixties*, 39-40
12. Lee Jackson, *Victorian London*, 58
13. Schlesinger, 51 and 54
14. Francis Wey, *A Frenchman Sees the English in the Fifties*, vl.org – Police and Policing – Perception Of – *Policeman's Beat*
15. Dickens (Junior), *Dictionary of London 1888*, 100
16. Thomas Burke, *The Streets of London*, 133
17. Sala, *Twice Round the Clock or Hours of the Day and Night in London*, 90-1

18. Ibid, 87
19. Doré and Jerrold, 27-8
20. Taine, 8
21. Mayhew, *London Labour and the London Poor,* vl.org – Publications – Social Investigation/Journalists – *Of the Number of Costermongers and Other Street Folk*
22. Adolphe Smith and John Thomson, *Victorian London in Pictures*, 75
23. Bennett, 34-6
24. Doré and Jerrold, 155
25. Richard Rowe, *Life in the London Streets or Struggles for Daily Bread,* 285-6
26. Ibid, 73-4
27. Bennett, 34
28. Smith and Thomson, 37
29. Mayhew, *The Morning Chronicle Survey,* vol.5, 4
30. Bennett, 44-5
31. Flora Tristan, *The London Journals of Flora Tristan,* 84

4. *Transport*

1. Schlesinger, from Jon E. Lewis, *London the Autobiography,* 239-40
2. Nathaniel Hawthorne, *The English Note-Books, December 8th 1857,* vl.org – Weather – *Fog*
3. Schlesinger, 155-6
4. Sala, *Twice Round the Clock, 6.p.m.,* 219
5. Charles Dickens, *The Last Cab Driver, Sketches by Boz,* 170-1
6. Bennett, 90
7. Sala, *Twice Round the Clock, 9 a.m.,* 87-8
8. *The Queen's London,* 368-9
9. Sala, *Twice Round the Clock, 7 a.m.,* 62-4
10. Schlesinger, 169-70
11. Dickens (Junior), *Dictionary of London 1888,* 38
12. *Cruchley's Handbook*, vl.org – Thames – Bridges – *Chelsea Suspension Bridge*
13. Dickens (Junior), *Dictionary of London, 1888,* 250

5. The River Thames

1. Friedrich Engels, *The Condition of the Working Class in England*, 59
2. Schlesinger, 136-7
3. Dickens (Junior), *Dictionary of the Thames*, 45
4. Ibid, 237
5. Londonist.com-Forgotten Disasters – *Steam Boat Explosion near Waterloo Bridge.*
6. Ibid, *The Worst Maritime Disaster in the Thames History*
7. Dickens (Junior), *Dictionary of the Thames*, 205-6
8. Ibid, 11-12
9. Liza Picard, *Victorian London*, 278-9
10. Bennett, 13
11. Ibid, 158
12. https://www.rmg.co.uk/national-maritime-museum/attractions/prince-fredericks-barge
13. www.portcities.org.uk – Arrivals and Departures – *Embarkation at Gravesend of Prince and Princess Frederick William of Prussia*, 2.2.1858
14. Ibid – *Arrival of Duke and Duchess of Edinburgh at Gravesend*, 7.3.1874
15. Schlesinger, 90-1
16. Picard, 16-17
17. Doré and Jerrold, 59-60
18. Bennett, 100
19. Taine, 7-8
20. *Mogg's New Picture of London and Visitors' Guide*, vl.org – Buildings – *Customs House.*
21. *The Queen's London*, 18

6. Shops and Shopping

1. Sala, *Twice Round the Clock, 8 a.m.*, 76-7
2. Cunningham, 422
3. Henry Colman, *European Life and Manners*, quoted in Sheppard, 355
4. Frederick Willis, *101 Jubilee Road*, 38-9

5. Charles Knight, *Knight's London*, vl.org – Shops and Shopping – *Bazaars*
6. *The Queens' London*, 290
7. *Cruchley's Handbook*, vl.org, – Shops and Shopping – *Arcades*
8. Schlesinger, 23-4
9. Ibid, 17
10. Charles Manby Smith, 331
11. Dickens, vl.org – Shops and Shopping – *Marine Stores.*
12. Dickens, *Sketches by Boz*, vl.org,- Scenes – Chapter 6 – *Meditations on Monmouth Street*
13. Doré and Jerrold, 153
14. Mayhew, *The Morning Chronicle Survey*, vol.1, 249
15. Ibid, 249-50
16. Mayhew, *London Labour and the London Poor*, 12-13
17. Rowe, 122-4
18. Mayhew, *London Labour and the London Poor*, 84-5

7. *Entertainment and Leisure*

1. Taine, 13
2. Schlesinger, 105-7
3. Taine, 22
4. Dickens (Junior), *Dictionary of London 1888*, 250
5. Bennett, 331
6. Doré and Jerrold, 74-5
7. James Greenwood, *Unsentimental Journeys Through the Modern Babylon*, 30
8. Wey, vl.org, – Entertainment – Clubs – *Reform Club*
9. Mary MacCarthy, *A Nineteenth Century Childhood*, 105
10. Taine, 214
11. Yates, vl.org, – Entertainment – Gardens and Spas – *Cremorne Gardens*
12. vl.org, – Entertainment – Gardens and Spas – *The Eagle*
13. J. Ewing Ritchie, *Here and There in London*, vl.org, – Entertainment – Theatre – *Penny Gaffs*
14. Ibid
15. Mayhew, *London Labour and the London Poor*, 324

16. Willis, 49
17. Bennett, 43
18. Cunningham, 348
19. Sala, *London Up to Date, 3 p.m.*, 168-9
20. Dickens (Junior), *Dictionary of London 1888*, 217
21. Taine, 187
22. *Mogg's Guide*, vl.org, – Entertainment – Museums, Public Buildings and Galleries – *Soane Museum*
23. Cunningham, 562
24. Dickens (Junior), *Dictionary of London 1879*, vl.org. – *Sanger's Amphitheatre*
25. *Mogg's Guide*, vl.org – Entertainment – Theatres and Shows – Dioramas and Panoramas – *Burford's Panorama*
26. *Punch* Online Archive, July to December 1851
27. Bennett, 61
28. Schlesinger, 267
29. Taine, 216-17
30. Dickens (Junior), *Dictionary of London 1879*, vl.org. Entertainment – Drinking and Drugs – *Opium Dens*

8. *The Great Exhibition*

1. J. R. C. Yglesias, *London Life and the Great Exhibition 1851*, 14
2. www.queenvictoriasjournal.org, 18.2.51
3. Ibid, 1.5.51
4. Yglesias, 42
5. Jon E. Lewis, *London The Autobiography*, 231-2
6. David Bartlett, *London By Day and Night*, 323-4
7. Taine, 188-9

9. *Health and Medicine*

1. James Greenwood, *Unsentimental Journeys Through Modern Babylon*, 3,5,6
2. Picard, 183
3. Dickens (Junior), *Dictionary of London 1888*, 128
4. James Greenwood, *The Wilds of London*, 147-8

5. *Times History of London*, 97
6. Dickens (Junior), *Dictionary of London 1888*, 119
7. *Cruchley's Handbook*, vl.org – Health and Hygiene – *Hospitals*
8. Smith and Thomson, 24
9. Ibid, 26
10. Bennett, 4-5
11. *Punch* Online Archive, July to December 1848
12. Charles Dickens, Letter to the *Times*, quoted in Jon E. Lewis, *London the Autobiography*, 243
13. Smith and Thomson, 22
14. Jackson, 65
15. Bartlett, 95-6
16. *Mogg's Guide*, vl.org, – Death and Dying – Cemeteries – *Kensal Green*

10. Religion

1. Dickens (Junior), *Dictionary of London 1888*, 68-78
2. The Queen's London, 254
3. Ibid, 316
4. Pamela Horn, *The Rural World 1780-1850, Social Change in the English Countryside*, 160
5. Dickens (Junior), *Dictionary of London 1888*, 78
6. Molly Hughes, *A London Family, 1870 -1900*, 68-71
7. Dickens (Junior), *Dictionary of London 1888*, 78
8. Taine, 11
9. Ibid, 11-12
10. Bennett, 110 -111
11. Dickens, vl.org – Entertainment – Holidays – *Sundays*
12. *The Queen's London*, 162
13. Taine, 10-11
14. 'Uncle Jonathan', vl.org, – Religion – Methodist – *City Road Chapel*
15. *The Queen's London*, 181
16. Bartlett, Chapter 8, 184-6
17. Taine, 190-1
18. Hughes, 67 and 71

19. Ibid, 72
20. Willis, 70
21. Richard Elman and Albert Fried (editors), *Charles Booth's London*, 244-5
22. Ibid, 245
23. Christopher Hibbert and Ben Weinrib, *The London Encyclopaedia*, 528-9

11. Crime

1. Francis Sheppard, *London 1808-1870, The Infernal Wen*, 368
2. *Times History of London*, 98
3. *Routledge's Popular Guide to London*, vl.org – Crime – Beggars and Vagrants – *Warnings to Travellers*
4. Dickens (Junior), *Dictionary of London 1888*, 49
5. Peter Quennell, *London's Underworld*, 199-200
6. John Murray, *The World of London*, vl.org – Crime – Thieves – *The Swell Mob*
7. Quennell, 168
8. Ibid, 169
9. Dickens, *On Duty with Inspector Field, Selected Journalism 1850-1870*, 308-9
10. Ibid, 310
11. Doré and Jerrold, 140
12. Greenwood, *The Seven Curses of London*, 87-9
13. Tristan, 175-6
14. Bennett, 32
15. Greenwood, *The Seven Curses of London*, 152-3
16. Quennell, 239
17. Bennett, 250
18. Quennell, 291
19. Michael Paterson, *Voices from Dickens's London*, 246
20. Dickens, *On Duty with Inspector Field, Selected Journalism 1850-1870*, 309
21. Taine, quoted in Sheppard, 367
22. Quennell, 100
23. Ibid, 102

24. Burke, 111
25. Schlesinger, 51
26. Quoted in Paterson, *Voices from Dickens's London,* 245
27. Sala, *Twice Round the Clock, 3 a.m.,* 390-1
28. Sheppard, 374
29. W. Pett Ridge, *A Story Teller – Forty Years in London,* vl.org – Prisons – *Newgate*
30. Thomas Archer, *The Pauper, the Thief and the Convict,* 145
31. Ibid, 124-5
32. Ibid, 175
33. Schlesinger, 60

12. *Street Children*

1. Quennell, 133
2. William Locke, *Report of the Standing Committee on Criminal and Destitute Juveniles*, vl.org, – Education – Education for the Poor – Ragged Schools
3. Mayhew, *London Labour and the London Poor,* 185
4. Archer, *The Terrible Sights of London,* 279-81
5. Mayhew, *London Labour and the London Poor,* 282
6. Ibid, 61
7. Ibid, 210 -11
8. Ibid, 211-12
9. Ibid, 278
10. Ibid, 291
11. Anon, *London Fogs and the London Poor, Continental Magazine,* October 1862
12. Booth, 34
13. 'Uncle Jonathan', vl.org – Childhood – Children – *Poor Children*
14. Greenwood, *The Seven Curses of London,* 126
15. Quennell, 218
16. Ibid, 303
17. Dickens, *A Visit to Newgate*, *Sketches by Boz,* Neil Philip and Victor Newburg, 61
18. Dickens (Junior), *Dictionary of the Thames,* 47

19. Dickens, *The Prisoners Van, Sketches by Boz.* Rosalind Vallance, *Dickens' London, 85*
20. Mrs Barnardo and James Marchant, *Memoirs of the Late Dr Barnardo,* 325
21. Archer, *The Terrible Sights of London,* 187
22. 'Uncle Jonathan' vl.org – Childhood – Children's Homes – *Dr Stephenson's Home*
23. Waifs and Strays Society, *A Chronicle of the Church of England's Waifs and Strays Society, 1881-1920,* 84-5
24. Barnardo and Marchant, 243-4

13. *The Imperial City*

1. Rowe, 106
2. Burke, 132
3. Ibid, 130-1
4. Ibid, 130
5. Dickens (Junior), *Dictionary of London 1888*, 130
6. R. D. Blumenfeld, *Diary*, vl.org – Dates and Events – *Queen's Golden Jubilee*
7. Edward Owen, *Select Narratives, Annual Events During Twenty Years of Police Service in Hyde Park*, vl.org – Dates and Events – *Queen Victoria's Golden Jubilee*
8. queenvictoriasjournal.com, 209-215
9. Willis, 16

BIBLIOGRAPHY

Notes on Sources

A number of primary sources have been found on www.victorianlondon.org, a vast resource on Victorian London containing the texts of many books now out of print or difficult to obtain.

Official Papers

Report of the Select Committee on Criminal and Destitute Juveniles, 1852

Books, Articles, Letters, Newspapers, Periodicals and Websites

Anon., *Toilers in London or Inquiries Concerning Female Labour in the Metropolis* (1889) (victorianlondon.org)

Archer, Thomas, *The Pauper, the Thief and the Convict* (1865) (Dodo Press Reprint, 2009)

Archer, Thomas, *The Terrible Sights of London* (1870) (victorianlondon.org)

Barnardo, Mrs and Marchant, James, *Memoirs of the Late Dr Barnardo* (1907) (Kessinger Legacy Reprint, 2009)

Bartlett, David, *London By Day and Night* (1852) (victorianlondon.org)

Bennett, Alfred Rosling, *London and Londoners in the Eighteen-Fifties and Sixties* (1924) (Dodo Press, undated)

Beresford Chancellor, E., *The Nineteenth Century in London* (B. T. Batsford, 1920)

Blumenfeld. R. D., *Diary* (1883-1914) (victorianlondon.org)

Booth, William, *In Darkest England and the Way Out* (1890) (Salvation Army Social Services Centenary edition, 1984)

Burke, Thomas, *The Streets of London* (B. T. Batsford,1943)

Burke, Thomas, *Travel in England* (B.T. Batsford, 1943)

Clout, Hugh, (editor), *The Times History of London* (Ted Smart,1999)

Colman, Henry, *European Life and Manners* (1849) (quoted in Francis Sheppard, *London 1808 -1870*)

Continental Monthly Magazine

Cruchley's London in 1865, A Handbook for Strangers (victorian london.org)

Cullwick, Hannah, Diary, (quoted in Jon E. Lewis, *London the Autobiography*)

Cunningham, Peter, *Hand-Book of London, Past and Present* (1850) (Forgotten Books, Classic Reprint series, undated)

Dickens, Charles, *Selected Journalism, 1850-1870* (Penguin Classics, 1997)

Dickens, Charles, *Sketches by Boz* (Penguin Classics, 1991)

Dickens, Charles, *Sketches by Boz* (1839) (victorianlondon.org)

Dickens, Charles (Junior), *Dickens's Dictionary of London 1879* (victorianlondon.org)

Dickens, Charles (Junior), *Dickens's Dictionary of London 1888* (Old House Books, 1993)

Dickens, Charles (Junior), *Dickens's Dictionary of the Thames, 1887* (Old House Books, 1994)

Doré, Gustave and Jerrold, Blanchard, *London, A Pilgrimage* (1872) (Dover Publications, 1970)

Elman, Richard and Fried, Albert (editors) *Charles Booth's London: A Portrait of the Poor at the Turn of the Century Drawn From "His Life and Labour of the People of London" (Pelican Books, 1971)*

Engels, Friedrich, *The Condition of the Working Class in England* (1845) (extract published in Jon E. Lewis, *London the Autobiography*)

Ewing Ritchie, J., *About London* (1860) (victorianlondon.org)

Ewing Ritchie, J., *Here and There in London* (1859) (victorianlondon.org)

Grant, James, *Sketches in London* (1838) (victorianlondon.org)

Grant, James, *Lights and Shadows of London Life* (1842) (victorianlondon.org)

Greenwood, James, *A Night in a Workhouse* (1876),

Greenwood, James, *The Seven Curses of London* (1869) (Kessinger Rare Reprint, undated)

Greenwood, James, *Unsentimental Journeys Through Modern Babylon* (1867) (Ward, Lock and Tyler, 1867)

Greenwood, James, *The Wilds of London* (1874) (victorianlondon.org)

Hawthorne, Nathaniel, *The English Note-Books* (1857) (victorianlondon.org)

Hibbert, Christopher and Weinrib, Ben (editors), *The London Encyclopaedia*, (Papermac, 1993)

Hogg, Ethel, *Quintin Hogg, A Biography* (Archibald Constable and Co., 1904)

Horn, Pamela, *The Rural World 1780-1850* (Routledge, 1980)

Hughes, Molly, *A London Family 1870-1900* (1946) (Oxford University Press, 1981)

Humphries, Steve, and Weightman, Gavin, *The Making of Modern London 1815-1914* (Sidgwick and Jackson, 1983)

Illustrated London News

Jackson, Lee, *Victorian London* (New Holland Publishers, 2004)

Keating, Peter, *Into Unknown England 1866-1913, Selections from the Social Explorers* (Fontana, 1978)

Kerr, Robert, *The Gentleman's House* (1871) (victorianlondon.org)

Knight, Charles, *Knight's London* (1842) (victorianlondon.org)

The Leisure Hour

Lewis, Jon E., *London The Autobiography* (Constable and Robinson, 2008)

Mayhew, Henry, *London Labour and the London Poor* (1851) (Penguin Classics, 1985)

Mayhew, Henry, *The Morning Chronicle Survey of Labour and the Poor; The Metropolitan Districts* (1849-50) (Caliban Books, 1982)

MacCarthy, Mary, *A Nineteenth Century Childhood* (1924) (Constable, London, 1985)

Moggs' New Picture of London and Visitor's Guide to its Sights (1844) (victorianlondon.org)

Murray, John, *The World of London* (1843) – *Blackwood's Magazine* (victorianlondon.org)

Owen, Edward, *Hyde Park, Select Narratives, Annual Events etc, during twenty years Police Service in Hyde Park* (1906) (victorianlondon.org)

Paterson, Michael, *Voices from Dickens' London* (David and Charles Ltd, 2007)

Pett Ridge, William, *A Story Teller, Forty Years in London* (1923) (victorianlondon.org)

Philip, Neil and Neuburg, Victor, *Charles Dickens, A December Vision and Other Thoughtful Writings* (Continuum Publishing, 1987)

Picard, Liza, *Victorian London, The Life of a City 1840-1870* (Weidenfeld and Nicolson, 2005)

Porter, Stephen, *London A History in Paintings and Illustrations* (Amberley Publishing, 2014)

Punch Internet Archive

(The) Queen's London: A Pictorial and Descriptive Record of the Streets, Buildings, Parks and Scenery of the Great Metropolis in the Fifty-Ninth Year of the Reign of Her Majesty Queen Victoria (1896) (Cassell and Co., 1896)

Quennell, Peter (editor), *London's Underworld*, Selections from Volume 4 of Henry Mayhew's *London Labour and the London Poor* (Bracken Books, 1983)

Routledge's Popular Guide to London (1873) (victorianlondon.org)

Rowe, Richard, *Life in the London Streets; or Struggles for Daily Bread* (1881) (Kessinger Legacy Reprint, undated)

Sala, George Augustus, *London Up To Date* (1895) (victorianlondon.org)

Sala, George Augustus, *Twice Round the Clock or Hours of the Day and Night in London* (1859) (victorianlondon.org)

Schlesinger, Max, *Saunterings In and Around London* (1853) (Nathaniel Cooke, 1853)

Sheppard, Francis, *London 1808-1870; The Infernal Wen* (Secker and Warburg, 1971)

Sims, George, *How the Poor Live* (1883) (victorianlondon.org)

Smith, Adolphe and Thomson, John, *Street Life in London* (1877) (reprinted by Dover Publications as *Victorian London Street Life in Historic Photographs*, 1994)

Smith, Charles Manby, *Curiosities of London Life or Phases Physiological and Social of the Great Metropolis* (1853) (victorianlondon.org)

Smith, Charles Manby, *The Little World of London* (1857) (victorianlondon.org)

Taine, Hippolyte, *Notes on England* (1860) (Thames and Hudson, 1957)

Timbs, John, *Curiosities of London* (1867) (victorianlondon.org)

The Times

Tristan, Flora, *Promenades Dans Londres* (1842) (translated by Jean Hawkes and published as *The London Journal of Flora Tristan*, Virago, 1984)

'Uncle Jonathan', *Walks In and Around London* (1895) (victorianlondon.org)

Vallance, Rosalind, *Dickens' London, Selected Essays of Charles Dickens* (Folio Society, 1966)

Waifs and Strays Society, *The First Forty Years: A Chronicle of the Church of England Waifs and Strays Society 1881-1920* (SPCK 1922)

Wey, Francis, *A Frenchman Sees the English in the Fifties* (1935) (victorianlondon.org)

Willis, Frederick, *101, Jubilee Road* (1948) (Phoenix House, 1948)

Yates, Edmund, *Edmund Yates: His Recollections and Experiences* (1885) (victorianlondon.org)

Yglesias, J. R. C., *London Life and the Great Exhibition 1851* (Longmans, Green and Co., 1964)

www.citymetric.com
www.digitalpanopticon.org
www.Londonist.com, *London's Forgotten Disasters*
www.portcities.org.uk
www.queenvictoriasjournals.org
www.rmg.co.uk/attractions
www.workhouses.org.uk, Salvation Army Establishments

INDEX

Also available from Amberley Publishing

Available from all good bookshops or to order direct
Please call **01453-847-800**
www.amberleybooks.com

Also available from Amberley Publishing

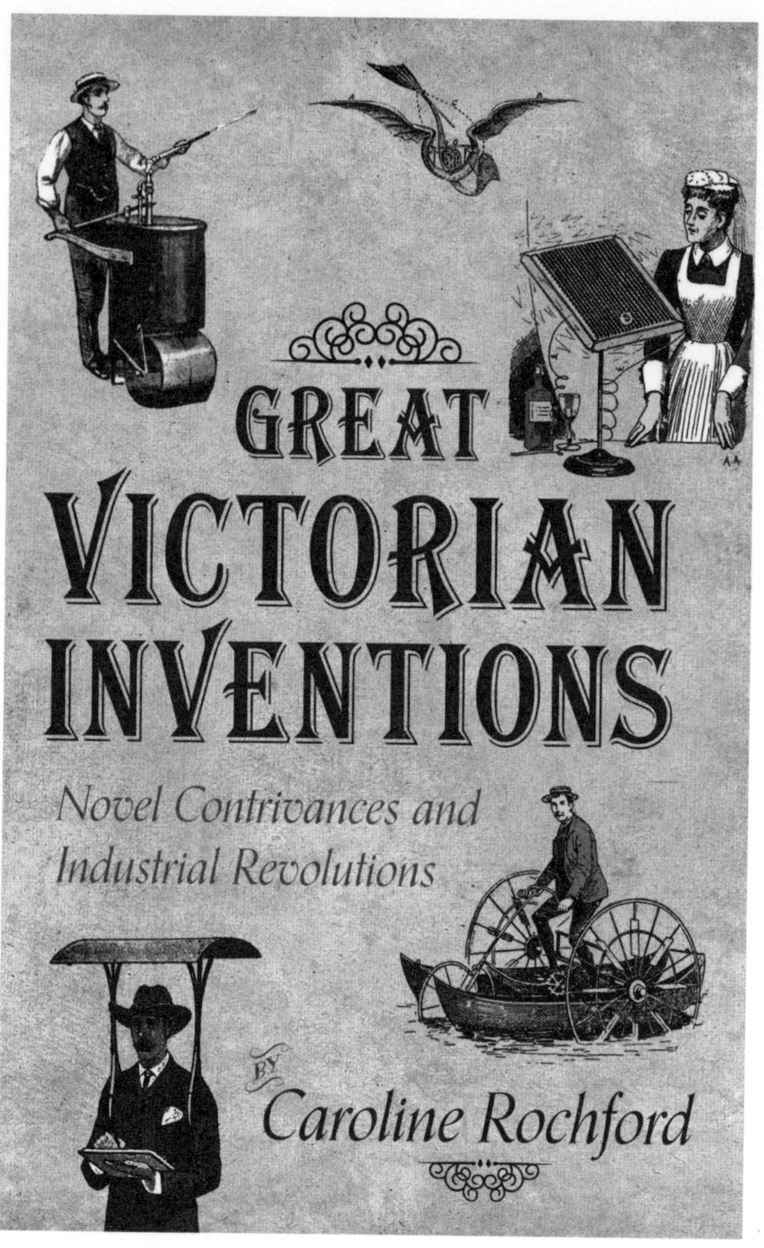

Available from all good bookshops or to order direct
Please call **01453-847-800**
www.amberleybooks.com